# 25 YEARS OF HELL

Curtis Brown

Fulton Books, Inc.
Meadville, PA

Published by Fulton Books 2020

ISBN 978-1-64654-042-6 (paperback)
ISBN 978-1-64654-043-3 (digital)

Printed in the United States of America

# FOREWORD

Twenty years ago, Curtis Brown was a stranger to me. We met, as Curtis was in desperate need of legal help and, by chance, he found me in an online search. In the last twenty years, Curtis went from stranger, to client, to friend, to close personal relationship. Never in my life have I met a man of such grit and determination to never give up; never just simply walk away, even when walking away is the exceedingly easier path. Curtis did not need to endure twenty-five years of hell. He could have walked away from it at any time. But that is not Curtis. When life throws you the worst nightmares possible, it is too easy to run and hide from them. For Curtis, the man I have revered and respected for twenty years strong, the tackling of those nightmares is the only way to know they haven't broken him. I am honored to write this foreword and to be included in Curtis' book. I wish it was a novel, as that would make Curtis an incredible story teller. Unfortunately, it as an accurate account of racial hell in a maximum security prison. While Curtis was not physically behind bars, he was trapped in a world of racial discrimination and injustice, the lengths of which go beyond the realm of insanity. And yet, somehow, he survived. He survived because he never gave up, never gave in and never just simply walked away. Curtis—you are one of the finest people I have ever known. Thank you for sharing your story.

Marc W. Garbar, Esq.
Head of Employment Law and Business Litigation Group
Brandon J. Broderick, Attorney at Law

# ACKNOWLEDGMENTS AND THANKS

First and foremost I must thank my Lord and savior Jesus Christ and God almighty for the many blessings that have been bestowed up me and my family. For the hedge of protection that was placed around me during my 28 years of service as a New York State Correctional Officer. Thank you Lord for all that you have done and for all that you continue to do in my life. I would like to thank my mother and father, the late Willie and Nancy Brown for the life lessons, values, and work ethic shown and taught to me as a child and for support. Thank you mom and dad! You are forever loved. To my beautiful, loving, and supportive wife Cheryle. I say thank you for being so supportive and understanding during our 36 years of marriage. For your undying love and support during my 28 year career as a Correctional Officer. I LOVE YOU from here to the moon a billon times over, God has truly blessed me with a soul mate. Thank you for being my wife. I would also like to thank my daughter Tiffany who helped finish the final edit corrections in the book, thank you baby for the help, I love you, and always remember to shoot for the moon. To my family and friends thank you for all the love, and support over the many years through prayers and encouraging words that helped to inspire me and gave me hope thank you. I would like to thank my Attorney for staying the course from the beginning to the end. For pursuing justice against the injustice and representing me in my quest for justice. Thank you for the great representation and thank you for being a friend. I would like to give a special thank you to Officer Q. My sincere gratitude and thank you isn't enough. I would like to thank you for being your own man and for your honesty and integrity. I am more than honored to call you a friend. Thank you!

L et's see where I start for better more where any reasonable person would start with beginning to describe in detail *twenty-five years of hell*. My name is Curtis Brown. I'm from a small town in upstate New York called Elmira. Yes, I was born and raised here, and I also raised my family here. I was born in 1963, to Willie and Nancy Brown. I, along with my other four siblings, me being the youngest. My father was a factory worker all his life—he worked in one of the well-known factories for forty-two years before retiring. Elmira is a small upstate New York town nestled in the valleys of the Finger Lakes region of the state. The last census report estimated there to be approximately twenty-nine thousand people living in the Elmira area. They use the inmate population at Elmira Correctional Facility as part of the census, a small town with two max prisons located only a few miles apart. I guess Elmira can be described as a prison town. We often laughed and said the prison was built and the town was built around it. The Elmira CF was called the Elmira Reformatory at first. It opened in 1876. Its inception was a direct derivative of the civil war. The Elmira area had what was known as one of the largest confederate prison camps better known as Hellmira, where many of those confederate soldiers died from disease. From the top of the hill on which the Elmira CF sits, if you look to your left as you walk up the hill just through the neatly pruned trees and the manicured lawn of the Woodlawn national cemetery, you can see a glimpse of the tombstones of the buried military veterans' section. This is also the civil war section of the cemetery. Our family home is located in Elmira. Our house in located up the street from one of Elmira's well-known residents, John W. Jones, who was a free slave who buried many of the confederate soldiers located in Woodlawn Cemetery.

His home is now a museum. At one time in the 1950s, our home was owned by a man that was a secretary at the Elmira Reformatory.

After working in the same well-known area factory as my father for five years, I took the test to become a New York State Correctional Officer. In October of 1988, I became a correctional officer. Becoming a correctional officer was the farthest thing from my mind. I don't think any young kid in my generation growing up said, "When I grow up, I want to be a correctional officer." I know I didn't, but with limited job opportunities and only one year of college under my belt, factory work was easily available, so I chose to become a correctional officer. My upbringing more than enough prepared and equipped me with all the necessary tools to do so. I was raised on the eastside of Elmira where the city housing projects were located. I saw a lot growing up and did a lot as well. I wasn't your typical kid from the east side. My first memories of growing up started on the south side of town. Back in the 1960s, majority of that side of town was white while the east side was majority black.

It was the third grade, I had just left my school on the south side, where I went to school with a majority of white kids, which I don't remember having a problem. After being dropped off in the office area of Thomas K Beecher Elementary by my mother, ten minuets later I was being escorted to my new classroom by one of my classmates that was sent down to show me to my new classroom.

After exiting the office area and walking down a long hallway, my new classmate and I, who didn't even introduce himself to me exited, the hallway into a small stairwell area leading to the second floor. Once out of view, my classmate began my greeting party. As I began to follow him up the steps, he turned and punched me dead in the face. I didn't know what the problem was, but he found out he had hit the wrong one because the fight was on. We fought for sometime in the back stairwell with neither one of us feeling satisfied on who won. We both arrived at the classroom with our clothing in disarray from the grabbing and rolling on the floor. The teacher never said a word, just asking me my name introducing me to the class and pointing out my seat in the classroom. That was my first day at Thomas K. Beecher elementary, School of Hard Knocks, as we called it. The kid who I fought earlier that morning later introduced himself on the playground along with the rest of his posse who were standing off to the side. He introduced himself by saying "My name is_____, I *run* this school."

With that said, we went on to have many—and I mean *many*—more fights while growing up. I also learned that he had purposely escorted me to the back hall to beat me up because the shortest way to the classroom were the front steps, not the back. I also learned the back steps was where a lot of things went down. Growing up in the seventies on the east side of Elmira, you'd better know how to fight. Hey, don't get it wrong—you could not come in our neighborhood and put your hands on anyone without getting a hell of an ass beating by many. We all played ball together from sand lot, little league to junior high to high school. Man, did we play ball.

I left public school after attending middle school at Ernie Davis Junior High School, I went on to attend high school at Notre Dame Catholic High. So I left a school system that was racially mixed for a school where I was one of six African Americans who attended. Some people would think that would be a problem—it wasn't. It was one of my most memorable experiences in my life, and it gave me insight and understanding.

I was called a nigger one time to my face while attending Notre Dame. It was on the football field. This kid who had gotten himself in some serious trouble, his parents decided it would be good for him to play football. This kid had never played football before, and many of the players didn't want him on the team. Me, it didn't matter to me. They all thought it would be a good idea for me to give him his christening hit during our hitting drills during practice. Now you have to remember this was the late seventies, bull in the ring was still legal contact in high school football. It wasn't the bull in the ring—it was that one-on-one drill: one man with the ball, the other tackles him, both men lie on their backs, heads facing each other, and when the whistle blows, you both get up as fast as you can. The guy with the ball tries to run through the tackler, which was me.

With the rest of the team watching, the coach blew the whistle, and all hell was released onto the newcomer. I hit him so hard one of his shiny new white football cleats came off as he was wadded up in a heap on the ground. As he got up while the whole team was laughing at him, the first words he uttered out his mouth was "You Nigger!." I was surprised, completely taken aback by what he said. It seemed like the words were coming out in slow motion, with every syllable emphasized driven with hate and anger for what he just felt on the field. Before I could react to his racist comment, I was pushed aside by my teammates, who were yelling, swing, kicking this poor soul off the football field and team for disrespecting me. And think this was in the late seventies. Man, I miss those days.

It came to be a great benefit to my life having had the opportunity to go to a private school, which was primarily white, and living in a primarily black neighborhood. It was truly the best of both worlds. I could hang out with anybody—my social world was unlimited. If we are given the opportunity to only interact with our own during our time of development, we are limited to our understanding of others cultures, races and religion, as well as understanding others dreams and aspirations in life. I wish that the many correctional officers I worked with had this same opportunity.

I'll never forget my first day reporting to the New York State Department of Corrections Training Academy, which was located on the campus of Keuka College, nestled in the beautiful Finger Lakes Region in Upstate New York. I was lucky to get this training facility because it is only an hour and twenty minuets from home. I arrived during the evening, as I was ordered to do so. Once on campus, I was directed to the training academy. Once I arrived and got out my car, I felt as if I truly stepped into the Twilight Zone or some would say "The Unknown—.

Stepping out of my car and walking in the department's training academy would change my life in so many ways. As I walked in the door, I was assaulted by glares from the training staff who immediately started screaming at the top of their lungs trying to compete with who could be the loudest. This didn't intimidate me or scare me as they could see as I gave them my name and information. I looked to one side—they had some poor guy in the lean and rest position. For you that aren't familiar with the military—that's a push-up position with your arms locked out holding it as ordered to do so, and may I add he had his suit on as we were ordered to report dressed in a suit. Lucky for them they hadn't ordered me to get in that position in my good suit.

After checking in, I was escorted out of the lobby area and to the dormitory area. There were some rooms that were four-men rooms and two-men rooms. After arriving late that evening, we were issued our uniforms, which were gray khakis. That evening, we were left alone to get our rooms and state-issued clothing together and time to meet each other. The training group for a cycle was called a session. In my session, there were approximately sixty or so recruits with six or seven of them being African Americans.

Later in the evening, the instructor who was the equivalent of a military drill instructor came back to the dorm area and ordered lights out. Early that morning, we were awakened by loud yelling: "Let's go get up and get outside. You have ten minutes." We dressed in our khaki gray uniforms and black boots. The mad rush was on to get to the bathroom and get dressed to get outside. Most were rushing around and unprepared. I had my gear—my khaki gray uniform, socks, boots, and underclothing already from the night before. I shot to the bathroom and quickly dressed and was outside for the first of many session formations. This is when everyone in the session lines up in a column-type formation. I was one of the first outside, ready to go after lining everyone up and informing us of what was expected of us and what we could expect. I was then made the session leader.

We were marched down the road to breakfast. We ate in the same dining hall as the students that attend the school. After breakfast, we were escorted around the area, which the department was using for training and given paperwork to fill out. Later that day, I was pulled aside, and my session leader position was explained to me. Now remember, I didn't ask for this, nor was I expecting to be thrown into this position, but I could clearly see I had no other choice but to except and embrace the newfound position that was bestowed upon me. As a session leader, you are leading 50-60 men and women and all eyes are on you. You have to lead by example and be responsible for those that are around you.

During the course of our training camp, some people dropped out for several reasons. They ranged from; not being able to qualify shooting a 38, AR15 and Remington 780p shot gun, issued by the state at the firing range. Others wouldn't be able to run a mile in a set time. Some would violate rules and would get kicked out. Then there were some that realized, corrections wasn't for them. Some of the people in our session quit late in the game after a field trip to the Auburn State Prison to get a real feeling of what Prison truly felt like. Some quit after their field trip. I remember one African American male recruit who was built a little thick in the backside area almost had an anxiety attack for fear that the inmates were going to talk about the size of his ass, which they did.

I remember entering the Auburn Correctional Facility, which was built in 1817, making it the oldest prison in the state of New York. The facility sure did look its age. I remember entering the dark, musty, cold, old prison and being escorted around the facility. When we walked into the cell block area where the inmates are housed. The cat calls and insults started flying out of the mouths of the convicted felons. These insults were directed at us in the form of putdowns about our looks, clothing, and just any little thing they could find to try and get under our skin. The black guy with the thick backside got it real bad. You have to remember these inmates have twenty-four hours a day to think of bullshit, and they just unloaded on him, screaming about the size of his ass to the shape to what they wanted to do to him. I remember talking him out of quitting and sticking it out after returning to the training facility the instructor at the training academy were correctional officers.

I later learned how they got those jobs that afforded them the opportunity not to have to work in the prisons. They did a lot of hop knobbing, ass kissing, and God only knows what else. Being the session leader only had one benefit, and that was a single room to myself. Other than that, I was being held responsible for every mishap or mistake my session made. Hell, where I'm from, we call that the fall guy.

Well, after the majority of us did finally graduate, those who stuck it out and wanted the job were sent back home for OJT, which stands for on-the-job training at a facility close to home for one month. My training facility was the Elmira CF. During this time, you were brought into the facility and taught the inner workings of prison and your job as a correctional officer. My uncle, my mother's brother, was a correctional officer who had worked at Elmira but had transferred to Southport when it had opened in 1988, the same year I came into the department upon arriving at Elmira. I was one of, I believe at that time, four black officers at the facility, but I was only there for OJT for a month.

While on OJT, you did the dirty work that the seasoned officers either refused or didn't want to do like frisk cells in the housing blocks of the facility. I remember one of the first cells I ever frisked was in G block at the Elmira Correctional Facility. The block was dirty—it smelled of body funk, shit, and garbage all mixed together. The group of trainees—or as the inmates called us, fresh meat or new jacks—were sent to the block to frisk for contraband. We started on the top gallery, wherein that block had a total of eight galleries.

I'll never forget going to the cell number I was given to frisk. Once there, I waited patiently for the door to open, and when it did and I stepped inside, I was slapped in the face with the smell of funk and garbage mixed together some of my fellow officers called it the mutt smell in reference to the inmates. As I entered the cell trying to hold my breath so I would not breathe too much of the awful smell in, I started to frisk the cell for contraband. I noticed a towel lying on the floor, which I picked up, and when I did—oh my Lord, I'm not exaggerating—there were approximately two hundred roaches that came running out from under the towel I had just moved. I jumped back in total shock and stepped out of the cell to gather myself. It wasn't the roaches that shocked me—it was the number of them. Remember, I was raised on the eastside of Elmira; it wasn't the first roach I'd seen. The year in which I was hired, 1988, there was a hiring frenzy, and the main reasons for this? The crack epidemic which ballooned the inmate population not only in New York state but throughout the country. The New York State Department of Corrections had a total of three training academies running, pumping out correctional officers as fast as they could to keep up with the high demand while on OJT, on-the-job training at Elmira; the trainees would all gather in the long corridor which connected one side of the facility to the other. During training, we wore a gray khaki-type uniform, but now we all wear the official correctional officer colors—a light blue shirt and dark blue pants which we could adorn after graduation. All you could see was a sea of blue shirts in the corridor. When it came time for the inmate movement, if it was rec time or time for the inmates to move to, turning out to chow and programs or turning in for the count.

Any time there were large numbers of inmates in the corridor, all the trainees would be there to frisk the inmates as they entered and exited. This was used as a divisive tool to intimidate the inmates to let them know who was in charge. While in the corridor with approximately fifty or more other officers, I myself would be the only African American officer. The only other African Americans all wear green pants and green shirts, making them inmates. Therefore, I stuck out like a sore thumb to the inmates. I was a fly in the milk, a house nigger, Oreo cookie, a sellout, an Uncle Tom. The inmates had a lot of deferent terminology or jail slang for the minority officers who showed up in a uniform that was other than green in color. I remember my first couple of days on OJT, I was standing in one of the four mess halls where the inmates ate. It was breakfast time, and I was standing along with my fellow officers. Still I was the only African American officer standing there when I was bombarded with a host of derogatory comments and words such as "Look at the new house nigger," "He's a fucking sellout," and "Token-ass Negro." This went on and on as I stood there amongst my peers and supervisors with none of them uttering a word.

Now I must remind you the only thing that looked like me in the mess hall all had on green. As I stood there feeling embarrassed and basically alone, I scanned the mess hall and spotted one of the Muslim inmates. He had looked in my direction, shaking his head in disagreement of the comments being unleased at me after chow was over. I had a chance meeting with this inmate, and he informed me that he didn't feel that way about me and there were a lot of other brothers who were glad to see someone that looked like them in uniform. I thanked him and asked if he could let the others who were speaking to me like that to stop disrespecting me and to let them know I was here for a job to feed my family, not to harass or put my hands on anyone. Either the brother was strong or the inmates felt sorry for me, but I never heard any more disrespectful comments come my way. The inmates would not talk to the white officers like that because they would take them somewhere and beat the life out of them. I was all alone like a wounded caribou in a pack being hunted by lions. Of course they were going to pick the easy prey.

While on OJT at Elmira, I was not welcomed with open arms by the almost entirely white workforce, security and civilian staff alike. I did notice they would watch me more closely than they would watch their own; it surely didn't take me long to catch on. They say the best cop is a street-smart person who knows their way around, and I was that person, as we would say in the neighborhood, hip to the game. After a month, OJT was over on the hill—that is what the Elmira correctional facility is referred to. Now the real adventure would begin.

After being home for a month and working just minutes from where we lived, we were now being sent to our new facilities through-out the state. The majority, if not all, were sent to Sing Sing, Mid Orange, and Bedford Hills, all facilities located down state. Four and a half to five hours from home, that day had finally come. Time to pack up and say goodbye to the wife and loved ones. Packing up the car with my uniforms and personal clothing along with provisions such as food that could be stored without refrigeration, reason being you didn't know if your vehicle was going to double as your new home away from home. It was like being sent into the wildness blindfolded. It wasn't like you were going down to your new facility, and the state had a nice place already set up for you. Finding a place to stay was your responsibility.

After the car was packed and I said my goodbyes, I got in the car and started toward my new facility, Sing Sing. Yes, I was assigned to Sing Sing. Out of the three facilities we were sent to, I would later find out it was the better of the three. Now you have to remember this was 1988. There weren't any cell phones. Cars were not equipped with all the fancy state-of-the-art technology. CDs and tapes were the media of the day. Riding down RT 17 the first time toward Ossining, New York, where Sing Sing is located was a long and daunting ride. Once I arrived in the wilderness by myself. I quickly went into survival mode and went looking for a place to lay my head for the night. After calling my wife and telling her I had made it safe and sound, I was in search of a hotel, motel, or even a Holiday Inn. What I found was a little dirty out-the-way motel outside of Ossining in White Plains, NY, where many have gone before me. In other words, a motel that was no stranger to correctional officers making the motel home. Once I checked in, I went to the room. I opened the door to find a dimly lit room that smelled of musk and mildew. I entered the room and closed the door and looked around to visually inspect the room. The carpet was badly stained, the bedding looked like it hadn't been washed in months, the bathroom smelled of funk and mold, and the floor was slipper with soap scum and dirt. Welcome to the wonderful world of corrections. I then went to retrieve my property from the car with daunting dilemma: bring my stuff in the room with the chance of something crawling into my things or leave a packed car in the parking lot to be vandalized. I chose to bring in the stuff that couldn't be hidden out of sight.

At bedtime, I remained fully dressed and placed a sleeping bag atop the made-up bed. As I lay there half the night looking up at the yellow-stained ceiling debating rather or not to stay or go, my thought was if I packed up now, I could be home by the morning and be at the factory. I had left to ask for my job back. I must have fallen asleep at some point because I awoke to the sound of the alarm clock I had brought with me. I got up and dressed in my state blue correctional officer uniform to start my tour of duty at Sing Sing correctional facility. After making the drive from White Plains to Ossining, as I drove up to the facility, I noticed the old stained concrete wall that surrounded the portion of the facility that was exposed to the street just outside. The facility sits right smack in the middle of town so much, so the train runs right smack through the middle of the prison if you have ever been in a prison, this goes without reason, a train running straight through the middle of the prison. Mind boggling, but with that said, I never heard of anyone escaping Sing Sing on the train. After riding around the facility to the employee parking area, I parked and walked toward the facility to a set of narrow concrete and lime stone stairs, which were attached to the large stone wall of the prison. The stairs twist and turn as you walk down to the bottom. It opens up to a lower parking area used for drop-offs, official state business, and the higher-ups like the superintendent, Deps, captains, and so forth. Oh, I later learned that weasels and butt kissers parked there too. This is also where the front entrance was located.

As I walked up to the entrance, I noticed the large aged iron gates on both sides of the door. I opened up the door. I was now a correctional officer at Sing Sing prison. After arriving I was shown the lineup room, where I met the other new jacks. We were split up in groups and shown the prison. One of the most memorable days in my time being a correctional officer was being escorted and showed the responsibility of the officers on the block. I was personally escorted by an older seasoned officer. During our rounds in the block, he stopped and told me, "Young man, whatever you do, just come in here and do your job—care, custody, and control. And don't come in here acting like a cowboy." He then went on to tell me he was in the B block riot that had taken place in 1983. He said he always did his job and only gave the inmates what they had coming from the state, and he is always fair, firm, and consistent with them. He then went on to tell me about his experience in the riot, in which he told me the inmates took the officers that they felt had disrespected they had harassed them and brutally assaulted them by beating them mercifully, hanging and dangling their body off the edge of the top gallery, which was approximately sixty feet or more in the air, threatening to drop them head first. He said they took some of the real tough guys and tied them to small tables face down and pants down with inmates lined up ten to fifteen deep, taking turns sodomizing them. He went on to say during the riot, they had punched him in his face, knocking out one of his teeth at which he opened up his mouth to reveal one of his teeth missing. He said after being punched in the face, he was dressed in inmate greens and thrown in a cell, where he stayed until after order was restored and the riot was over. It had only been five years ago that the B block riot had taken place. My take from the older officer's wisdom was fully received and understood. I never forgot that while preforming my duties as a correctional officer. It was a wonderment to me to see this officer still able to perform his job in the same block he was held hostage. His wisdom and advice didn't fall on deaf ears. This officer had a profound effect on how I modeled my career.

Some days later, I was still assigned to work in B Block. They were slowly cutting us loose from the cord to take on the daily task of running the block. The sergeant in charge of the block—we will call him Sergeant B—was African American. He ordered me to watch the B block front entrance gate that was controlled by locking and unlocking with a key as directed as the inmates came back in for the evening. As the inmates lined up on the gate, I would inform the other officers, and they would let me know whether to let them in or have them wait. All was running smooth until I was directed to let in a group by the officers standing there, and the sergeant became enraged and started screaming at me at the top of his lungs, belittling me as the other homeboys stood around, either laughing or sheepishly smiling as he did so. *Homeboy* is an officer who works at his home jail. After this happened, I stood there stunned at first, then my common sense and survival mode kicked in. I made sure the door was locked. I then handed the key to one of the home boys and walked over to where the sergeant was sanding and asked him if I could talk to him in his office. We then entered his office and shut the door. I then proceeded to tell Sergeant B he wasn't going to disrespect me and yell at me like I was his kid and he wasn't going to use me as entertainment for his homeboys. The sergeant stood there stunned, and his response was in agreement. We then stayed in the office, and we talked both of us, telling each other about one another. He did tell me he appreciated me coming to him like a man and not running up front and reporting him like other officers from upstate had done. We became close. He would sometimes buy lunch. He even invited me to his wedding anniversary in White Plains. I also learned he like a lot of other officers from the area had two jobs to offset their state pay.

Sing Sing was a great jail for a young officer to learn. While there on OJT, on-the-job training, the majority of the officers from Upstate New York immediately put their names on the transfer list for two other downstate jails that primarily had white employees. I stayed at Sing Sing for over a year, and while there it was truly a learning experience. I remember one incident where I was working in A Block, and I was on the red dot response team, where officers report to emergency disturbances in the jail such as; fights and various other situations. On this particular day, a red dot call came out from the SHU area in the jail. That is the area where inmates who break the rules in the facility are sent—in better terms, the jail inside the jail. When the call came out, I and eight to ten other officers scrambled to the area to help.

Once at the SHU door, we banged on the door for someone to open it. When the door opened, we were greeted by the sergeant. His white shirt and blue paints and face and hair were covered with a yellow dust-like substance. We asked what was going on, and his response was, "He's downstairs." We then scurried in and made our way downstairs. As we made our way down, we stopped in amazement, looking at the almost inch and a half of water that covered the floor. As we walked into the water and rounded the corner, we observed the situation at hand. One of the inmates had gotten out and was positioned in the corner with a dry chemical fire extinguisher, holding security staff at bay with it as he blasted anyone who came close in the face area. I found out when I too made an attempt to gain control of the inmate or the extinguisher. It went something like this—me walking up and saying, "Put it down," and the inmate gave me a blast of dry chemical from the extinguisher. It got in my eyes, mouth, and up my nose. I now looked like the sergeant who had greeted us at the door. After receiving my blast, I stumbled backward, unable to see. But once my sight was clear, the fight for the extinguisher was on. I looked around and found the source of the water that covered the floor. The officer had messed up and basically was at fault for allowing the inmate access to the extinguisher. He was standing there with the fire hose in hand. I took it from him, told him to turn it all the way on, which he did. Now I had my equalizer.

19

The hose was shooting a high-pressure stream of water. I gave the inmate the order to drop the extinguisher. He refused, and the fight was on. I sprayed him in the face then in his groin—face, groin, face, groin until the finale. He tried to throw the large extinguisher, and when he cocked it back, I put the water stream on his arm, causing him to drop it. He then fell to the floor. By this time, there were more officers in the area and the pack surrounded him. I remember holding the pack of angry officers off as we handcuffed the inmate. After the situation was over and reports had to be written, it was found out the new jack officer who was working in the area had discovered a fire that the inmate had set in his cell, and in doing so, he extinguished the fire and had sat the extinguisher down. Then letting the inmate out of the cell, he grabbed it and went on his rampage. I remember also one time, I was called to escort an inmate out of the MHU block (mental health unit).

To the hospital, when I arrived, there seemed to be no urgency. I was met at the door. Greetings were exchanged, and the sergeant said, "We got one that needs to see medical," and I was told to escort him over. Me along with the sergeant and a couple of the officers working the block walked around the corner where the inmates were. I noticed the inmate had a bloody towel pressed against his groin area. The sergeant then looked at me as I stood eyes wide and in a nonchalant manner. This one decided he did not want his penis anymore. The inmate had used a tuna fish lid can to try to sever his penis from his body. The penis was still hanging by a little piece of skin; a chill shot up my body just thinking of the pain. The inmate was escorted to the facility hospital and taken to the outside hospital where his penis was reattached. The inmate had done it because he was on human growth hormones, which the state was paying for, and he wanted the state to pay the bill for his transformation operation to have his penis removed.

On another occasion, I had the outside mobile patrol where you would ride around the facility, checking the outside wall area and parking lots. Well, doing so, one evening, I was ordered to report to the facility hospital door area, where I was met by a frantic sergeant and nurse followed by a stretcher with a body on it. The stretcher along with the lifeless body were placed in the back of the van, and I was ordered to drive as fast as I could to the area hospital. After being there a short while, the inmate was pronounced dead.

After working at Sing Sing for over a year, I transferred to the Sullivan correctional facility located in Sullivan County, where there were other officers from the Elmira area working there. Elmira is about a two-and-a-half hour drive one way. We carpooled every day; an eight-hour shift and a five-hour commute equals a thirteen-hour day. I worked at Sullivan for approximately seven months. Sullivan correctional facility at that time was a large PC jail. PC, Protective Custody, where the inmates are put there because they are scared or have enemies that are out to get them. It also housed high-profile inmates like the Amityville Horror Killer and Son of Sam. It was a quite max facility where there were hardly any problems.

In the basement area of the hospital, they housed the mental hygiene inmates, the mentally ill. One evening while working with two senior officers, I had the floor area, and they had the bubble area which controlled the doors on the unit. My job was to tend to the inmates and keep an eye on them. I was essentially locked in a room with the crazies. One of my jobs was to take a chow list on the unit, and this particular night, there was pork on the menu and some inmates didn't eat pork, so I had to asked each inmate if they wanted pork or the alternative, which was peanut butter and jelly. After making the list, I gave it to the other officers in the bubble, and they informed the kitchen area so they would know what to send. Later when the meals arrived, it was also my job to hand them out. While doing so, I got to one of the biggest inmates on the unit, a big white guy who stood about 6'8" and weighed about 350 pounds. I handed him his dinner tray, which was peanut butter and jelly. I was standing directly in front of him, looking up at him when I handed him the tray, and when he opened it to find the peanut butter and jelly, all hell broke loose. He lost his mind. He took a step toward me, yelling at the top of his lungs, "I didn't want this shit! I wanted pork." I turned to see if the other two officers in the bubble were watching. When I turned, they were practically bent over laughing at me.

I turned back to face the inmate, and my street survival skills kicked in. It was time to fight crazy with crazy. I pointed my finger at the inmate and yelled back at him, you said, "You wanted peanut butter and jelly, and that's what you got. Now get the hell away from me." The inmate took the tray and walked away. I turned to see the two senior officers stand with their arms folded, nodding in agreement, yelling, "That's right!" After chow was done, I was told by the other officers that the inmate was always trying to intimidate staff with his size. The inmate was incarcerated for assault on a police officer. He had fallen on top of a police officer and broke his leg while they were struggling to arrest him on the street. He was one of the biggest inmates I had come across in my twenty-eight-year career. Sullivan Correction Facility was the first time I'd seen a transvestite inmate while working in one of the blocks. One of the old timers or senior officers had me make a round in the horse-shaped block as he and other officers looked on.

As I was just finishing up getting to the last couple of cells, I was startled by a set of large breasts looking back at me. As I looked in the cell, I jumped back in astonishment, and the other officers looking on laughed as I did so. If I had been lighter in color, I'm sure my face would have been flushed or red. After coming downstairs after making the round, I asked them why the hell they hadn't warned me of the Transvestite that was in the cell. They just laughed. At Sullivan, there was way too much downtime, so the fellows played a lot of fun and games to pass the time. Tomorrow, it would be some other unassuming new jacks turn to be laughed at. The daily five-hour commute was really starting to take a toll. The only other alternative was to get housing in one of the apartments or houses. The other transient officers were renting, which I didn't want to do, which was later found to be a good judgment call. And the reason being a group of new officers living together were busted for drugs and fired from the department. Even carpooling came with a risk. I remember this one officer while riding with him and others with him at the wheel as we passed through the town of Sullivan. During the summer on our way back to Elmira, we passed through one of the Jewish communities where a large number of Jewish people from New York City came to spend the summer. While we passed a street crossing, a large number of Jewish people was attempting to cross the street minding their business going about their day.

He sped up and yelled out, "I'll run all their asses over." As they walked across the street in the crosswalk, the vehicle approached at a high rate of speed. The people in the crosswalk were running and jumping out of the way. As we rode through, the racist idiot at the wheel was spilling Jewish hatred from his mouth.

I was seated in the back and begin by asking him if he was crazy and told him if he had hit one of those people, his ass would be going to jail. I also told him, "Those Jewish people haven't done anything to you." All fell on deaf ears; the idiot just chuckled and the others fell silent. I was so glad. I never rode in the car again with him at the wheel. It definitely became clear that some of my fellow officers were outright racist and weren't afraid to show it. I was the only African American in the carpool. Hell, most of the time, after leaving Sing Sing, I was usually the only African American around.

After carpooling five hours a day for seven months, I was transferred to the Cayuga Correctional Facility located in the Finger Lakes region of upstate New York. I was now one hour and fifteen minutes from home. To move from jail to jail, you have to put your name on a transfer list and wait until your name is reached. The list is ranked in order of seniority. Once I reached Cayuga, I put my name on the transfer list to Elmira.

The Cayuga CF is located in a small town called Moravia, New York, with a population of around 3,800 people, give or take one gas station and two or three stores. The facility was built on top of a hill and was said to be built on a Native American burial ground. I had worked at two maximum security facilities, Sing Sing and Sullivan. Now I was working at Cayuga, a medium-security jail, from inmates in cells to inmates in large dormitories. There were around five other African American officers working there when I arrived. Almost all the facilities in upstate New York only had a sprinkling of minority officers in them. They all have primarily white officers and civilian staff working at them, and the inmate population is primarily black and Hispanic. It doesn't take long to see the overwhelming lopsided ratio of nonwhite employees working at these facilities. Now you have to remember, I got to Cayuga in late 1989 at the height of the crack epidemic hitting the country. The dorms at Cayuga correctional facility were fifty-man dorms, and that's how they were when I arrived. But a short while later after my arrival, the dorms at not only Cayuga, but all the mediums in the state were doubled. With that said, the dorms at the facility went from fifty to ninety.

Hell, when the dorms were busting at the seams and more space was needed, they took the gym, which was used for the inmates' recreation and put bunks in there. I think there were over two hundred inmates housed in the gym. With the gym taken away, the state brought in an inflatable building and installed a wood floor, which was used as a recreational building. The facility was literally busting at the seams. I worked a dorm at Cayuga, the same dorm for the approximately seven years. I worked E-1 dorm. There were a total of seven dorms. Each dorm had two sides—E-1, E-2, etc., all filled beyond capacity. Early on, it was mainly young guys ages eighteen to twenty-five which resulted in a lot of problems—fights, sexual assaults, and a lot of stealing among the inmate population at the facility. With the inmates so young, we were literally babysitting. I remember coming in one morning working my regular shift, 7–3, and greeted by inmates, all giving me a play by play of last night's events that had taken place telling of the poor young white inmate who had been raped during the night, just a few cubes from the officers desk. As he slept in his cube, he was raped by a number of what were reported as Hispanic inmates as the officer lay asleep at the desk just twenty feet away. I thought, *Hell, I stepped into a crime scene.*

First thing in the morning, the victim had already been taken off the unit by the time I arrived. The story from more than half of the inmates on the unit went like this. As the officer lay fast asleep at the desk area, a number of inmates low-crawled (lying on the floor and scouting or wiggling to move without detection), army or ninja style across the dormitory floor to their victim's cube, were they proceed to sodomize him. They went onto say during the assault on the inmate the officer was fast asleep. Afterward, the assailants were overheard laughing about their crime, and they laughed about using jelly on the victim to sodomize him because they had no other lubricant.

When I asked that officer whom I was relieving from the post on which this assault took place what had taken place, he said he was told not to talk about it and hastily exited the dorm. Later that day, some of the inmates and staff were going around referring to the victim as sweet buns because his attackers had used jelly to lubricate themselves to sodomize their victim. In prison, there is little or no compassion for those that are most vulnerable to abuse. This particular officer who was on duty at the time of the assault was asleep no doubt because the inmate that was assaulted was just twenty or so feet away. This took place on the night shift eleven to seven in the morning. This was a shift where most staff working tended to sleep on duty. Hell, there were officers sleeping on the 7–3 shift at times. This officer received no punishment for his lapse in security or the dereliction of his basic duties as a correctional officer, which is care, custody, and control. There were many incidents where staff were allowed to neglect their duties. Just like any jail in upstate New York, I would later find out.

In my later years as a correctional officer at Cayuga, there were only a few African Americans officers. At one time, I believe there were six of us and one Hispanic officer I had been there less than a year when—they all transferred out, going to jails closer to home.

At one point, after having ongoing problems with the large population of young inmates they changed the population by moving in older inmates to offset the younger population; in theory they were adult inmate babysitters. It had its good and bad sides. The older inmates would sometimes be able to keep the younger inmates in line by talking to them about doing time because a lot of the older inmates had come from maximum-security prisons with most of their time served enabling them to qualify for medium status. They would talk to the younger inmates. Some would threaten them, while others would extort the younger inmates for their personal property like commissary food from the facility store packages sent from home such as allowable food items and clothing.

One time, I remember I received a call from the facility package-age room for one of the younger Hispanic inmates to report to the package room to pick up his package. The inmate was sent to the package room, and after returning to the dorm, I observed him in his cubicle going through his package placing things in his locker. While doing this, an older inmate approached his cube. They talked, and after they finished speaking, the older inmate walked away with some items in his hands. He walked directly in front of the officer's desk area that was slightly elevated. When he was directly in front of the desk area, the younger inmate came up from behind him and hit him in the head with what appeared to be a ball in a sock. Because the first hit bounced off the older inmate's head like a ball, it was the second strike that hit home for him. Blood started gushing from the head wound he was stuffing with. By the time the inmate went to try to hit him a third time, I was able to stop him by grabbing him and calling for help.

During the investigation into the incident, it was learned that the older inmate that had been hit upside the head with one of the oldest weapons used in jail for protection and assault, the lock in the sock, was living on the unit extorting the younger inmates. The younger inmate didn't receive a harsh punishment for the fact that the older inmate was pushing up on the younger inmate. The older inmate was taken to the facility infirmary, stitched up, and a turban now adorned his head for all to see in the medium jail.

There was a lot of stealing because the inmates were in a dormi-tory-type setting, making it easier for the sneak thief to hit. See, you had the extorter, who took by power and threats, and the sneak thief who slithered around like a snake.

One officer came into work and inmates were giving him a hard time, and he was giving it right back. It was the 11–7 tour. He was at the officers' desk. Later into his tour, at some point, he got too comfortable and closed his eyes, and then from somewhere in the dorm, an inmate threw a can of jack mack, which is a can of fish. The can hit him smack dab in the head, knocking him out. When he was able, he called for help, and all hell broke loose in the dorm. Additional staff were called, and tactics of intimidation were applied to the inmates to gain knowledge of the inmate responsible for the assault on the officer. Staff turned the dorm upside down; that's when all the inmates in the dorm had their cubes frisked for contraband. There was inmate property sprawled out throughout the dorm. A number of inmates were cuffed and taken to the special housing unit (SHU) on suspicion of being the one who threw the can at the officer. The dorm, after an incident such as this, would be on the burn—punished for the incident. They would be last called to chow. The microwave on the unit for inmate use would be taken away. There would be no late nights on the weekends lights out early, etc. This would go on until someone at the top at the facility felt they had suffered enough.

There was another notable incident one day. There was a big fight in one of the dorms with multiple inmates involved. A group of officers responded while they were in the rec area of the dorm. While they were breaking up fights between multiple inmates, one of the inmates in the rec area, an older little person, his height approximately four feet tall, started mouthing off and threatening the officers. He the inmate was slapped, at which time they said the four-foot-tall inmate scurried off to the dorm area, only to return with a banger. A banger is a long, sharp weapon used for stabbing, usually made of metal, wood, or plastic—material found lying around or stolen or torn off something. The four-foot tall inmate's weapon was metal—he began to chase the officer who had allegedly slapped him. The officer ran as the inmate chased him until he along with others were able to subdue him and stop him. It was a dangerous situation, but later, all laughed and said the officer was chased by the little person who played on the old show *Fantasy Island*. You really never knew what the day would bring working in a prison.

There was one morning I was sitting in the dorm after the inmates had been let out to chow and programs when one of the inmates hastily returned to the dorm just ten to fifteen minutes after he had left, asking if he could come back to retrieve something from his cubicle. I told him he could enter, but if he did, he was subjected to a pat frisk. He agreed and entered. As I went to pat his pants pockets, I felt an object. I pulled from his pocket a fourteen-inch wielding rod sharped at one end like an ice pick. I had the inmate turn away from the wall he was leaning on. With sharpened rod in hand, I asked him what the hell he was going to do with this. His reply flooded me. He said, "It's not mine."

I then said, "I know, I just pulled it out your pocket."

He then said, "Come on, Brown, give me a break." The inmates would call some officers by their first names like friends and others by just last names as to leave off the officer to make it more personal or friendlier. After the inmate hit me with the most bizarre explanation and request, I ordered him to place his hands on the wall and help was called. The inmate was cuffed and escorted to the special housing unit (SHU). The inmates' cube area was searched by me, and a total of eight to ten other unsharpened wielding rods were found under a locker in his cube. The rod I pulled off him was long and sharp enough to go through two people.

Being a minority officer, you had to set parameters and boundaries with the inmate population if you were going to effectively and reasonably do your job. To communicate that back then, it was as simple as telling the inmates you were in charge of "Don't start nothing, wouldn't be nothing." Meaning the officer was going to do his job and the inmates were going to do their time, and if there was a problem, it would be dealt with. Later in my career, that all went out the window.

At one point, while working a Cayuga correctional facility, I carpooled with others back and forth to work; these guys were worse than the inmates. We all used to meet at a small store plaza to park and ride. While waiting, we would go into the store to get things for work. One officer, while in uniform, went into the store and stoled a tin of chewing tobacco and got caught by the store management. These same officer while in the parking lot after work on a separate occasion was in an altercation with another officer, during which I had to get in the middle and stop. What had happened was the thief had brought a new car—I guess from all the money he was saving on his five-finger discount. So he had this new car. We were carpooling in multiple cars usually parking next to each other while one of the other officers thought it would be a good idea to put his snow-covered boot on the bumper of the thief's new white car to tie his boot. When the thief observed this, he lost his mind, he grabbed him, and they started pushing and shoving one another. Threats were made by the officer with the ice scraper in his hand. I then got between the two of them and told them, "Someone is going to lose their job out here." They came to their senses and stopped. The officer that had the scraper in his hand was branded with a nickname that followed him the rest of his career.

Another officer in the carpool had his mind set. He was a race car driver. If you had the pleasure of riding with him, he would go at speeds of up to ninety miles an hour or faster on some roads traveled to and from work. He was a motor head who would be way too wired up early in the morning. He also unhooked the odometer on all his cars so they wouldn't record the mileage on his vehicles. He told this himself, and when riding with him, you could observe the odometer was not moving. The last time I checked, tampering with an odometer was illegal. After the exodus of the few African American officers, I myself remained as the only African American officer at the Cayuga correctional facility. Once by myself, problems started to be created by, at first, the homeboys, the ones from the area, and then from the officers from Elmira and the administration, including my direct supervisor.

On one occasion in the early 1990s still working at Cayuga, the facility was visited by a deputy commissioner. We will refer to him as Commissioner C. He was a tall, large African American man. During his visit at the facility, he made rounds on the dormitories escorted by the facility's higher-ups such as the superintendent, deputy superintendent, captains, lieutenants, and sergeants. Let's put it this way—the inter administration was running behind him with their nose up his ass, you know, brown nosing. The commissioner had started his tour at A-dorm and was now at E-1 dorm, the dorm which I worked for two years now, more or less my regular job, once on E-1 dorm with the entourage. The commissioner walked around the unit with me in tow. After completing his round, he stood in the middle of the dorm and said to the superintendent, "Hey, superintendent, let me ask you a question. How is it I just walked through all of the other dorms and I get all the way down here and this is the best-looking one I have seen?"

The superintendent had no explanation for his superior, so he turned to me and asked me, "Officer Brown, you tell me why this dorm is the best-looking dorm I've seen."

And my explanation was, "Commissioner, I talk to the inmates. I don't just order them around. I will first ask them to do something. I will then request for them to do something, and then when that doesn't work, I give them a direct order to do what I asked of them."

He seemed to be pleased with my answer. E-1 dorm was always clean from top to bottom. The inmates' cubes were always nice and neat. The inmates' bathroom and shower area stayed sparkling clean by jail standards. There was a small slap of white stone marble that separated the shower room floor from the day room floor, and that was the cleanest, whitest piece of white marble you would ever see. It was scrubbed daily with a scrub brush or toothbrush. The toothbrush scrubbing would be done by an inmate that had received a work detail for breaking a rule. This could be a facility rule or a rule out of the inmates' standard statewide rule book. Either way in the early nineties, there was a procedure in place. If an inmate broke a rule that was considered minor, he would have the option to volunteer for a work detail or receive a sanction such as loss of recreation time or loss of packages at that time. Most of the inmates, not all, would opt for the work detail. The work would be cleaning something usually, which all the young inmates knew. You didn't want a work detail with Officer Brown because you were going to do just that work.

After the commissioners' tour was completed, in the days following, I started getting dirty looks from my peers and higher-ups. There were phone calls on the unit with no one saying anything, my admitted supervisor now had a problem with the way I did my job. You see what had happened was by no intention of my doing a new standard was set for what the other dorms should look like at Cayuga correctional facility in the commissioner's eyes, and I was to blame for it. The administration was put under pressure by Albany higher-ups and my fellow officers were now being pressured by the administration to clean up the dorms. Hey, it wasn't my fault that others didn't take pride in the job and work areas, and the administration was well aware of the condition of the dorms, the reason being they periodically made round on them. As they made an attempt to get the dorms up to the commissioner's standard, I continued coming to work and doing my job—care, custody, and control of the inmates I was in charge of. I would now be subjected to my real first taste of discrimination, harassment, and retaliation for no more than doing my job...or you can say doing my job just a little too good for some's liking. They had already been taunting me before the commissioner's arrival by subjecting me to racist jokes and referring to me as *boy*, none of which ever occurred until the exodus of the other minority officers. To really understand prison, you really had to work in one. There is no other job on the planet Earth like being a correctional officer.

Being black definitely has its advantages when it comes to the inmates. For me, going to work in that dorm-type setting was literally like back in the days, going to the neighborhood community center with exceptions. All were convicted felons, and we were in a prison-type setting, and I was in charge. Being a correctional officer, I always said it was 99 percent communication skills, so with that in mind, I was able to effectively perform my duties as a correctional officer. To stop my ability to successfully carry out my duties, the other staff along with the administration would move inmates off the dorm I was in charge of and replace them with inmates that were problem inmates in the hope they would come on to the dorm and start problems. Now these same troublemaking inmates that they, my fellow officers, were having problems with came to the dorm I was working in, and in less than a week, the inmate was cleaning his cube, helping to keep the dorm clean and, most importantly, not causing any problems. I would observe how some of my fellow officers would speak to the inmates. It would be just outright disrespectful. A man is still a man. The staff would speak to the inmates like they were subzero, less than human—hell, like slave and master. That is why the majority of the staff couldn't get the inmates to do anything more than what they had to do. Now if you want a man to work and give it his all and more, show him some respect and talk to him like he is a man. That's how I would get the inmates to cooperate and keep the dorm clean and have minimal problems on the dorm. Staff would sometime add fuel to the fire with just the way they talked to the inmates. I would watch as a young twentysomething officer would speak to inmates twice their age like they were little kids for the simplest things just because they could. When the effort to disrupt and cause problems by sending the troublesome inmates to the dorm didn't work, the staff at the facility started harassing me more and more each day.

One of the officers in the car pool who was working the front gate area where you entered and exited the facility decided one day to ask me and only me to show ID to exit the gate area and while he was demanding to see my ID and no one else's, he was laughing and mumbling behind the thick bullet-proof glass. I didn't get a chance to see him after work, but the next morning, I saw him at the carpool area and asked him what the hell was that about yesterday when I was trying to exit the facility. Now remember I'm the only African American in the carpool and facility, so when I asked him, he became belligerent and stated talking to me like I was one of the inmates at the facility, which in no way in hell I was accepting. This was the same guy who unhooked his odometer on his cars. So he and the other carpoolers decided I could no longer carpool. Little did they know it had always been a clear understanding to me that they really didn't want me around at all, so from that day forward, I drove every day to work. Their plan was that I would lose my job having to drive every day.

Approximately one month later, my wife and I brought a new small compact car that was great on gas, so the carpool idea fell apart on them. The racial harassment and the discrimination persistent at the facility by the administration and staff were all over me. Being the only African American officer at the facility, I had a good working relationship with my peers until I myself became the target of unwelcome verbal and racial harassment and discrimination. Now here I am, working at an all-white prison located deep in the sticks in Moravia, New York. While working there, I never saw any other minorities in the town, in the stores, or just out and about. Only the inmates at the prison, truth be told. I had no problem being the only one. Remember, my upbringing had equipped me for that. I had gone to an all-white Catholic high school while living in the lower income part of town. I can't call it the slums because in the country or rural areas you don't have large slum areas like you see in the big cities, so growing up struggling to live also comes with its advantages. One, you tend to appreciate things more in life as you climb the economic ladder, such as a job. As my fellow officers and the administration set out on a mission to have me fired or make me lose my job by subjecting me to their unwanted daily harassment and discrimination, I set out on a mission to do everything to keep my job as a correctional officer. I would go to work, and my peers would watch me more closely than they would watch the inmates. And me—I was watching everything that was going on. It seemed to be the mind-set of the majority of the white officers. It was all right to harass me along with the administration and others. They would harass me daily. If it wasn't a verbal threat, it would be a physical threat of harm to force me to quit my job. When they weren't threatening me, they would give me the silent treatment, which I loved, not hearing all the stupid stuff that came out of some of their mouths. Their talk would be mostly of hate-filled anger toward the inmates, and at no time would they stop and think that the inmates were the reason that their stupid asses had a job.

You see, the white officers didn't believe that having a good state job with benefits is a privilege. They saw it as their God-given right, something owed to them, or something willed down to them. Some even had the attitude that the only place for minorities in the Department of Corrections was behind bars, wearing greens as an inmate, when many of them should have been locked up. Don't get it wrong or twisted—you had some outstanding officers in the department who would go above and behind the line of duty to perform their jobs, but one thing that the majority of them would not do was tell on another correctional officer who had done wrong. They would go as far as to lie to protect one another, but what they were really protecting was a culture and outdated ideologue of what they perceived to be their right to keep and hold on to old traditions and their time-honored right to the job of being a New York state correctional officer. You had a lot of guys whose fathers were correctional officers or guards back in the days. Hell, in the upstate prisons, they are run by families who have multiple family members employed at the facilities as officers, civilians and higher-ups, both in the facility and in Albany and were protected by an out-of-control union that seems to have more power than the people in charge in Albany, our state government, that is supposed to be in charge of the Department of Corrections. The union would bend over backward to protect my harassers. The union and some of the higher-ups literally gave those harassing me their blessings to do so, you know, carte blanche—do as you wish. My harassers would act as if the prison was their personal playground or personal land of which they themselves were the owners and I surely had no right to be there. Some of the staff would run around and act as if they had no home training or had never been shown right from wrong. They would talk to the inmates like a slave master would talk to their slaves, belittling grown-ass men for the most trivial shit sometimes, just because, and other times to get a rise out of the inmate. Or you would have an officer or even a higher-up in uniform yelling and scramming at an inmate about his attire, which was state greens, the uniform the inmates wore, and this same staff member doing the complaining, his uniform looked like he had pulled it from the bottom of the dirty clothing hamper. Most of the staff, with the exception of a few, would come to work with dirty, stained uniforms looking like they worked in a factory or grease pit, which was all acceptable. Their light-blue shirts would be dingy with stains. Their white T-shirt would be either a gray, brown, or pissy yellow or would have writing on it which you could see through the light-blue shirt. Their dark-blue pants which required tailoring would be just cut off at the bottom with fringes hanging and dirty. The pants were nicknamed Tom Sawyers. I would observe an officer in this state tell an inmate to clean his act up. The sad part about that was these officers were allowed to come to work in this state.

A lineup was held at the beginning of every shift and an inspection of each officer and his uniform, which in my twenty-eight years never happened. Instead, the lieutenant at these upstate prisons would use the lineup as their personal improv or comedy club. Fitness for duty and professionalism was low on the list. Instead, the lieutenant or whomever would laugh about assaults or altercations the inmates may have gotten into. If there was a cutting, they would laugh about the number of stitches an inmate may have received or how badly the inmate had been beaten. While still working at the Cayuga correctional facility, I continued to be harassed by my fellow officers and the brass. *Brass* is a sergeant or above in uniform at the facility up to the. First dep dep of security and so forth; the facility administration includes the superintendent, deps of administrational facility programs, etc. At upstate facilities, these were usually all white males who usually moved up the ranks by family connections or some other form of connection. I found out during my twenty-eight years that test taking was a small part of moving up the ranks. It is more of whom you know and if you're willing to play along to get along—in other words, if you were the type of person who could easily turn your head to wrongdoing, you could go far in the Department of Corrections. And I can say that because I have seen and experienced this firsthand.

While being harassed at the Cayuga CF, I was forced to make my complains of the harassment to a hostile administration—in other words, I was forced to complain to the same people that were harassing me. The officers and the administration were hell bent on getting my job, and I was serious and hell bent on protecting my rights and keeping my job. I was harassed verbally and subjected to differential treatment by not only my fellow officers but by those in charge. My immediate supervisor, who was a young sergeant, was from the area, along with the majority of the jail; they were homeboys those who lived in the immediate area, which was the Cayuga and Auburn area. Many of the correctional officers had previously worked at the Auburn Correctional Facility, as well as many members of the administration. To understand a prison in any area, you have to look at the mind-set of those in charge, and the people that worked in these facilities located in rural upstate New York towns. They were usually white males, uneducated, and had been raised or brought up around people that only looked like them, resulting in a narrow-minded way of thanking, and top that with no common sense. Then you put them in charge of a jail full of minority inmates, mostly African American and Hispanic inmates, and you have a problem. And those in charge saw the inmates as property of the state, just like in the slave days, when the slaves were property of the slave owner.

Prison is more or less modern-day slavery, where the guards are the slave masters or slave drivers and the inmates the slaves. It's a slave-master type of atmosphere. A lot of the inmates see the African American officers as house n———s. Back during the slave era, this referred to the slaves that were handpicked to work in the master's house to attend to his needs. The white officers would stick together no matter what because each other was all they had. If one lied, the other one would back the lie up, and they would be backed by a union and an administration who also had that same ideology as them, whether it was right or wrong. They would put themselves in a box with no opening to escape. I would watch as the white officers would put pressure on each other to do and say things that they knew was wrong but refusing to go along. Would get them ostracized from the rest. This is achieved by the threat of being called a rat if you didn't play along with the wrongdoers. So in essence, they controlled each other.

The majority of the African American officers I worked with were their own person and did their job, but I also worked with some that would play along to get along. After the exodus of the African American officers at Cayuga CF, it reminded me of a scene on *National Geographic* of the caribou being chased by a pack of hunger lions that had manage to separate one from the pack and chase him down, only this time I was going to make sure that the pack went away hungry and mad. They continued to harass me at Cayuga. My admitted supervisor would lie about me and write me up, and I would report him to the administration, and they would cover it up. At one point, he became so addicted to me. One day, on his day off, he waited down the road when I got off work. He was in hiding and chased me down a narrow winding wooded road and attempted to run me off the road. I stopped a couple of times and motioned for him to get out of his vehicle, which the coward refused to do. You see the cowards are only tough when they are with buddies at work. Now remember, the Cayuga Correctional Facility is all white and the town is all white, but if the sergeant would have gotten out his vehicle, I would have beaten him all the way back to the facility. He continued to follow me until I was out of the wooded area and on a main road. You see, the road he chased me down was littered with deep drop-offs, and if a car were to go off the road, it would tip over. The sergeant didn't want to fight by showing his refusal to exit his vehicle in the woods; his desire was to kill me.

Immediately following the incident, the African American commissioner in Albany gave me permission to carry my off-duty weapon to work and check it in and out of the facility arsenal upon arriving and leaving the facility. I remember the first day I carried my weapon to work. As I arrived, the entire shift of officers was waiting in the lobby to observe me as I checked my personal weapon into the arsenal. It was really unheard of for upstate officers to carry a weapon to work like the officers in the down state jails Sing Sing and others—the threat to my life was real. You would really have to be uneducated and have no common sense if you thought I was going to be harassed by a prison full of racist, out-of-control guards and do nothing to protect myself, so I informed those ultimately in charge of the department, and inform I did.

The atmosphere in these upstate prisons is like high school. Some can't be trusted with too much responsibility; it's like a college frat house where one parties all the time with a carefree lifestyle. The sad part about it is it's not just the lower echelon, but the higher-ups were the same. It's like the coyotes being allowed to watch the hen-house while the wolves look on to guide them. That's as simple as you can put it. An out-of-control atmosphere where all wrongdoing is covered up with a lie and backed up by higher-ups and those in charge. I will be the first to tell you your loyalty should be to your employer. As long as your morals and your good faith are not on the table for an offering for acceptance into their exclusive club. So yes, your acceptance comes with a lot of strings attached, such as your willingness to lie, your willingness to back other officers even though you know what they have done is wrong. And your willingness to look the other way.

Our uniform state-issued shirt even has a patch on it with the state crest with the word *Excelsior* on it, which means "of superior quality." Also, the department says it follows the military uniform detail and some of its traditions. The department only uses this statement in court and other proceedings it stands in front of to give the illusion that it is buttoned down and standing tall. They can literally say anything they want because the truth is shielded from the public with a closed-door policy and by tightly monitoring the media with lies.

Before I continue let me say that all that I express here in this book is the truth. If anyone doubts me, I'm willing to take a polygraph, voice stress test, or any other lie-catching technology. The United States prison system is a billion-dollar industry that uses human beings as commodities as a means of profit, taking full advantage of its poor and minority citizens by warehousing them and keeping them in the prison system to maximize the full worth of their incarceration. The longer the stay, the more money for the system. As I continued to wait, the wheels of justice turned to address a problem not started by me but by the intolerable system which denied me the right to be free of harassment for no other reason than the color of my skin. And the retaliatory action by those in charge allowing my peers to harass and threaten me with the hopes of attempting to silence my cry for justice. They say the wheels of justice turn slow, but the wheels grind fine. I didn't have anyone at the Cayuga CF standing along my side. It was truly a David and Goliath fight, and at times, it seemed like it was me against the world. The harassment and retaliation continued for years.

One winter, we had a major snowstorm in the area. Approximately a foot and a half or more. By the time it was over, when it became time to leave work for the day. As I exited my post, I climbed through the snow for the walk up front. I noticed everyone was huddled in the front lobby. The commuters, the ones that were carpooling and driving a distance back and forth to work, were being told they would have to stay the night at the facility, me included. No one could order me to stay, and with that in mind, I exited the front door and searched the parking lot for my vehicle. Once I found it, I unburied it. While doing so, the many faces of those huddled in the lobby were smashed against the large lobby window to observe me. As I set off down the road, some of those who were in the lobby came out to watch me leave the parking lot for the main road. As I started my journey home with the snow almost covering the tires on my small compact car, I said a prayer. It usually took an hour and twenty minutes from the jail to my doorstep. As I drove down the snow-covered back roads, which were more than treacherous, I made it to the snow-covered main roads. I continued driving. I counted only two other cars on the drive home, which took me only forty-five minutes longer, and ironically, my vehicle got stuck in the snow in the large apartment parking lot where we lived. Thank God, I call that truly riding on a prayer. There was no way in hell I was staying the night at the Cayuga CF where my harassers were.

Driving alone came with privileges, such as not depending on others, and no one make a decision like "Shall we stay or shall we go or riding with an intoxicated driver?" I remember one guy during my carpool days on the 3–11 shift. He would stop and get a twelve-pack of beer and offer the three riders a beer, and by time we got to the carpool drop off, he would consume the remainder of the beer by himself. Talk about dangerous, and you have to remember the ride was only an hour and twenty minutes. He wasn't the only one—you would also go to work and smell booze on officers all the time with no one in charge doing anything about it. Remember, the sergeants and lieutenants who were immediate supervisors were cut from the same cloth. And the ones that weren't were too scared to stand up and do their jobs for fear of being labeled a rat for turning in one of their own, so you see, that's how the wrongdoing is allowed to continue.

After being harassed and threatened over and over again, I continued to report this treatment to upper management. That would be Albany, one of the deputy commissioners. He gave me his direct number to his office, and I would call him periodically to inform him of the persistent problems. The administration didn't take kindly to my access to the commissioner, and neither did the facility phone operator from the way she would respond to my request. From the unit I was posted on, I would pick up the phone, dial the operator by pushing 0, and ask her to get me the commissioner's office. At which time her attitude would be rude and obnoxious to my request by yelling in my ear. You have to remember these people that worked at the facility were all connected to each other—if not by blood, by their hatred for me or their loyalty to each other. After the operator on duty did what she didn't want to do and I was connected, I would inform the commissioner of the behavior I was being subjected to. He would listen and ensure me he was working on a fix, but this would only put them at bay and put their bloodthirsty cravings on hold. The constant harassment was being done with the hope I would respond physically by hitting one of them. When they first started harassing and threatening me, I knew that their goal was to get me to assault one of them so I would be fired, so with that in mind, I knew this would have to be a nonviolent protest, and besides, my goal was to keep my job. You know what, they say the pen is mightier than the sword or, in this case, the mouth.

As I patiently waited for my transfer out of Cayuga, it started to look like there was no end in sight. I thank God for my wife, my family, and my friends who supported me and encouraged me to keep up the good fight for justice. I eventually was forced to seek legal counsel, which became a daunting task. Even the law offices in the area weren't interested in helping me seek justice. One thing I quickly learned I was in a web, and these law firms in the area were not about to help me in filing a lawsuit against the New York State Department of Corrections. They basically shooed me off. You would think after a lawyer passes the bar and takes an oath, they would be willing to help those seeking justice. I'll be the first to tell you that's not the case. Upstate New York has a biased, racist element to it. The justice system in the area helps to protect and shield those who perpetrate discrimination and hate. You have to remember these jobs in law in enforcement are inherently given to white males and it would almost seem that these jobs are willed to their offspring. In these prisons in upstate new York, there are families that have generations of family ties to these facilities, especially the older facilities like Auburn, Elmira, Attica, and Clinton. All these jails are ran by families that have been allowed to deeply imbed their heels into these facilities for years, from the administration to the correctional officers and civilian jobs, and they control who is allowed to work in these facilities—and the reason for this? It's so the old ways of doing what they want or running the jail in the manner that they wish is kept alive, passing down the old, traditional ways of doing things. So by only hiring family and friends, the chances are less likely that they will be exposed for wrongdoing by an outsider that will witness their out-of-control behavior. In my twenty-eight years of service, I witnessed these over and over—that is why the same problems persist. The newer facilities are like this—the workers who get the civilian jobs are usually family and friends, and the security staff is a mix of old and young officers and the same with the brass such as the sergeants, lieutenants, captains, and deps. The younger staff are trained by the older officers who have adopted the ways of the old guard or traditions that have caused chaos and confusion in the department for years. And they are protected by higher-ups that have been given jobs at the top of the Department of Corrections through nepotism, which is alive and well. This is one of the biggest problems—the department has systemic nepotism that has been allowed to go unchecked for decades, allowing these upstate jails to be ran like an independent company or plantation where the only people allowed to be employed are their own.

Case in point—how is it that all the state-run maximum security prisons are all run differently with respect to rules and each one is allowed to implement their own policies and procedures? The inmates, upon entering the New York state Department of Corrections, are issued the same rule book in every state-run facility, but each superintendent is allowed to run the facility as he sees fit. Look at Attica CF. Here it is 2018, and the inmates incarcerated there are still paying for the Attica Riot with unfair treatment, what any reasonable person would see as cruel and unusual punishment. I have to emphasize *reasonable* because the staff there are direct descendants of some of the staff that worked at Attica during the 1971 uprising. Approximately forty-seven years ago, I believe at present there are one or two African American officers employed there, but the remainder of the six hundred plus security staff is white, with an inmate population of mostly African American or Hispanic inmates. What do you think goes on? In fact, the only reason I or any other minority was even allowed to work in the system was a direct effect of the Attica Riot. Right before I retired in 2017, an inmate there viciously and brutally attacked. The photos taken of the inmate looked like he had been run over by a bus, and the staff lied and covered up the assault that took place at their hands, and the racist union helped them in doing so.

Why can I say the union is racist? Because during my twenty-eight years of service, I had more than my share of dealing with the union and they have always protected the white or Caucasian officers, shielding them from prosecution. You really have to wonder who is in charge of the Department of Corrections. Is it our state officials or is it the racist union? Because all I have seen and experienced over the many years of working in the prison system, the union has more power and say over what goes on. Now this is from my observation and opinion. I think the state more or less gave the department over to the union years ago giving them the power to do as they wish and running the department as they wished, freeing up the state from the responsibility of doing it themselves. Once again, the coyotes are overseeing the wolves watching the henhouse.

As I waited for my transfer out of Cayuga CF to either Elmira CF or Southport CF a new superintendent arrived. For some reason unknown to me, he summoned me to report to his office. Shortly after his arrival, once there, he introduced himself as the superintendent and then more or less attempted to threaten and intimidate me. I ensured him I wasn't threatened by him, and I was going to continue to report to Albany and him the harassment and discrimination I was being subjected to.

Shortly after my introduction to the new superintendent, the facility was experiencing a drug problem. One of the older inmates on the dorm I was regularly assigned to came to me and said he was having problems with the younger inmates who were using drugs. At least that is what he told me, so I asked him if he knew who was getting the drugs into the facility, and he said he knew one of the heavy hitters. Remember I'm street smart, so my first instinct was to think if it was the inmate he owed money to and couldn't pay, so I took the information to a lieutenant that I had a good working relationship with. He then asked me if I thought I could get the inmate to make a buy from the inmate selling the drugs. The drug in question was cocaine. I did what the lieutenant had requested of me and spoke to the inmate, and he said he would be willing to make the request for drugs from the inmate selling. The lieutenant then took this information to his boss, the captain. For the inmate's corporation, the lieutenant paid the inmate with cigarettes and ensured me I would get a letter of accommodation in my file.

Approximately two weeks later, a large bust took place at the facility, which netted an ounce or more of cocaine. After it was all said and done, I never got that letter of accommodation, and the captain took all the credit for the bust. This same captain was also involved in the harassment that I was being constantly subjected to. The inmate who had made it all possible asked me if I received a letter of accommodation, and I told him no. He then went on to say that he had only done this because of me. A week or so went by, and I once again had to call the commissioner regarding the treatment I was being subjected to at the facility, and I informed him about the captain's hijacking of my efforts to rid the jail of drugs.

Days later, as I was leaving for the day, I observed the captain moving boxes from his office to his personal vehicle. The captain was sent back to the Auburn CF, where he came from originally. There is and has always been a drug problem in the prison system, and it's a known fact that all the drugs aren't brought in by just the visitors there. I remember one incident while working my regular job post, which was E-1 dorm, one of the troubled inmates from another dorm moved in. I received a call from the area sergeant, he ordered me to strip-frisk the inmate because he was being suspected of having drugs on him. Once the inmate was in the dorm, I ordered him to come with me, and I escorted him to the laundry room, which was used for strip-frisking inmates when the need arose. Once at the door area of the laundry room, the inmate took off running back toward the dorm. Once in the dorm, he proceeded to run around the dorm with me in pursuit. Before I started the pursuit, I notified the facility arsenal by calling on my radio officer, "Brown, E-1 dorm in pursuit of inmate in dorm area." Then I and the inmate ran around and around in the large dorm area with me yelling for him to stop. If it wasn't for the fact that he had drugs on him, I would have just watched until help arrived. As we ran around and around, he bent down and attempted to throw the drugs under one of the cubicles in the dorm, which I reached down, secured, and told him, "Like I just didn't see you do that." It was almost comical because the inmate had nowhere to go but around and around the dorm area. After help arrived, he was taken off the dorm. Even the inmates in the dorm laughed. The inmate was charged with possession of marijuana.

In 1996, I was finally transferred to Southport Correctional Facility located in the Elmira area by high-ups in Albany. Southport is a maxi, max or supermax where inmates with disciplinary problems are housed. The inmates are locked down in their cells for twenty-three hours a day and let out for a one-hour rec period. Their rec is in a large blacktop-paved area with a number of steel cages where they are locked in. Each cage holds one inmate. These cages are side by side in what is called the rec yard. There were a few—and I mean few—other African Americans at the facility. I remember the first day I reported to the facility for duty. It was a cold and unwelcoming atmosphere. One would had needed a winter coat to chase the cold away. One of the few African Americans was my uncle, who had over twenty-five-plus years on the job. He was one of the more senior officers. He was actually the reason I chose to go into corrections. I remember growing up and watching my uncle. I thought he worked for the FBI because of the many uniforms he wore. He was a correctional officer in the early seventies. He quit and became a capital security guard, quit that, became a mailman, quit that, and ultimately went back to being a New York state correctional officer. Yes, my uncle wore many hats in his time. He was afforded many opportunities. As I arrived at Southport where my uncle was at, I never had that opportunity to work alongside him. He had one of the transportation jobs, although I would see him and his partner in passing, and what a pair they were. They were like an old married couple by the way they spoke to each other, and you could tell they had a lot of respect for one another. At Southport, I was allowed to work the day shift for approximately two weeks. My uncle gave me the heads-up about who was who and who to look out for, and he also let some of the main players know that I was his nephew. You know, in other words, "Don't mess with my people." As I got accustomed with my new surroundings and received the cold shoulder treatment by the Caucasian officers who tried to put me in a corner, which I wasn't having. I continued to get to know the facility. The minority officers, which included the Caucasian female officers, welcomed me and showed me what was what and explained the operational function of the facility, while the others harbored their ignorant, self-serving, uneducated feelings about me, which preceded my arrival. You see, the state had what is called the grapevine before the internet era. The grapevine for the state went from one end of the state to the other, and news and rumors were spread by word of mouth as officers traveled from one end to the other, either by officers going from jail to jail dropping off or picking up inmates or officers traveling back and forth to work and home. One thing correctional officers do a lot of is talk. You have to remember, the majority of these officers' obligation is to each other, not their employer, the Department of Corrections. So they only followed each other, and the leader was usually the officer harboring the most racist tendency along with out-of-control behavior that the rest of the uneducated officers follow. Some of the followers are unable to make their own decisions and think for themselves. Others felt peer pressure, and some don't want to be ostracized. From my upbringing and good faith-based knowledge, if you allow any person to think for you, that person is living your life for you. For example, if one of these officers had a problem with an inmate, everyone else was supposed to have a problem with him. It might have been just a personality clash between those two individuals, but these guys saw it as a way to cause chaos and confusion as they set a trap for that individual inmate they had chosen as a mark or target to harass to no end. From my upbringing, no one will ever tell me how to treat another person, and I could care less who you are or what your status is in life. My thoughts, my feelings, are just that—mine and mine alone. Also, my integrity and obligation was to my employer, not to the idiots running around causing problems.

Prison is truly a beast of its own. Most of society sees prison as a cesspool full of undesirable citizens who have broken the law, which has put them in their current situation, when one really has to step back and look at the whole situation, and while you're looking, remember one thing that no man or woman is exempted from prison. We are all just one bad decision from incarceration, and black and brown people have a higher chance of being incarcerated than any other race in the United States of America, and that is a well-known fact. The inmates have categories: there is the guilty, the innocent, those that border on the line of guilt and innocence, and those who more than desire to be incarcerated—murders, rapists, along with child molesters, who make up those that society sees as the most undesirable individuals. In prison, it's hard for most correctional officers to look past an inmate's crime. To be able to successfully perform your duties as a correctional officer, you have to try to look past that undesirable individual and remember you are only here for care, custody, and control. As a correctional officer, we aren't the judge, jury, or executioner, but the majority of the officers run around the facilities, calling other staff members, seeking out information on an inmate's charge to ultimately use as justification to deny an inmate what the state has given him during his incarceration or to harass and intimidate the inmate because of his crime. That is why I would try not to know an inmate's criminal history during my career with the exception of an inmate working in an area where civilian female staff was working, and I was responsible for that area. Other than that, an inmate was an inmate, and my main mission was care, custody, and control, and all inmates were treated fairly, firmly, and consistently so as to not jeopardize my integrity and my responsibility to my employer. Even though I would do this, other officers would make it their business to share the information they had obtained on a particular inmate, which was then usually shouted out by that officer, telling of some savage, unthinkable, horrific crime that the inmate had committed. And after hearing of this, it would turn even the most even toned person's attitude into a sour note. And then, when having to deal with that particular inmate that the officer had exposed, a bitter note would ring out and ill feelings would usually surface in many of the officers. One only has to be alive to know of the horrific crimes that are committed in today's society and all that goes on. After being home and working at the Southport correctional facility for a couple of mouths, the state decided it would not go to court with me and opted for an out-of-court settlement for the harassment that had occured at the Cayuga CF. The settlement was the state's ideal and was negotiated through a local attorney that I had. I really wanted my day in court so that the citizens of New York would hear what really goes on inside these correctional facilities, but that would never happen with a lawyer looking for a quick buck, and the state, looking to keep the harassment quiet, they made a settlement offer. And taking my lawyer's advice, I took the settlement.

While working at Southport. There weren't a lot of jobs to get assigned to. The majority of the jobs were what you call rec, short for recreational jobs, which were the officers that took the inmates out of their cells for the one-hour recreational period. The rec pin, were literally called dog runs. The cages were built just like a dog pin or run you would find at your local animal shelter or someone's backyard. Soon after entering the Department of Corrections in 1988, the Southport correctional facility opened up. Shortly after its opening as a maximum-security prison, it operated as a functional max prison, meaning it had programs and jobs for the inmates within. Soon after, the programs stopped, and it was announced that the facility was stopping its operations as a regular function facility and instead was going to operate as a SHU facility, which stands for "special housing unit." You know, some call it the box, the hole, a twenty-three-hour-a-day lockdown. Soon after the facility was converted into a SHU facility, a riot broke out where staff were taken hostage, and some of the staff members were assaulted. Sections of the jail were taken over by the inmates, and the inmates held hostage as they tried to negotiate with Albany. The inmates were complaining about the treatment they received from the guards, and the officers were complaining about the understaffing at the facility. During the time of the riot, I was still working at Cayuga Correctional Facility, but I lived in Elmira, New York, just minutes from the Southport correctional facility. During a conversation with a commissioner, he asked me what I thought went wrong at the Southport Correctional Facility, and my response was, "If you put a dog in a cage and poke a stick at him all day, what do you think he is going to do when he gets lose?"

Now Southport Correctional Facility is the belly of the beast, a facility wherein as you ride up to the jail, you can feel the tension. The inmates housed there were inmates with disciplinary problems such as assault on staff or another inmate, weapons charges gang activity, drugs, or a host of other violations they may have committed at other facilities. So you have the worst of the worst that are in the system, and majority of them were African Americans or Hispanics, housed all together in one place, and then you have a workforce of 95 percent white males, some of whom had never had any interaction or dealt with anyone other than their own race. What would one think the outcome would be? It is an easy assumption to make that problems of all sorts would arise, and they did and do. One of the main reasons for a lot of the problems in the upstate prison system is the lack of diversity and nepotism, which is allowed to persistently exist within the system, something that has been known for years and never addressed. While at Southport working, I was ultimately placed on the midnight or 11:00 p.m. to 7:00 a.m. tour so as to be out of the way. Most of the interaction with the inmates took place on the day shift or the 7:00 a.m. to 3:00 p.m. I had never worked midnights while employed with the department, so it was something new. I was informed by a supervisor the midnight shift was laid back, and I did find this to be the case. In fact, it was so laid back the officers would get undressed out of their state-issued uniform. —yes, the uniform. The state issued to us to do our jobs to sleep in their makeshift bedding, this bedding included and wasn't limited to state property such as new sheets and blankets out of the facility supply or even a state mattress. Some even brought items from home to make their rest more comfortable then it already was. They would make their sleeping quarters underneath the control counsel in the bubble or control room, which was in each block and manned by any officer.

Seeing I was a man with low seniority working on the night shift, I was assigned a roundsman's job which was making rounds to the block areas in the bubbles and galleries where the inmates were at sometimes. The shift would start with a 10:45 p.m. lineup or roll call. After lineup, we would report to our post and relieve the 3–11 officers. Shortly after the relief was made, a round was made and paperwork was filled out for the count, and the fake fire and a safety report was done and a little idle chitchat, and after the first count was in, it was lights out by twelve o'clock—the Southport CF was fast asleep. When I made rounds to the block areas, I was greeted by a weak correctional officer, some of them dressed or half dressed, T-shirts and underwear. When I entered the bubble, I would observe their sleeping accommodations. You could tell by their bedding if they had been doing this for a while. The guys with time had the more comfortable-looking bedding. When I had to work in a bubble with one of the sleeping dead, I would stay up reading or listening to the radio. While they slept, I would occasionally catch them looking at me out the corner of their eye. Because I wasn't asleep at one point, they thought I was IG, the investigation unit for the department. I remember my uncle stopping me in passing one morning, and he said, "Hey. Curt the lieutenant stopped me and said he wanted to talk to me about you." He said the lieutenant, the night shift watch commander, had told my uncle, "Hey, I like your nephew. He's the only one around here awake at night." My uncle said he laughed and told him he would let me know I would never close my eyes in a prison. It was truly amazing to observe what acceptable behavior by the department was. Now you have to remember Southport. The inmates were in their cells for twenty-three hours a day so you could make a round at 3:00 a.m. and walk past many of the cells in the block where inmates were wide awake because they had slept all day. Also, that twenty-three-hour idle time for a lot of the inmates was just time to plot their next move. The officers would teach the inmates that they didn't like or care for by withholding food supplies, soap, toilet paper, and most of all, writing paper. The inmates used to write up the harassing staff. Some of the inmates that didn't care would taunt the staff by yelling obscenities at them some would even throw feces at staff. I say some didn't care because after the harassing of staff or the throwing of feces, the inmate knew he was going to get a beat down from staff, but some inmates couldn't care less about a beatdown and had the attitude of "Bring it on," so you have the officers going after the inmates and the inmates going after the officers. This would play out day after day. It was like a state of perpetual evilness bordering on the line of anarchy. Even though there were rules in place for staff, they would be broken at a whim to justify some sort of retaliation against an inmate who had wronged them and would be covered up by the masses to show their support for fellow staff at any cost. I say this because it wasn't just the security staff that would have issues with the inmates it would also be the civilians such as councilors, medical personnel, or any other non-uniformed employee. For example, a counselor could be on rounds seeing the inmates on their caseload, and either the inmate would ask the councilor to do their job as far as providing them with paperwork or seeking information from the councilor, and the councilor seeking a signature from the inmate on some state form the councilor would need to turn in, and just from that interaction, it could all go sideways with the inmate and councilor, turning it into a shouting match with the inmate ending up getting the short end of the stick. Same thing with medical—the medical staff would be on rounds, and the inmates would be seeking medical attention, and the inmate and the nurse would have issues or the escorting officer would chime in and insert his dislike for the inmate and help prevent the inmate from being seen by medical, that's when they would lose it with the inmate writing up the nurse or officer and the nurse or officer writing up the inmate. A lot of the staff members are very invested in one another though marriage or family, friends, or socially, to the point of if one has a problem with a particular inmate, they all have a problem with him. There would be orders put out in the blocks by staff members who had a problem with a particular inmate. "He is on the burn" meant no staff was to help the inmate, and the inmate was denied his recreation, chow, and any other state right he may be entitled to. This

50

would play out over and over through the years. Southport was a facility with a lot of downtime. The only interaction the officers had with the inmates was during the one-hour recreation and when the chow is served and the limited showers, this gave correctional officers a lot of downtime. They had too much time on their hands to think of bullshit to do to continue the constant chaos and confusion, just as the inmates do when all they have is time on their hands. You see, the inmates have an agenda, and so do the officers. Most of the inmates want what the state department of corrections has entitled them to, or some try to run a game of manipulation while they are incarcerated, and most of the officers have the attitude or belief that the inmates deserve nothing during their stay. So with this in mind, you can just imagine the day-to-day problems that this creates with the officers and the inmates.

After approximately nine months or so, I was transferred to the Elmira CF, a.k.a. the Hill. I had previously worked on the Hill during my OJT, on-the-job training, approximately eight years ago. Yes, it took eight years of up and down the states' vast highway system to finally make it to the facility that I had number 1 on my transfer list. By the time I made it back to Elmira, I was a very well-seasoned officer once again. Just as the Southport Correctional facility, I was welcomed with cold shoulders and threatening glares by not only my peers but also by the supervisor staff and the administrational personnel. It was hard to find a friendly face. The facility houses approximately 1,700 inmates with a security staff of approximately 480 correctional officers with the majority of those officers being white. Out of 480 officers, there were five African American officers, and the majority of the inmates were African American or Hispanic, just as the majority of all the upstate prisons. They were run by a majority of white staff and controlled by families that have been allowed to deeply in bed themselves into these upstate prisons. These family members held positions as high as superintendents all the way down to the lower position in these facilities. Job vacancies are quickly filed with family and friends, and this is done to keep control of the narrative and control these facilities that they run. The atmosphere at these facilities can only be described as indescribable—an atmosphere that one would truly have to experience themselves to even begin to imagine what goes on behind those walls, fences, and bars, The prison system in whole is no more than the equivalent of modern-day slavery. The days of slavery, you have to remember, ended with mass numbers of African American men and boys being denied their freedom by being incarcerated in Americans' new form of slavery known today as are modern-day prison system. Elmira CF is truly one of those prisons that have evolved out of the days of slavery. Before the Elmira CF, there was a place called Hellmira—it was a civil war prison camp, so yes, Elmira was cast directly out of the flames of the civil war in 1864. The civil war prison camp in Elmira, New York, a.k.a. Hellmira, opened up. It took in some twelve thousand prisoners of war. It was ultimately given the name Hellmira for the fact that many of the prisoners died from the harsh conditions such as lack of medical treatment, food, shelter, clothing, sanitation, all of which were contributing factors in the high death toll of the confederate soldiers imprisoned.

Some twelve years later, during the reconstruction years of the United States, during its rebuilding and healing years. In 1876, the Elmira Reformatory was opened, the first of its kind, and would become a model for prisons throughout the country. Reform of the criminal was the goal of the day. Many of the other states adopted the standers and teachings of the Elmira Reformatory. The facility name was changed to the Elmira Correctional and Reception Center in 1970. To date, many of the locals or people who knew of the prison referred to simply as the Hill. Although my reception was cold, I navigated my way through the thick, foggy layer of hate, animosity, anger, and ignorance that filled the Elmira CF. The one thing I had going for me was I was from Elmira. Some of the people that worked at the facility I had grown up with or went to school with at one of the local high schools. The point that most correctional officers or law enforcement personnel failed to understand was that this was a job. It's not a family—it's not a way of life—with the exception of providing you and your family with an income. It's not an inclusive club where those that worked in the club decided another man's or woman's entrance to the club. It was a job. A lot of the officers didn't have this viewpoint. A lot of them had the attitude that the facility was theirs. It was willed down to them or the state wasn't doing them a favor by employing them. They were doing the state a favor by working there. And they do as they please and backed by a heavily membered union with more power than the state department of corrections. Its self—yes, the union seemed to be running the department. I was told of stories of the racial problems that existed on the hill. I had heard stories of African American officers being harassed verbally by the Caucasian officers. There were a few local African American officers working at the facility, and the others were from the down state New York city area during the time. Officers who came from other parts of the state and were not born in the area were called (carpetbaggers) and were labeled as such by the (homeboys), those who were from the immediate area. These officers from other parts of the state were harassed, ostracized, and shunned for no reason other than not being raised in the immediate area. These officers would usually move from downstate NY to rural upstate NY to escape the city life, which was associated with a higher cost of living and a higher crime rate. Many of the officers who had worked downstate at facilities such as Sing Sing, Bedford Hills, Fishkill, Otisville, Sullivan or any of the other downstate facilities and were from upstate New York where a wealth of information to the downstate officer thinking about relocating to upstate when I was working at Sing Sing. I was always questioned or quizzed by the officers from the city about the Elmira area like housing, schools, and questions one would ask if they were thinking about moving to the area. I myself was hoping that the ones who asked me about the area were seriously thinking about moving to the Elmira area. The prison was surely in need of some more officers of color. The homeboys would truly make the out-of-towners feel unwelcome. They also felt that they were coming upstate taking a job away from one of the homeboys. They truly had a territorial and predatorial nature about what they perceived to be their prison, plus no outsiders were welcome. Remember, the scenario had to be controlled, and this was one way it was done—by only allowing or accepting those that they have chosen into their world because behind the walls, fences, and bars existed a world of its own. In these small populated upstate towns, the prison's population could match or exceed the town's own population, so in essence, these prisons were small towns within the town.

During my career on the hill, T-shirts were printed and sold by staff to memorialize the fact that the facility was a world of its own. The T-shirts were printed with the words "Welcome to our world," seeing the prison world was different from the world outside of it, a world that was shadowed and shielded from the public's eyes like a bride with a veil concealed and hidden from the groom.

When I first arrived at Elmira, I had to work the 3–11 shift. I remember an incident in one of the larger blocks where I was working with other officers who had been working the block regularly as their bid job. A bid job is a job wherein an officer bids on against other officer and jobs are awarded by seniority. Officers without bid jobs are considered extra and fill-ins were needed. Being new to the jail and shift, I was an extra while working in G-block. Prior to reporting to the block, I was stopped by a fellow officer I had known growing up, and he warned me about the staff in the block being laid back a little too much and that security was lax.

When I arrived at G block, I was informed of my job duties, which was an eight-gallery officer. There are eight galleries in the block. As I worked 8 gallery, I had a clear view of the bottom floor. After working max jails downstate, I knew the only inmates that were supposed to be out were the gallery porters, but in G block, there were inmates running all over the block, most of them on the lower level. When I observed this, I made sure that the gates on the gallery were secure front and back. When the inmates saw a new officer working in an area, some of them started the con game where it usually started off with small talk, trying to get familiar with the new officer and obtain as much information as they could possibly get voluntarily from the officer. The rest they would pick up by listing to the loose-lipped staff as they spilled their idle chatter about the new guy or woman. Some of the inmates would even go as far as to tell a new officer how to do his job if he wasn't sure about what he was supposed to be doing. While I was working G block eight gallery sticking out like a sore thumb, a new officer and African American, one of six out of approximately 460 security staff, I stuck out all right to the inmates and the staff.

With that said, the inmates attempted to try me. It started with one of the porters, an inmate that is allowed to walk the gallery and look after the inmates in the cells, such as getting them water and sweep and mop the gallery, but that usually turned into basic bullshit. The inmates would usually just hang out and attempt to pass contraband from one inmate to another, and you as the officer would have to be smart enough to catch them. The porter on the gallery where I was assigned asked me if he could run downstairs and get something from one of the inmates downstairs who was running around. There were approximately ten inmates' cells open, and they were running around the block from floor to floor. I also observed and heard him and another inmate in a heated exchange. The porter's request to be let off the gallery was met with my usual response to bullshit: "You must have lost your rabbit-ass mind." The inmate wasn't authorized to be off the gallery. His job and his cell were on 8 gallery, and I learned early in my career by observing the wrongdoings or slip-ups of other officers not to fall for the bullshit; an inmate's bullshit wasn't worth me and my family's livelihood. So if it wasn't any and everything that had to do with their rights or privileges given to the inmates by the state and honored by staff, it would be immediately shot down by me as a request.

After denying the inmate's request, a short while later, I went downstairs to use the bathroom. I exited the bathroom to find chaos erupting—inmates and officers scurrying about and a whole lot of blood drippings on the floor. I immediately headed upstairs to find the eight gallery front gate opened wide and the gallery porter suffering from multiple wounds—and that was putting it lightly. The inmate was cut up so bad he had lacerations all over his body, including the crack off his ass. It looked like Edward Scissorhands had attacked him and he was bleeding profusely. There was blood all over the place. A medical emergency was called, and the inmate was immediately rushed out of the block myself, and other staff ran with the stretcher. We were running so fast one of the older offers could not keep up, and he ended up being dragged along the floor as he held tightly to the stretcher. The rush was because this inmate was bleeding so bad he could have bled to death.

Once the inmate was in the facility infirmary, he was immediately transported via ambulance to the outside hospital. After the inmate was placed in the hands of the medical staff, it was then time for the investigation and paperwork. My first question to the G Block sergeant was how did the gate which I locked become unlocked while I was in the bathroom. Just prior to going to the bathroom, the inmate who had stood behind the locked gate on eight gallery had just asked me if he could go downstairs to retrieve something, and I told him no, he couldn't, and he was now cut up. An answer I never did get.

Now let's see—I had walked away from a locked gate that I had checked before walking away, and to the best of my knowledge, the inmates had no key to the gate. The blood trail started on the ground floor and trailed to the top floor onto 8 gallery. It was more than an observation that someone had opened the gate for the inmate and allowed him to exit the gallery while I used the bathroom. Let the report writing begin. I assured the sergeant that gate was locked. Reports were ultimately written and turned in to the watch commander for review. Sometime later, the true story came out about what had happened. The inmate had owed money to one of the dope-dealing inmates that was locked on the lower level or flats area of the block. The inmates down below keep yelling up to him, trying to get him to come downstairs. Once I went to the bathroom, one of the other officers opened the gate so he could get out, and he went downstairs and didn't have what he owed, and for that, he was sliced and diced. It was never revealed who did it or how the lock gate became unlocked, but later on in my career while working at the Elmira CF, I found out there were many things that were unexplained—no explanation needed or given.

The inmate ultimately sued the state for the attack and injuries he sustained. I also found out that yes, some of the staff in G block were way too close to some of the inmates in the block—overfamiliar, which is a direct conflict of interest to a correctional officer. There were staff members that would allow inmates the freedom of running around the block and would bring and give them things—for example, frying pans and hot plates. Now a visitor could never smuggle those items into the jail. They are not sold in the jail. When the inmates come to the jail, their property is searched and contraband is seized, so where do they come from? They come from the corrupt, incompetent, and poorly supervised staff that have gone astray. My thought was always if you would bring an inmate something, you could bring him anything, including weapons and drugs.

After the incident in G block, I tried to avoid the area, but not having a bid job, you would be at the mercy of the chart sergeant who filled the empty job slots. This was in 1996. Now you have to remember I had just arrived at the facility and already I had witnessed firsthand corruption of staff and inmates. This was surely nothing new. After working the 3–11 shift for a while, I was able to bid a day job so I could be home with my family. The job I was able to get as a young officer was the mess hall / kitchen area, a job the more senior officers didn't want at Elmira. There were a lot of senior officers with time. As a correctional officer, time is everything to the job. Time dictated the jobs you bid in a lot of the facility's vacation time off and overtime pay because of two reasons—you made more with more years on the job and the older officers would be given preferential treatment for that over time. And time was needed for the most important thing of all: retirement. You would hear a lot of officers who had time tell the younger officers, "Go get some time," "You don't have any time," "You wish you had my time," and the all-time favorite, "You no-time bastard." This would be said by the older officers if the younger officers pissed them off about something.

I secured my first bid job—mess hall number 3–4 kitchen officer, which was a relief job for the officers who would work a bid job in only mess halls 3–4 and kitchen officers' job. Slowly but surely, the jail began to warm up to me. As I went about my duties as a correctional officer, I became very acquainted with not only my immediate area but with the facility as a whole. Behind those walls, fences, and bars existed a world only known to those who directly exist in it. It is unknown and nonexistent to others. The mess hall kitchen area was a desirable area for the inmates to work. A lot of the inmates would put their names in to work in the area, and at the time, there was a long waiting list for some of the inmates. The job was needed for their survival—for instance, if the inmate had no outside help from family, friends, or others they would be solely dependent on the New York State Department of Correctional Services for survival, and that would mean you were ass out. But access to the food service area, mess hall, or kitchen, as an inmate, you would be able to eat. The inmates would take full advantage of what they could by also stealing food from the facility's food supply. There were inmate workers in the mess hall or kitchen area that would have deferent contracts in the facility blocks. For example, one inmate would have a contract to sell the sugar he would pilfer from the kitchen area and another for the meat that he could pilfer and so on and so forth.

But it was not only the inmates pilfering the kitchen or mess halls; it was also the officers. They were all robbing the place blind. I didn't have direct knowledge or access to the facility budget, but I could only imagine it was very high with the loss of so much food. It was obvious to me that someone had crunched the numbers and they didn't like what they had seen because shortly after my arrival, a crackdown was enforced on the inmates' thievery but staff were given a pass. The staff just wasn't as brazen; a little more shade was put on the act.

In my daily duties, I was speaking with other officers and brass about the different things for the officers in the facility like the honor guard group, which was a group of officers that practiced military-type ceremonial traditions and were used at facility events and funerals for fellow employees. I was approached by the sergeant that supervised the honor guard, and he asked me if I was interested in being on the honor guard. He, the sergeant, explained to me that he was having trouble finding officers who had the desire and who had neat and tidy uniforms.

Most correctional officers' uniforms look a mess. Over my career, I have seen it all under the watchful eye of the supervisors of the department. Officers are allowed to take a pair of scissors and just cut the bottom of their pants to fit to length, not hemming or tailoring them but just cutting them, leaving fringes at the bottom. Some just let their pants drag the floor. Light blue shirts are worn so long the color fades out. There are stained and soiled shirts. I've observed officers who would come to work with the same soiled shirt they had worn the day before.

The supervisory staff was no better. The majority of them didn't care how their uniforms looked. You did have some officers and supervisors who took pride in their uniforms and were what they would call in the military "squared away." I say the military because the department says it follows military protocol or tradition in its use of uniforms and departmental use of ceremonies it performs such as the honor guard, yet the majority of the security staff was allowed to look a mess with no one telling them otherwise with the exception of the notification that would be put out to staff when someone from the department's upper management from Albany was coming. They basically told staff to clean themselves up. The thing that got me was why would you have to tell a grown adult to clean him or herself up. They, the administration, would also put pressure on the sloppy supervisory staff to pressure the officers to pressure the inmates to clean up the facility, and the heads of the department would give notice to the facility that they were coming. Other than the times when the cry went out that Albany was coming, it was business as usual, so whenever a commissioner or higher from Albany would come to inspect the facility, it would be wrapped and concealed under a vile of deception to hide its true appearance.

My uniform was always clean and pressed. I remember only once in my twenty-eight-year career coming to work with a wrinkled uniform, and that was New Year's Day 1990. I always took great pride in my appearance on and off duty. You know the old saying, your first impression is a lasting impression when you meet someone. While working in the kitchen area at the time, I was the youngest officer with time and age. The area sergeant was the laid-back type, the type that officers would call spineless, meaning that the officer didn't think that the sergeant had their back when confronted by the administration about one thing or another.

When I first started working in the kitchen area, there were a total of seven officers and an area sergeant, an officer in each of the four mess halls, a kitchen officer and a rear kitchen officer and a scullery officer. The scullery is the dishwasher area. The officer who ran the kitchen area was quite a character. At his post in the kitchen was a desk that stood approximately three feet high and four feet wide with a high stool behind it for sitting. He would never sit; he would stand poised behind the desk with his hands clenching either side of the four-foot-wide desk, looking like a bulldog ready to defend his territory if required. His look was grimacing, his attitude repugnant. We will call him the Major. He was soft-spoken and quick to anger. The Major had been in the kitchen area for many years and seemed to be more in charge of the area than the sergeant himself and was very, very close to one of the superintendents we had at the facility in charge for years. He seemed to be a legend—yep, in his own mind. The Major had piss-poor communication skills with the inmates and staff alike. If one was to ask him a question, it was met with a quick, blunt response, usually with one of his hands pointing in the direction he wanted you to go, which was away from him. The Major had so much influence over the superintendent and higher-ups. He was allowed to have a pet at work. He had an inmate that he kept that was allowed to work the Elmira CF kitchen area for over seventeen years. Yes, that inmate was allowed to remain in one area of the facility for more than seventeen years, something I later protested to not only the area sergeant but also to the higher-ups and the union. They ignored my request to remove the inmate for being way too familiar with staff and his work location. You can see the problem this poses—overfamiliarity between staff and inmates is what made the escape from the Clinton Correctional Facility possible. Just as I was ignored, someone probably notified higher-ups at Clinton in advance of the escape, but they too were shooed away and ignored as I was. It always felt like bullshit trumped common sense.

This inmate was so familiar with his surroundings. He would tell staff that were unfamiliar to the area how and what they had to do in the area. Basically, he would tell staff what their job was. The inmate had no real job in the kitchen area. The inmate would position himself in the hallway that connected the four mess halls in the middle just across from the Major's desk area in the kitchen, and from there, they would stare at one another. The inmate would also be tuned into all the conversations that the major had, either with staff present at the desk area or over the phone; the inmate was always just an earshot away from the major. This is the type of inmate that truly had taken advantage of his situation and was allowed by those in charge to do so. The inmate was more like staff than an inmate. And no one was going to change this as long as the Major wanted his pet because someone had anointed the Major the owner and proprietor of the kitchen area, and by all means, bullshit trumps security. His pet would try to get close and friendly with me to get favors and special treatment, but he was unable to do so. He was the type of inmate you had to keep an extra eye on.

During my twenty-eight years, I treated all the inmates the same. They were treated fair, firm, and consistent while I performed my duties of care, custody, and control as a correctional officer just as the State of New York had hired me to do. No more, no less. I was never looking for an inmate pet to give preferential treatment to, which would have clouded my judgment and impeded on my integrity and would render myself basically useless in a prison setting.

Whenever I questioned a supervisor about another officer's interaction I had observed that was questionable and dealt with integrity, they would say, "Well, you know it takes all types to work in here," and that was that. The major's pet wasn't the only inmate kept in the facility. There were others as well that were close to staff. Likewise, I remember one incident that surprised the hell out of me. Early in my career, there was an officer—we'll call him Officer O. One afternoon, in the late nineties, as chow was being run in the mess hall, Officer O entered the mess hall with his group of inmates. As the sergeant stood watch in the mess hall, he observed Officer O pass something to an inmate. The sergeant had the inmate patted down, and a razor blade was found in the inmate's possession. The sergeant himself had witnessed the officer give it to him. The officer was ultimately fired but never criminally charged even though in the state's own policies and procedures it should do so if found guilty of promoting prison contraband. As serious as this was, a reasonable person with no law enforcement background could see the severity of handing an inmate a razor blade not used for shaving. I have to say that because razor blades are issued to the inmates in the housing blocks on a one-for-one exchange for the purposes of shaving. The blade given to the inmate in the mess hall was a weapon that could have been used on me or anyone else in the facility from the inmates to the staff. Officer O's reason for given the inmate the weapon was never revealed, but as a correctional officer, your job is to prevent violence in the prison system, not promote it and take part in it.

Contraband is a major problem within the New York State Department of Corrections and Community Supervision. The problem has been allowed to exist though poor management, which results in poor supervision, which trickles down to staff who have been allowed to roam free inside these prisons unchecked and do as they like and backed by a union. You remember that is more in charge of the New York State Department of Corrections and Community Supervision than our own state government itself. Now if I would have seen and reported this incident of an officer giving an inmate a weapon, I would be called a snitch, rat, or some other derogatory term the bad guys come up with to keep good people with integrity from revealing the truth, or hell, I would be brought up on some type of trumped-up charge myself. That is how it works in the New York State Department of Corrections and Community Supervision, brought to you by NYSCOBA, the union in charge. The giving of contraband by staff to inmates is what fueled and ignited the escape at Clinton Correctional Facility. I'm quite sure a lot of head turning and covering up went on both before and after the escape. Once again brought to you by NYSCOBA, the union in charge.

I only keep saying this because all that is wrong in the department can directly be attributed to the union, from the refusal to have officers that are guilty be disciplined to the objection of implementation of rule changes that bring with them more accountability of its members. I have personally been the victim of the union's retaliatory nature. When reporting one of its members for wrongdoing, I would watch as an officer is charged with a disciplinary infraction of some form or another. The union, although the officer is guilty and the whole facility knows what he did, would fight tooth and nail to keep this officer's job. Hell, they would put the union up as collateral for them if they had to. This is why those that do things such as being too close to inmates and bringing or introducing contraband into the facility feel comfortable doing so—because the union is going to protect them and it would be all covered up.

Take the coverup of a cocaine-dealing lieutenant while I was working in the mess hall. I was one of the few officers who would always be on their post. Well, one morning while standing in the doorway of the mess hall I was running, this lieutenant walked past me and ordered me to keep the door locked for no other reason than to order me to do something. Really, you had people that would be on a power kick with some and a party with others. I would observe this same lieutenant early in the morning when I would arrive at 5:45 a.m. coming out of the supervisor's locker room moving a mile a minute, talking fast and jittery. After observing this behavior, I said to another officer, "Hey, you know, coffee alone doesn't get you moving like that unless you eat the whole can," and we laughed. The other officer asked me what I thought it was, and my response was cocaine. It was the midnineties, and the cocaine epidemic was at its height. He also concurred with my suspicion.

One morning, I had to ask the lieutenant a question, so I was face-to-face with him. He was trying everything he could do to avoid eye contact with me. Inside, I was laughing; his eyes looked like they had been sprayed with a glossy finish. After speaking to him, I again told that same officer of my suspicion of the lieutenant high on duty in the jail. Approximately two to three months later, he was busted coming back to the Elmira area on the highway with a large amount of cocaine. He was locked out of the facility. It was funny because the word in the jail was he was the runner. He would go get cocaine not just for himself but was also selling to other officers at the facility, so the plot thickened. There were officers worried they were going to be exposed as the lieutenant awaited his court date and his sure demise. A funny thing happened—the evidence, the cocaine that was found, came up missing from the outside police agencies' evidence locker. It was said that his father was connected with the department and the union, and he made it happen.

Me, I don't know. All I know the man was charged with a large amount of drugs one day and was ordering me around the next. Everyone I know in the city of Elmira charged with a large amount of cocaine was doing time in state prison, not working there as a supervisor.

That in no way was this the end of the lieutenant's cocaine obsession. Just months later after he dodged that bullet, he was busted again. This time, it was said to be a federal charge and old Daddy dearest and others couldn't pull any strings and manipulate the justice system this time. He was ultimately fired from the department this time, and to think he was a supervisor, the one I would take my orders from.

There was this one sergeant who worked the kitchen 3–11 who used to give me a hard time and undermined the day sergeant by accusing the day shift of not doing their job. It seemed he used to go out of his way to find me before I was relieved by one of his 3–11 officers or one of his henchmen or loyal soldiers. One of his solders was a tall, skinny guy about six foot tall, and he weighed about ninety pounds soaking wet. His duty belt could have fit the average ten-year-old. He along with the sergeant would come and attempt to harass me regarding the mess hall. The day shift was responsible for the breakfast and lunch meals, and the 3–11 shift only had the dinner meal. But the 3–11 shift would try to pawn off their duties such as setting up the mess hall for their shift. So each day, the sergeant would come in, eyes glazed over, along with his henchman, the skinny, frail beanpole that smelled of liquor on most days. It was said he was an alcoholic and had a real bad drinking problem. Each day, I would have to prepare myself for the bullshit to come from these two losers while wishing they would go away.

And one day, my prayer was answered. The loudmouth, know-it-all sergeant was busted for growing marijuana in his backyard. It seemed the sergeant was growing marijuana, his own supply of pot. It was said that his neighbor had observed him tending to his crops, and the neighbor called the authority and he was charged and fired. His sidekick, the skinny alcoholic, soon vanished. He was sent off to rehab or what they called whiffle ball camp. Those in charge, the state—or shall I say the union in charge—would know these individuals had a problem, and they would allow them to continue to come to work unstable because it was surely not hard to spot someone high on drugs or alcohol.

There was one officer who worked F block when I first arrived back at the Elmira CF in the midnineties. I will never forget my first interaction with this officer. I reported directly to F block after lineup. Once there, I stood around the desk area with the other officers, waiting for the first officer to hand out the keys, which he did so after the regular block officers who had bid jobs in the block got their equipment from the first officer. I approached him and stood about an arm's length away from him but was hit with the smell of alcohol as if I were a dentist in his mouth checking for cavities. The second thing I noticed was his head would not hold still. He was like a bobble head.

After speaking to him, I left the desk area and asked an officer whom I knew if he realized that the officer at the desk was drunk. He laughed and so did the others who had heard me ask the question. One of the officers responded, "He drinks vodka and orange, and he brings it in his thermos." They all laughed. It was no lie this man had liquor in his thermos in a state prison and all were aware. But nothing was being done to stop the officer from bringing contraband in the prison or to help this man and his out-of-control drinking.

He wasn't the only officer with a drinking habit. There were many with out-of-control drug and alcohol addictions. Many of them would get DUIs or DWIs and a slap on the wrist. Many of them had multiple DWIs or DUIs. When the law was passed in New York state making it a felony to have three or more convictions for the offence, that didn't stop some officer who already had multiple offences for driving drunk to take their roll at the system, testing it to the limit by racking up more drunk driving convictions. There were inmates housed at the Elmira CF convicted of just that—multiple drunk driving convictions, which made them eligible to do time in a New York State Prison. There was one officer who had four convictions for drunk driving, but because he had money—and you would have to believe that because he was a state correctional officer—he was able to avoid jail or prison time and keep his job. This kind of stuff went on all throughout my career—officers breaking the law. Granted, it's a large organization of what is supposed to be a state agency, which some think would contribute to the large number of misfits and derelicts, but there are larger companies and organizations that hold their employees to less of a standard and their employees are not acting under the jurisdiction of the state's government and an oath that do better with their employees because they discipline their employees for misconduct.

After being at Elmira for a short while, I learned about the CERT, team which stood for Correctional Emergency Response Team. I learned of this during a conversation with other officers and members of the team. It was described as the response team that they called in to corral large disturbances and uprisings that may occur at Elmira or elsewhere throughout the state I was also informed the team met once a month for training above and behind what a correctional officer is mandated to have to be certified as a correctional officer. I liked what I had heard and was sold on the CERT team. My bid job or my regular post was still in the mess hall. I worked alongside two officers who were close to the sergeant who was shift supervisor in the mess hall. These two officers both had more time than me. I remember one afternoon after the mess halls had finished running and the inmates were cleaning up in their areas, I came out of the mess hall. I was in charge of looking for the sergeant to ask him a question. I found the sergeant standing at the desk speaking to the Major. I approached the desk area and started to have a conversation with the sergeant. The Major had joined the conversation.

As we stood and talked, out of the corner of my eye I thought I observed a hand moving quickly. To my dismay, when I turned to see what was happening, I observed the two senior officers in the area standing in front of the mess hall three door area, one on each side of an inmate worker from the mess hall they were in charge of. As I turned, I observed the inmate slapping up the two officers. He would slap one back away from him as the other approached, trying to keep the two of them from both bouncing on him at the same time. I was approximately thirty feet from them as I turned. I immediately started running on an all-out sprint like a sprinter going out of the blocks on a hundred-yard dash. As the inmate dealt with the two officers, I hit him from the side like a linebacker on an illegal blind side hit that placed him on the floor and me on top asking for handcuffs to restrain him. The sergeant immediately rendered his assistance by helping me place the inmate in cuffs. The two officers that had been slapped up by the inmate both stood there, stunned. One of the officers was about 5'10" and 130 lbs. and had a mouth on him like he was King Kong. His action was all the indication and varication I needed to see he was all mouth and no action. We will call him Loose Change. The other officer was 6't and 240 lbs. with no knuckle game but would always talk a good game. The inmate was 5'11" and 180 lbs. and had slapped them both up. Boy, I knew at that moment if something were to break out in the mess hall area, I would have to wait for help to come because these two were worthless. It was later learned during the investigation that the inmate had refused to do his job, so the two officers had brought him out back to lock him up and send him back to the block, but before doing so, they tried to tip the inmate over by belittling him with verbal taunts, which worked by the reaction they got out of the inmate, slapping them both up at the same time. The littler of the two, a.k.a. Loose Change, was the main instigator. He was all mouth and no action. Later in my career, I had problems with him harassing me.

After the two officers were done starting trouble and the inmate was escorted out of the area, as we were walking to the infirmary to be checked for injuries, the officer called Loose Change said, "Man, I never thought a black man would come to help me," referring to me. Getting that inmate off his dumb, stupid, racist ass, I just looked at him and was forced to remain silent. After the incident, it was all over the jail how the black man, as I was referred to by the dumb-ass officer, had helped break up the incident in the mess hall. When you come into the department, it is said over and over again in training, "There are only two colors inside the prison, and that is blue and green." Which as you can tell by the reaction and the surprise of Loose Change that color is at the forefront of the way he thinks a correctional officer would or should perform his job.

Now for me, there were only two colors: blue and green and right and wrong. Those things were always at the forefront of the way I preformed my duties as an officer. It didn't make a difference to me if you had blue or green on inside the jail—wrong is still wrong.

A short while after the incident, my application to join the CERT, the Correctional Emergence Response Team, was accepted, and that made me the first African American correctional officer to be on the Elmira CF CERT. I was quickly thrown onto the team with the other officers. There was another officer of a different race that was on the team and a sergeant of a different race as well. Other than that, it was all Caucasians.

After joining the team, I found out you were paid overtime for training. At first, everything seemed to be all right. You know, you had some guys who were standoffish and had little or no conversation for me or would give me that look of disgust like I was invading their domain. I soon found out they were the punks or cowards on the team. They couldn't beat themselves out of a wet paper bag if I started the hole for them. They were weak. Being on the team and working in the jail, you may have to come into to restore order. It was another thing I was told not to talk openly about, being on the team, and members weren't to identify as a team member while on duty in the jail. So it was mighty funny. Inmates questioned me about my CERT status immediately after I became a member of the team.

I wonder how that happened. I'll tell you how. Correctional officers are truly their own worst enemies in the jail with their mouths always talking just to talk and most of the time openly around the inmates that pick up on their conversations, whether the inmate is in his cell or out and about. If they can hear your voice, someone is listening always. You know the old saying "Loose lips sink ships," so the inmates know because my fellow officers told them so. Now the whole jail knew Officer Curtis Brown was on the Elmira Correctional Facility CERT, team but mum was the word for the rest of the team.

While on the team, the training could have been better if you truly had someone who was in charge. I would sit back and watch the backbiting and power struggle that went on between the so-called leaders of the team that seemed to make training more of an overtime money grab and hangout then an actual learning experience. During one training session for the CERT team, one of the older members who acted more like he was a supervisor than a correctional officer along with a couple of others who acted just like him were allowed to take the lead in a training exercise on entry of a building. In the exercise, the door had to be breached with a cutting tool. I was standing where I was directed to stand, and there was this dumb-ass idiot know-it-all who considered himself God's gift to corrections—you know one of those guys who just thinks he knows everything. Well, as I stood there. the dumb ass revved up the large cutting saw that he had in his hands, and instead of cutting the door hinges to breech the door, he attempted to cut my leg off by hitting my leg with large saw that he was in control of. And then after the idiot did it, he then tried to justify it as my mistake. Lucky for him, I was quick enough to jump away from the saw which had ripped through my pants and caused a small laceration to my upper thigh area; it just nicked the skin. I couldn't say if he did it on purpose or if it was an honest mistake because like I said, there were many of the team's members that resented me, an African American correctional officer, for being on the team. Hell, from the way some of them acted in the jail, they resented me being a correctional officer altogether. They seemed to act as if that was a job just for Caucasian males.

After being on the team for a while and observing the workings of the team, I quickly came to another conclusion of why the dumb ass almost took my leg off. It was a good chance he may have been drunk. You see training took place after hours. It was after work, so team members would go home and return in the evening after some had eaten dinner, and some had a liquid dinner in the form of alcohol. During training sessions, I had smelled alcohol on him and other members of the team.

While on duty in the jail, other officers not on the team would often ask me why I wanted to be on the CERT team. They would refer to the team as "the sorry-ass CERT team" or "the Squirt team," in reference to the size of some of its members. Some were the size of an average-sized eighth grader, and it seemed to me for them being a member made them feel more powerful while working inside the jail.

There was one who surely had a little man's complex. Other officers would tease him about his short stature, and in return, he would take his frustration out on the inmates or spout off to other staff members, trying to redirect his anger over being teased about his statue or size. He was one of the littlest guys on the team with the biggest mouth. He was also one of the officers who would look at me with discontent or anger for me being a correctional officer and a team member while a member of the CERT team. I was also a member of the honor guard that participated in ceremonial events and funerals for staff members when called upon to do so. I saw these things as a way to stay involved in the facility which I called home, seeing I would be there until I retired in twenty years at the time. Also, it would look good to have these things under your belt when it came time for advancement in the department. I also enjoyed learning new things, all of which were valid reasons for me wanting to belong to these two teams.

There are so few minorities working in these upstate prisons that it becomes difficult for the majority, which are Caucasians, to entertain or conceive to the fact that minorities have the same rights as they do to hold the job of being a correctional officer, when all they see is minorities in green as inmates. This has happened because of a non-diverse workplace that has been allowed to exist for many years. You have a prison that houses 80 percent minority inmates run by a 99 percent Caucasian workforce, and that has the backing of a union that only caters to the majority of its members that happen to be Caucasian. What would one think the outcome would be? Chaos on all fronts.

In or around 1998, we had a major fight that broke out among the inmates. At the time, there were four mess halls, one that held approximately four hundred, one that held three or so, and two other smaller ones that held half or less than the other two larger mess halls, and they were located in the large corridor area that was the length of two football fields. On the day of this incident, chow was running, everything was going smoothly, and then out of nowhere, fighting among the inmates broke out in all four mess halls. The inmates that were in the corridor that were leaving and coming to the mess hall started fighting. The inmates that were in the housing blocks that were being let out started fighting. There were so many fights going on you didn't know which one to run to. You would break up one, and two other fights would jump off. Officers were running up and down the corridor, breaking up fights.

I remember one particular inmate who was fighting around the rollup door area where there is a gate to let vehicles pass through the corridor. He had just been placed on the wall by this older thin officer who had the inmate in the yoke, his arms around the inmate's neck to choke him out. A sergeant and two other officers were all standing around the inmate. As I approached, the officer that was holding the inmate around his neck was yelling. He tried to stab me with what appeared to be a broken piece of wood as he looked to the floor in front of him. The inmate managed to speak out as he was being choked and was saying he had it for the other inmate. He was fighting as the officers got ready to put what's known as the boots to the inmate. I grabbed the inmate by his shirt and loudly yelled out, "Hey, Sarge! You want me to help escort him to the box?"

With all the chaos going on, the sergeant ordered me to escort the inmate to the box, (special housing unit), where the inmates go for breaking facility or state rules. As I escorted the inmate down to the box, I asked him if he had lost his rabbit-ass mind and asked him if he was trying to get himself killed. He responded by assuring me he wasn't trying to attack the officer—he was going after another inmate that was after him. I couldn't stand there and be part of a beatdown on an inmate. The officer wasn't injured, and I was trying to keep the inmate the same. Remember, my only job was care, custody, and control inside these walls, no more, no less. After escorting the inmate to the SHU, I exited the large heavy red steel front door of the SHU unit, which put me right back in the middle of the chaos. As I exited other inmates were being brought in. The door was painted bright red to stand out, and the inmates were reminded on a daily basis about taking a trip to the red door if they got out of line. It seemed as if the chaos went on forever, but in all reality, the whole thing lasted about seven minutes before order was restored to the facility. In my twenty-eight years, that was the most chaotic chaos

I witnessed firsthand. There were many other smaller incidents that took place, but none of them were on this scale.

Prison is, by nature, a violent place. You have inmate-on-inmate violence, you have staff-on-inmate violence, and you have inmate-on-staff violence. With all that during my career, I watched how the violence from both staff and inmates spiraled out of control to the point where it was acceptable and expected the change from the eighties to the millennium years. In the eighties, most officers would not put their hands on an inmate over a look or from feeling like he had been in some way disrespected. I say *most* because you did still have some who would take the smallest of incidents to the extreme, but nowadays, if an inmate looks at one of these what I call cowards the wrong way, that inmate might get beaten down, or if the inmate says something to one of the cowards, they might get beaten down. These were cowardly beatdowns; you would hear stories from both staff and inmates.

I remember one incident that I caught. One morning, while on my post in Mess Hall 3, as I checked off workers coming into the food service area to work, I heard a scuffle taking place out in the larger corridor just outside the front doors of the mess halls. I looked out the door to find an inmate on the floor and approximately ten correctional officers standing over him. They were kicking and stomping on an African American inmate. I observed feet being raised as high as they could without losing their balance and stomping down on every part of the inmate's body. All the other mess halls had closed their doors to keep the inmates from seeing what was going on. As I stood in the hallway unaware to those committing this outright assault, I stood approximately forty feet away when one of them looked up and spotted me standing with my hands on my hips with the "What the hell are you doing?" look on my face.

He quickly motioned to the others to stop and said, "Brown is watching." Then and only then did they stop, and the sergeant who had stood by and watched it all came out from the recessed door opening to also observe my presents. The inmate was quickly grabbed off the floor and dragged down the long corridor out of view.

This type of violence would and could break out at any time. You had staff members who were notorious for putting their hands on inmates. A guard could assault an inmate and would merely deny it or justify it by saying the inmate had attacked him, which would be backed up by other staff, both security and civilians, and the inmate would be made to look like a liar and receive more punishment by receiving time in the special housing unit or keep locked in their cell with loss of privileges. That, in some instances, would include the basic human necessities for survival—food and water. Yes, there were employees that enjoyed watching human suffering. Some would even go out of their way to start a conflict with an inmate and recruit other staff members to go along just to get a negative reaction out of an inmate in the form of the inmate, either receiving a disciplinary infraction or a beatdown. They would call that *tipping an inmate over*. I witnessed both security and civilian staff speak to grown men like they were their kids, just because they could if the inmate was trying to find out information about one thing or another or if they were trying to obtain something that the state had given them the right to have while incarcerated. Those employees didn't want to see the inmates have what little rights we allowed them to have such as visitations, correspondents, along with packages both from home and allowed authorized vendors and some, conjugal visitation.

I remember in Elmira CF in 1996, an inmate was having a conjugal visit in one of the trailers located inside the prison walls, toward the back of the prison. He killed his wife by strangulation and committed suicide by hanging himself, all while their young child lay sleeping in another room in the trailer. I remember this incident, and that day had started out like any other day. I was still working in the food service area of the prison. On this particular day, I had the desk area, which was at 4:45 a.m. to 1:00 p.m. On this post, you would open up the kitchen area along with one of the civilian cooks and the early kitchen crew of inmate workers. The conjugal trailer area was just one building down from the food service area. There was nothing out of place. The day started quiet and uneventful until a little after 6:00 a.m. when the gruesome crime scene was discovered by the FRP officer during his count in the area. The trailer area is the FRP

73

area, the family reunion program. It was told that the officer went to knock on the trailer door to rouse the occupants, the inmate, his wife, and their child. When no one responded, he opened the door and discovered the crime scene—the wife dead, the inmate hanging, and the young child in a corner, balled up, crying. What appeared to be a quiet start of a day in prison turned into a double homicide. Prison is surely a place of employment that is ever volatile, and when it erupts, it's never good. That was the first time in the conception of the family reunion program (FRP) that anyone had been killed.

After the incident, the staff were all saying, "I bet they'll close that program down now." The program didn't shut down, and it still exist today. The program is designed to help the inmates try to keep a family bond and reward those who try to do the right thing. While incarcerated, the true loser in all of it was the young child who awoke to the horror of finding his parents both deceased. After the incident and time went on, the outcry to close the program down grew quiet until it was muted altogether. Was it looked at as one of those things where the benefit outweighed the risk? Or was it the possible relationship of the inmates if the program was stopped? Who knows?

From 1996–1999, three years of my career were quiet and free of harassment as I worked at the Elmira Correctional Facility. I continued working in the food service area, and I was on the CERT, the Correctional Emergence Response Team, and the honor guard. I had thought that I had the respect of my fellow officers. Some would go out of their way to say "Hello," "Hi," or "What's up." Some of these officers would see me out and about around the center gate area of the prison that was located in the middle between the facility, where most of the inmate movement took place back and forth to programs. Some of these officers would be as far as seventy-five yards away, yelling my name, "Hey, what's up, Brownie?" Even though my name is Brown, the majority chose to call me "Brownie," which I accepted. I would wave or yell back to my fellow officers, returning the greeting. All—and I do mean all—of the inmates who were at the jail know my name.

I remember an incident where my name tag had broken off my jacket that day, and this miserable, broken-down sergeant questioned me about not having a name tag, and I responded by letting him know I didn't have it on because it had broken. His response was I needed it so I could be identified. I asked the sergeant if he really believed that, which he confirmed as I stood next to the sergeant. Alongside us, a few of my fellow officers and a large group of inmates passed by, going to chow. I stopped a Caucasian inmate in the group, and in front of the sergeant I said to the inmate, "Do you know my name?"

The inmate smiled and said, "Everyone knows your name, Officer Brown."

The officers standing with me laughed as the sergeant's face turned beet red with embarrassment. I turned and said, "See, Sarge, everyone knows me."

As I walked away, I felt like a fly in a bowl of milk, unmistakably noticeable. At the time, there were only three African American officers working in the prison, one on each of the three shifts. I could not hide who I was even if I wanted to. The sergeant was just being a wise ass because he surely wasn't critiquing any of the other officers' uniforms that looked a hot mess, just mine. I guess he didn't care for flies in his milk, and may I remind you my uniform was clean and pressed every day. Hell, my uniform looked better and neater than the sergeant's. The real reason the sergeant felt the need to say anything was that it was me. Him addressing the Caucasian officers about a name tag wasn't happening. They were never singled out by the almost entirely white supervisory staff about anything. Being the only African American around had its challenges, pitfalls, and benefits, mostly the latter of the three.

As a member of the CERT team, during the year 1999 around the fall time, chatter among the staff was that the higher-ups had received information from around the state prison system that there would be a major disturbance or uprising on the upcoming millennial New Year 2000. As the date approached, the CERT team was activated. On New Year's Eve 1999, the CERT team, on the ready for any problem that could arise at any one of the two local prisons or statewide on New Year's Eve. The team was assembled at the facilities training room, where we dressed in our CERT uniforms and gathered other equipment. When I arrived, I was met with some stares and glares from those who felt I didn't belong. When I approached my locker, I found the word *token* written on my locker. I stood back and took a long, wide-eyed stare, making sure I had a good mental note of this hateful, disrespectful show of racism that had been plastered on my locker for the world to see, but only I saw it, no one else, including those in charge, the supervisors.

We were then transferred to a local army recruitment center that would be our home for the next three days, placed on standby, awaiting a call for any disturbance or uprising. I was the only African American there. I had just been subjected to racial intimidation back at the facility by someone or person's place. The word *token* on my locker was with the blessings of them all because no one said "Don't do it" or no one took it off before I got there, and I was one of the last to arrive. Little did I know this was just the start of the racial harassment.

After arriving, we were shown around the recruitment center. It was a well-maintained facility with a large room for staging or drill inspections that was used as our main room for sleeping and storing our equipment. There was also a large kitchen area just adjacent to the large staging area; downstairs was a locker room along with showers. After getting acquainted with our new environment and securing a spot to sleep and storing my equipment, people were just hanging out between the main area and the kitchen. I tried to mingle around and keep my distance from those that had made it obvious they didn't want me around. I happened to make my way into the kitchen area, where guys were just hanging out, talking. One of the guys happened to be well-connected to the superintendent. As soon as this guy spotted me, he immediately made me the center of attraction by talking to me like I was stupid because I was complaining about coming down with a cold. He suggested I put an unpeeled orange in the microwave to heat up the juice for consumption to help with a sore throat.

The others in the room got quiet after hearing his suggestion. I guess he thought black people didn't own microwaves. I thought about it and said to myself, *I'll play his game*. I watched as this grown man' s eyes light up like a child on Christmas Day filled with excitement as I placed the unpeeled orange in the microwave to explode from the pressure. When the orange finally exploded from the pressure, all laughed, but none as loud as me as I exited the kitchen.

This man wasn't right in his own mind. He would come to work two hours before the start of his shift and was allowed to be on his post in the prison. They say he wasn't being paid overtime, but as I said, he was very close to the worthless superintendent, this same guy would help frisk the inmates as they entered the food service area in the morning. I and others would watch as he helped frisk through the inmates' dirty clothing in the net bags that they were bringing to work to be picked up by the facility laundry workers. We wore plastic gloves as we frisked the inmates and any property they had with them as they entered the food service area to work. In the summertime, the main corridor where this took place would be extremely hot from the brick construction holding the summer heat. This man would take his gloved hands that he had just run though the inmates' dirty property which contained dirty underclothing and other soiled clothing items. Without removing his soiled gloves from his hands, he would run his gloved hands from his forehead to his chin to wipe away the sweat that had built up. I wasn't the only one that noticed this disgusting, unhygienic act. Another officer once said he was acting like a bloodhound getting a good sniff of the inmates' dirty clothing so he could get on their trail—how disgusting is that?

The superintendent at the time had been brought up from the ranks and felt his officers could do no wrong and would do anything to protect them. He also liked his ass kissed, so he didn't like me because my motto was and is "I kiss no ass before its time and it's never going to be time," so I wouldn't light up when he was around or laugh at his stale humor. Others would have their lips glued to his ass, waiting for a pat on the head like a little kid. These grown men would need confirmation from another man to make them feel good about themselves, not I. He was like the majority of these superintendents that worked at Elmira. They walked around most of the time with their heads down. I was never sure if it was from shame or just not wanting to see what was right in front of them. Most of the superintendents I worked under at the Elmira Correctional Facility were worthless. They would not stand up to what was right. They would cater to injustice and cover up for wrongdoers, and they had no integrity. There was one superintendent during my career who had integrity and did his job his way by being fair, firm, and consistent. All the others catered to the masses.

After the encounter with the idiot in the kitchen, I went back to the main area, where we were using to sleep and store our gear. We all had a spot with an army-issued cot. I watched as those who thought they were elite officers walk around and attempt to give orders to other officers. One short drunk ball-head officer who thought he was tough walked around threatening to place a coat hanger down the throat of anyone that was caught snoring. I watched as he walked by the other officers, informing them of his intent. When he got to me and said that same dumb shit, I informed him if he put that hanger down my throat while I was sleeping, I would beat his ass, and those were my exact words. This guy was one of those guys that couldn't beat his way out of a wet paper bag if I started the hole for him. There are a lot of cowards like him in the department, and his type is a cancer that plagues the department. Don't get me wrong—there are tough guys, but he definitely wasn't one of them, and besides, the tough guys were quiet and not troublemakers. It was the punks like this loudmouth that caused problems for everyone else.

It was New Year's Eve, and all was quiet at the prison, and none of the other facilities were reporting problems. Late in the night, some of the guys brought the party with them and drank the night away. They would slip outside for a smoke and a drink while others watched out for them and vice versa. Their personal vehicles were parked in the parking lot, so the fellas had their stash in the car, all liquored up and ready to go. *What a joke*, I thought to myself. If something did happen and the inmate decided to become unruly and we had to respond, we would have been responding with a bunch of party revelers.

The morning light brought the morning. After cleaning up and eating chow, we were ordered to report outside. Once there, we were lined up and given a briefing of the current situation. We were told to get comfortable because we would be here a couple of days. We were also told about the status of our facility, and around the state, it was reported that there were only a few minor incidents on New Year's Eve. This was reported by the CERT commander. He also informed us a small group of officers was going to be selected to go to the facility to frisk and move a few inmates. We were then also told we were doing some training while we were outside. We were then broken into a few smaller groups and performed different tactical formations. We usually lined up in these formations by height, and that usually put me toward the front of the formation. The different formations were used when the team was moving inside the prison toward its intended target, mainly a group of inmates. While performing the different types of formations, one of the racist coward punks that was at the rear of the formation yelled out at the top of his lungs, "Hey, Brown, tell them here comes the house nigger!"

Now from what I know of the term *house nigger*, it's a term used to identify a black man that receives special privileges from the white man that other black men don't receive. I can't tell you what this man was thinking when he decided to say what he said, but I can say that he knew the exact effect of what he said. Why? Because he was a grown adult. Children are the only ones we excuse. Why? Because they don't know what they say. I was taken aback and stunned by his racist remark. The reaction to all within an earshot was quiet—crickets.

The formation practice was ended, and everyone dispersed, walking away. I myself was taken back—yep, to slavery—and wanting to stun this loudmouth racist bozo, the clown-looking dude, with a punch in his loud mouth. During the rest of the day, I tried to keep my distance and keep to myself, but in closed quarters it is impossible. Yes, the only African American was trying to become invisible.

Later in the day, that group of team members the commander said he was going to take to the facility were rounded up and told to put on their CERT equipment. Of course, I wasn't chosen to go. I don't remember how many went, but I think it was twenty or less. After, the group was sent off to the facility to move a few inmates the facility felt were troublemakers and to frisk a few more. The members left behind were left trying to find something to do until their return.

When the team returned from our facility, the Elmira Correctional Facility, they arrived walking through the door with big cocky smiles on their faces, and the first thing out of the littlest one's mouth was, "You should have seen the look on those niggers' faces when we walked in there." He looked around smiling after his ignorant, backwoods, racist statement to find me standing there looking at him. I shook my head and walked away.

Now let's recap my three-day CERT millennium emergency standby. I first arrived to find *token* written on my locker. I was then spoken to like black people are stupid by the superintendent's very, very close friend. I then had Bozo the Clown yell out during a team drill, "Hey, Brown, tell them here comes the house nigger," topped off with "You should have seen the look on those niggers' faces." That was all said to me or done to me in three days. Yes, the ugly truth was exposed—my fellow team members were a bunch of ignorant racists, and they wanted me gone.

After we were ordered to stand down and the millennial threat of some form of disruption within the department by the inmates was over, we were let go, and the next day, we reported back to our regular jobs, and I immediately informed the CERT commander I was resigning. He didn't ask me why. He asked me to remain on the team, at which time I informed him of each of the despicable, hateful, ignorant, racist comments made to me or directed at me and my African American heritage. The lieutenant who was the CERT commander was well aware of all that had transpired during the team's activation. He continued to ask me to remain on the team, which I declined by resigning from the team effective immediately.

After my resignation at around 10:00a.m, it was all throughout the facility by 10:15a.m. I had other officers asking about what had taken place, at which time I referred them to basically ask the members of the CERT team what happened. That cat was soon out the bag also. Over the next few days, I was accosted by Bozo the Clown himself trying to justify why he had yelled out, "Hey, Brown, tell them here comes the house nigger." I told him he was a grown man and knew exactly what came out of his mouth and this guy was a loudmouth that needed his mouth shut. He was always talking like a tough guy but was one of those guys who couldn't beat his way out of a wet paper bag, unless I started the hole for him. He was an outright racist, confirmed by his comments and actions. He didn't come to me to apologize; he came to me so I could make him feel better by telling him it was all right, which in no way in hell it was.

I was also accosted by the little loudmouth guy who himself was a minority who attempted to explain why he felt it was all right to yell out at the top of his lungs "You should have seen the looks on those niggers' face when they saw us." His explanation was as follows: "Well, Brownie, they call me a sand nigger because I'm of Middle Eastern descent."

I couldn't believe what I was hearing out of the mouth of this idiot. I then asked him, "Who calls you a sand nigger?"

He said, "Guys on the team and some of the officers here at the facility while I'm on duty."

I told this man he was out of his mind if he thought I was going to stand for anyone addressing me in such a disrespectful manner, not now or ever. I also told him he should be ashamed of himself for allowing others to disrespect him and his race. I then told him I would rather be respected than liked. This man came to me to convince me that it was okay to yell out the word *nigger*. He was playing along to get along. I will never forget the conversation I had with this man at the end of our conversation. I told him, "I don't care how you allow this guy's to talk to you or treat you, but no one is going to treat me like that."

After my departure from the CERT team, there was all kinds of chatter throughout the jail. The bozo who had yelled out "house nigger" started bringing me gifts to work. He knew like a lot of other people I was a big fan of the Chicago Bulls and Michael Jordan. Hell, even my license plates were Chicago Bulls sports plates with CB23 as the tag number, so Bozo started to bring me Michael Jordan figurines and hats and would try to make nice with me. I took his trinkets and threw them in the trash. As much as I liked Mike, I liked me more, and there was something in me not wanting to see Bozo with a figurine of a black man. And I wondered if he had one of those black jockeys holding a lantern at his house to greet his guests.

It seemed that everyone in the jail had an opinion about what was going on with myself and the CERT team. The writing of *token* on my locker was still a mystery, but that too was revealed later on. I continued coming to work and preforming my duties as a correctional officer just as I had been, but now my fellow officers had openly showed their racist ways to me. I had remained on the honor guard after resigning from the CERT team when one of the younger officers became ill and passed away. He was a very liked guy, and also there were other family members who also worked at the Elmira Correctional Facility. It was a sad and somber time.

During his service, the facility honor guard was called upon to be present. I and the other members of the honor guard all met the night before the funeral at one of the local funeral homes in Elmira, New York. Once there, we met up with the sergeant in charge of the honor guard detail, and he informed us where he wanted us to stand. Some were inside, and some were outside. I was outside with a few others, as the large procession of mourners paid their respect for the fallen young officer. After standing outside for approximately two hours, toward the end of the service, when the long line of mourners had passed, members of the honor guard filed in to the funeral home.

As we made our way through the crowd, I was stopped in front of a lieutenant who yelled out, "Hey, I didn't know they let niggers in here!" Some of those standing around him were stunned by his statement. As I looked around the room, some heads and eyes dropped toward the floor in shame, as the just-retired lieutenant stood three feet away from me with a wide smile on his face after making his disrespectful, racist statement, which was directed at the only African American standing there—me. My first thought was to punch him in his mouth and knock his false teeth out, but that would have made me look just as ignorant as his ignorant, racist ass. After his comment, I continued to make my way through the conjoined rooms to the room where the young officer's body rested. After paying my respect and giving my condolences to the family, I exited the funeral home.

A few days later, I had a conversation with the sergeant who was in charge of the honor guard. I informed him about what had transpired at the funeral home. he acknowledged he had already heard what had transpired. I then notified the sergeant that effective immediately I would resign. Just as the lieutenant, the sergeant requested I remain on the honor guard, which I also declined. It was clear the writing was on the wall—or in my case, on my CERT locker—when some racist wrote *token* on it.

After resigning from both the CERT team and the Honor Guard, I thought that the racial discrimination and harassment would stop by me not being on any of the extracurricular activities. While working in the mess hall or kitchen area, I and a few of the other officers seemed to have a good working relationship, to the point a couple of the officers invited myself along with my family to join them and their family at the local hockey game. Elmira NY had just gotten their first semi pro hockey team. A lot of the staff at the facility went to the games. I myself had never seen a live hockey game, so I and my family went to the game. Once there, we all sat and enjoyed the game. At the intermission or break in the game, I and another officer went to get refreshments for ourselves and others. While we were making our way down the stairs toward the concession stands, an officer from the facility who was on the CERT team spotted us and yelled out to the white officer I was with, calling him by name, "Hey, I see you brought your porter with you," referring to me as an inmate that cleans up in the facility.

The two stairways were separated by a large opening. He quickly took off in the crowd. The guy I was with looked at me, stunned by his comment. He then said to me, "He is an asshole." When I had the opportunity at work, I saw the little loudmouth troll of a man and confronted him and asked him who the hell he was talking to at the hockey game. He then became loud and boisterous to bring attention to us. Before this, I told him not to harass me and leave me alone. It was found out that the little troll was the one that had written *token* on my CERT locker. This guy was known as a troublemaker. He stood about five feet, six inches tall with his lifts in his boots. Yes, the man had the short man complex and everyone knew it. Other officers laughed at him for being on the CERT team. Because of him and a couple of other guys on the team who were short in stature, the team's nickname was known as the Squirt Team. This was one miserable bastard.

I remember one day, me and a few officers were talking about some tragic event that had taken place in South America, where a number of people had died. He overheard us saying how awful it was and he interjected with, "F—— those people. I don't care about them, they're not Americans." We all walked away, shaking our heads. Shortly after confronting the troll over the hockey game incident, I found a picture of a disheveled black man with a wild hairdo, and written on the picture were the words "This is your black ass brother." This I found stapled to my time card. I was surely being pushed into a corner. I warned those individuals that had their minds set on harassing me to stop, which they ignored.

I soon was forced to report all the harassment I was receiving to the higher-ups at the Elmira CF and the state division of human rights, who were all the while aware that the facility had a problem when it came to minorities. Elmira Correctional Facility was already under a federal court order for discrimination in the case *Santiago vs. Miles*. This was a case brought by the inmates for being treated unfairly when it came to how housing, jobs, and programs were being given to the inmates. The court found that the white inmates were being given preference over the best jobs, programs, and housing even though the black and Hispanic inmates outnumbered them by a disproportionate amount. After reporting the many racial incidents I was subjected to, you would think it would have settled down, but it only fueled them up and emboldened them to harass me even more. Some of the racist officers started saying, "Brown is playing the race card" once I reported all the racist incidents. No, I wasn't playing a race card. I was playing the hand that these racist out-of-control officers had dealt me when they started all this. They were well aware of my stance on discrimination, which was "Don't start nothing, won't be nothing."

The little racist troll who had harassed me at the hockey game and had written on my locker and time card was fueling the fire after he was questioned regarding his actions, so after, he started harassing me whenever he saw me riding down the street or just out and about. Elmira, New York, is a small town, and unfortunately, he lives just two streets over from me. He would make it a point to see me and my family and find some way to harass me. My hands were tied; I couldn't do anything to him to make him stop, so I started documenting everything. I started keeping a daily diary of everything. When he couldn't get a physical reaction from me, which is what he wanted, he enlisted the local law enforcement. His brother-in-law was an Elmira, New York, police officer. The next thing I knew, I was being harassed by the police. I was stopped while driving and had multiple false reports made by the racist troll to bring the police to me and my family's home, which ultimately resulted in my false arrest. Now let me remind you, I hadn't had any negative interaction with the local law enforcement. I couldn't even remember a traffic stop by them, but now after reporting the racial harassment that was taking place at the Elmira Correctional Facility, I became local law enforcement's top priority. This harassment became so pervasive I contacted and pleaded my innocence to the detective bureau of the Elmira Police Department, which had one of the other local law enforcement agencies administer a lie detector test to me and the racist troll, and the results were I passed and he failed. But even though he failed the test, they didn't charge him with filing false reports. If I would have failed the test, there is no doubt in my mind I would have been charged with multiple charges.

After he failed the lie detector, he stopped using his brother-in-law and the Elmira Police Department as a tool to harass me, but this wasn't the end. It was only the beginning of a campaign of unrelenting harassment at work that would span well into a decade by my fellow officers, the administration, and the union NYSCOPBA.

After the incident with this troll who had used the Elmira Police Department to harass me, I immediately contacted the state division of human rights to file a complaint to protect my rights and job. After doing so, all hell broke loose. My job as a correctional officer now became questionable. The officers and supervisors who were named in my complaints became very hostile and aggressive. I was one of four black African American correctional officers working at Elmira. I was the only black officer on the 7–3 shift. The supervisors and officer that were harassing me seemed set on trying to make my life a living hell. They recruited other employees, both security and civilian staff, to ultimately join their campaign to harass me with the hope of me either striking back physically or quitting my job. I had always said if they would have only come together as a collective to accomplish the department's goals for the good the way they came together collectively against me, the facility would have ran like clockwork. It was clear they wanted me gone for reporting their wrongdoing.

As I continued to work in the mess hall or kitchen, some of the officers bid better jobs so their jobs were bid by other officers who were working the evening shifts in the mess hall or kitchen. These new officers, along with the area supervisor, began to harass me. This harassment included verbal, physical, and outright violations of the departmental rules and regulations, also including and not limited to criminal offenses. One of the officers was a washed-up bodybuilder to whom it seemed that rules didn't apply. He truly thought he was the Boss more in charge than the supervisors themselves. You know he thought he was *jefe*. He along with his followers would also get together with the civilian workers to sabotage my job in the area. They would short the mess hall I was in charge of food rations so it would run short, causing all kinds of chaos such as the mess hall being run late, delaying the running of programs and other time aspects of the facility. I and a few others that cared about what was going on and were set on doing our jobs could see what was happening, but the supervisors would turn their heads to the problem that were being created or orchestrated by those set on harassing me and others.

I wasn't alone as a victim of the hateful harassment, although I was the only staff member being racially harassed. You had others being harassed by these rogue racist officers. There was one civilian who worked in the food service area that was subjected to relentless verbal harassment and threats by the washed-up, crazed weight lifter that was allowed to have crazed outbursts where he would literally tip tables over and threaten people with personal harm, acting like he was having some form of rage. The civilian was eventually transferred out of the facility and his job filled with another who feared no better against the raging out-of-control officers and his posse. I remember an incident where before he and the others came to the day shift, he had come in the mess hall where I was working to relieve me for his 2–10 shift. He came in and threatened me and started yelling and screaming at me. He then told me to step into the small broom closet. To settle his dispute, I ran into the small broom closet and told him I was waiting. It was just me and him. He decided against coming in that broom closet with me. If he would have, I was going to shut his punk mouth for him—I knew this guy was all talk. He and the others in his posse that were under his control, I kid you not, I have never seen so many loudmouth cowards in one spot. They were all talk, and they would only get tough around their buddies. Like I said, there were guys who could handle themselves. They were usually not troublemakers.

The cowards continued to harass me. One of the henchmen for the ragging, washed-up weight lifter, was a large, big-mouthed biker whom I nicknamed the Bucktooth Rabbit because his false front teeth were bucked. He was approximately 6'3" and three hundred pounds. He would attempt to threaten me. There was an incident in one of the mess halls when he threatened me in front of a group of inmates, where I stood toe to toe with him literally. As he attempted to intimidate me in front of the inmates, I told him, "I wish you would put your hands on me." He wasn't crazy; he knew I would fight him. Nothing happened.

In another incident with him, he attempted to have one of the inmates who worked in the kitchen / mess hall area assault me. I was working in the scullery or dishwashing area early one morning that was attached to two mess halls. As I sat in the room alone waiting for the workers, this same officer came into the smaller of the two mess halls, followed by an inmate that had a known mental illness and had violent outbursts. I had written the inmate up a few times previously in the last few months for different rule violations. As I sat there, the two stood behind the serving line in the mess hall, discussing something. The next thing I knew, the inmate walked into the room where I was at, looking crazed in the eyes. He was just walking around the room, pretending to look for something. I looked out the door to find the officer with his eyes glued on the door like he was waiting for the action and was acting as a lookout. When I ordered the inmate to leave the area, he immediately flew off the handle and started threatening me, yelling very loudly. As I looked around and looked out the door, I found this officer, one of my harassers, looking in on me and the inmate, and he was just standing there watching as the inmate threatened me. This inmate was stone-cold crazy and had assaulted staff in the past. I again attempted to order the inmate to leave the area, and he again refused by remaining in the room just feet from me, screaming. I again looked for assistance from my fellow officer who stood there looking on as to say, "You're on your own."

My street instincts kicked in, and I fought crazy with crazy. I begin to pace around the room, telling him to get out. There was a mop bucket close by with a large metal ringer attached to the side that I had grabbed hold of to protect myself against the inmate and rogue officer. I didn't carry a baton, so it was the next best thing. As this was going on, it was disrupted by other staff and inmates entering the area. I observed the bucktooth rabbit scurry out the locked door away from his lookout post. As the others entered the other mess hall from the other side, I and another officer handled the inmate, who was written up and locked up again by me. This officer had conspired with an inmate to assault me.

I reported this to the administration, which covered it up. The administration was embedding themselves with my harassers. In my long quest for justice, there were many incidents like this. My harassers would use many tactics to harass me, such as using the inmates in the food service area. My harassers along with the area supervisor would bring in food and other items for the inmates. The food would be cooked, and they would all share in the bounty in return for the inmates doing whatever the rouge staff would tell them to do. There were civilians involved also. They would have the inmates write false grievances against me, and I would have to respond to their outlandish or false accusations. There was a time where I would receive four to five grievances or complaints a week made by the inmates at the request of my fellow officers and civilian staff, which I adamantly complained about to the area supervisor and the administration, which was ignored and covered up, but that soon fell apart for them when a Hispanic inmate that I had warned the area sergeant about being too close to a female officer wrote a grievance and accuse me of using racial slurs at him. The area sergeant came to me one day with a smile on his face handing me that grievance and ordered me to give him a response in writing immediately, something told me to look at the grievance closely, and I did I read the three or so lines of lies over and over while looking at the paper for the proof of the lie. After a while, I found it—the date and time the inmate accused me of. His lie was on my day off, my RDO (regular day off). I immediately asked the sergeant if the inmate was mistaking me for another officer, at which time the sergeant looked at me like it was impossible to do so. Why? Because at the time I was the only African American officer working the day shift. I asked the sergeant if he could check with the inmate to ensure it was me. He returned and said, "The inmate said it was you on," and the sergeant then said the date.

I laughed and told the sergeant that would be impossible for it to have been me because I didn't work on that day. The sergeant didn't return the grievance to me, and they stopped using the inmates to write me up. The inmate who had written this grievance whom I had warned the sergeant about his close involvement with the female officer working in the food service area tuned out to be dead on the female officer and the inmate were having an affair. They found letters in the inmate's cell from her to the inmate and other unauthorized material during my twenty-eight years.

This same problem played out over and over at the Elmira Correctional facility. It seemed there was at least one incident a year of some form or another of staff having sexual relations with inmates. There was one incident where a female civilian staff member was having sex with an inmate, officer, and high-ranking security staff member. You had staff members who seemed to be trusted employees who would wind up mixed up in some form of sexual activity with an inmate—you couldn't trust anyone.

My harassment from staff heated up after those who insisted on harassing me found out I wasn't intimidated. I truly think they thought I was scared because I was the only African American officer on the day shift. They were sadly mistaken. I wasn't going to quit my job, and I had my mind made up to survive their outright discrimination and harassment.

Not long after filing charges with the EEOC and the state division of human rights, I was given an NOD. One of the officers in the food service area started harassing me and verbally threatened me. As I was heading up front to report this, I was stopped on the cage floor by the sergeant who had worked in the food service area that day. I had been relieved from my post as I walked onto the cage floor (main area where you enter and exit the facility), also were the watch commander and the chart sergeant Officer is located.

As I stepped on to the cage floor, I was met by this thinly built sergeant who had attempted in the past to intimidate me. He literally ran upon me, blocking my path and started screaming at me, asking me where I thought I was going. When he did this, he was inches in my face. There were approximately eight to ten officers hanging out on the cage floor. It was like a social gathering place for those officers trying to skip out on doing their jobs, when he the sergeant screamed in my face. I stood motionless and turned my head away to keep from smelling his breath. I felt a spit droplet hit my chain. That's when I lost it. I turned my head back around to face the sergeant, cocked my head back, and shot it forward, giving the sergeant the hurricane hippo holler. I screamed back in his face, "Get the hell out of my face, don't you threaten me!"

The sergeant's eyes shot wide open, and he stepped back out of my face. I know the sergeant got spit droplets on him off my tonsils. After yelling back in the sergeant's face, all the officers hanging out scurried off. It also brought the watch commander and the chart sergeant out of their offices to see what was happening. As I was continuing up front to the administration office, I was stopped and ordered into the watch commander's office, where the lieutenant questioned me and threatened to fire me, which he had no authorization to do.

After listening to the lieutenant misrepresent himself as the sole person who did the hiring and firing for the New York State Department of Corrections, I left his office and attempted to report the earlier incident with the officer threatening me and the one that had just occurred. The administration didn't want to hear about it, and in the next few days, I was suspended without pay, one of many suspensions I received for reporting discrimination at the Elmira Correctional Facility.

As I sat waiting for a hearing regarding my suspension, I now knew that I needed an attorney. I began to make calls to damn near all of the local law offices in Elmira, which all refused to help. I then started to call law firms in the upstate area such as Ithaca, Rochester Binghamton, and Syracuse, also with no luck. It seemed that the local law firms were like a web of protection to local law enforcement, so I took my search outside the web and compiled a list of lawyers in New York City to call. It seemed like I made five or so calls down to lawyers in New York City when I found myself speaking to attorney Marc Garber a young lawyer who sounded very energetic and enthusiastic. He wanted to meet, so my wife and I took a trip down to meet him. His office was located in Manhattan. We sat down and talked, and he sounded very understanding and sympathetic to my plight. As we talked, I described to him in detail about the treatment I was receiving. After we finished, he agreed to represent me. Neither one of us would have thought this would be a ten-year journey for justice. Over those years, I and my attorney have built a relationship. We have shared good times and bad times together just as friends do. Yep, I can still remember the day I met attorney Marc Garber who took my case. I was able to have the time to find an attorney because of my suspension without pay.

The department was now using the arbitration system as a tool to harass, intimidate, and punish me into submission to their racist treatment. Let's think about it—you disrespect me and my race, talk to me like I'm a slave back in the 1800s, and I'm supposed to keep all this quiet and not tell anyone what you're doing? I think that's right! Is that what I was supposed to do? Let my fellow employee disrespect me in any and every way they felt like? No self-respecting

person would allow another person to treat them with such disrespect. I didn't start this nor did I ask for this, but one thing I did
know—if those who chose to harass me thought for one minute that
I was going to allow them to intimidate and harass me into quitting my job, they should have thought different. My fellow officers
had declared war on me for reporting the discriminatory harassment
and treatment that they bestowed upon me. After, as the NOD or
suspension played out, a phony investigation was already being conducted. As I had stated, during the incident with the sergeant getting
in my face, there were approximately ten or more others who witnessed the whole incident, but all chose to become deaf, blind, and
mute to what truly transpired, those putting the sole assumption of
guilt on me.

You see, the sergeant wasn't being charged with anything. I and
I alone was being charged for the sergeant's disrespectful treatment of
me. I didn't see the sergeant before or after this treat any other officer
in which the manner he had disrespected me being just inches in my
face yelling about me reporting the discrimination and harassment
I was receiving. I did make it perfectly clear to all I spoke to investigating or questioning my action, "No man is going to get that close
in my face and not get the reaction the sergeant received, and I don't
care who they were." And I ended it with, "Including the president
of the United States." If the sergeant would have yelled in my face
this same way in the street, away from work, he would have surely
gotten knocked out.

It came time for the arbitration hearing the trial for my false
NOD, which is a dog and pony show where the state, union, and
arbitrator have already come to some form of conclusion to your
guilt or innocence. Now remember I'm one of three black officers
out of around 460 officers, and I'm charged with a NOD in retaliation for reporting discrimination. My lawyer, the lawyer for the
state, the judge, my accuser, all the witnesses the state had gathered
to lie, and the stenographer were all white. I could only watch while
an orchestrated circus starring the dog and pony show played out in
front of me. If this arbitration was being conducted in the name of
justice, then justice has no shame. The sergeant lied, and so did the

witness for the state that was backing the sergeant's lies. My fellow officers were doing me just like they do inmates when there out to get them for one reason or another. The department of corrections was showing me just how racist it was.

After the arbitration hearing ended, I remained suspended without pay, awaiting the outcome of the arbitrators' decision, which we already knew wasn't going to be in my favor. After the lackluster representation I received from the union lawyer and the lie-riddled testimony given by the state's witnesses against me, I was given a decision of Guilty, and the state took over six months' pay and benefits from me for punishment for reporting outright discrimination and harassment. It was clear retaliation. I was allowed to return to work after my suspension.

The arbitration system was just one of many tools my harassers used to harass me. For instance, they used my car as a tool to harass me. One morning, I arrived to work, parked my car in the facility parking lot, and I was on my post in the mess hall working when an officer entered the mess hall with a group of inmates and the officer came up to me and said, "Hey, Brown, your truck has a flat."

I then said, "What did you say?"

He then repeated, "Your truck has a flat." I then went to the area sergeant and reported what I was just told and asked to be relieved to check out my vehicle that was parked in the employees' parking lot. As I was waiting to get relieved, the officers that were in the mess hall were all quiet like they had known something. I also remember thinking, *How did this officer know what kind of vehicle I drove anyways?* But see, that was the thing about being the only one, *uno*, the one and only black officer on the day shift at the Elmira CF. Everyone thought they knew me, and I couldn't tell you half of the employees' names on the day shift, let alone tell you what kind of car they drove.

After being relieved from my post to go check my vehicle. I made my way up front and to the parking lot, where I found my two rear tires flat from lashes. I reported this to the dep of security, and while speaking to the dep of security, he seemed more upset at me than at the person or persons who had damaged my vehicle. As we spoke, he had the attitude like he really couldn't care less about me or my personal property. As we spoke, I informed the dep this was clearly retaliation for me filing a complaint against those that were and are harassing me. I then went on to say. "Hey, Dep, I'm not putting my hands on anyone's property around here, and I don't appreciate anyone putting their hands on mine."

His reaction to my statements put him in full protection mode, making it clear to me that there wasn't anything going to be done about it by saying to me, "So what do you want me to do?" It was clear that the facility administration was unconcerned about my vehicles' tires being slashed.

I then informed the dep of security that the police should be notified, which didn't happen. I then had a local auto garage come to the facility to tow my vehicle. I was then sent home and suspended from work. Yes, that's right—my tires on my vehicle were slashed by some crazed racist nut and they suspended me for it, but wait, wait on it! They also made me go see a state psychiatrist to get cleared to return to work, Now if that's not retaliation, what is?

I remember going to see the state psychiatrist. The doctor asked me why I was there, and I responded with, "I thought you knew why I am here," and the doctor confirmed that he didn't know. I then told the doctor that I was at work being discriminated against and my tiers were slashed and I was suspended and ordered to see him before I could return back to work.

The doctor looked shocked and stun at the statement I had just made. He replied sharply with "You shouldn't be here," and said "Good luck when you go back to work." That was the length of our conversation.

Days later, I was allowed to return to work, which I did. Neither the administration or the union offered me no explanation for the suspension for getting my tires slashed. Also, I never parked my vehicle on state property again while on duty. There was no doubt my fellow officers and the department and union were all out to punish me for reporting discrimination. My vehicle was just one tool my harassers were allowed to use. They also used my state time card to harass me. I would put my time card in the time card slot just like every other employee at the Elmira correctional facility, and my harassers would take my time card and either destroy it or discard it. I would then be ordered to fill out a new time card after it happened three or four times and I was summoned to the time and attendance lieutenant's office and given an order to fill out a new time card that had been taken from the time card rack by someone intent on harassing me. Once again, just as my tires, the lieutenant spoke to me just as the dep, trying to make the missing time card seem as if it was my fault, placing the blame on me. As I sat there listening to the lieutenant threating me with disciplinary action for the missing time, I did not take kindly to the lieutenant's threats for some idiot taking my time card out of the time rack, and he was making it my fault.

I interjected with a stern but respectful response to the lieutenant's threat. I first told him he wasn't going to sit here and threaten me and that it wasn't my fault for someone taking my time card, and if he felt like he wanted to write me up go ahead but I had had a time card until someone took it, and he needed to find that person and write them up, not me, and I wasn't going to make out another time card. This time, I was refusing to comply. It wasn't an order given with common sense nor did it have integrity. What the lieutenant was giving me was a threat, and I was refusing to obey his threat.

Days later, I was summoned to the dep of security's office and once again questioned about missing time cards and asked about the conversation I and the lieutenant had. I stopped the Dep and corrected him and said, "You mean when the lieutenant threatened me with disciplinary action for someone else's neglect by using my time card as a tool to harass me."

Once again, the dep became defensive of the lieutenant's action, the same way he had done when my vehicle was vandalized. He was speaking like he was trying to convince himself that it was all right for some idiot to take my state-issued time card out of the employee's time card rack and it was all right for the lieutenant to threaten me with disciplinary action. Just as I did the lieutenant, I respectfully told the dep I wasn't making out any more time cards and expressed to him what I had expressed to the lieutenant. The dep seem to take a different tone after that when I also told him he wasn't going to make me responsible for some idiot taking my time card. He then tried to offer me solutions to the problem, none of which would have solved the problem of me having my time card taken by someone insisting on harassing me, for reporting and filing charges of discrimination against those individuals, and the administration at the Elmira Correctional Facility that had harassed me and discriminated against me. I ended up coming up with a solution for the problem. I informed the dep I would be keeping my time card on my person and not in the time card rack along with everyone else. He agreed, and from that day on, I carried my time card on me. The time card rack wasn't just a place to store and display time cards. It also functioned as a security tool. After punching in, it was placed in a rack to acknowledge all the security staff that was on duty in the facility on that shift. The dep authorizing me to carry my time card on my person and not place it in the time card rack broke security procedures, but the dep would had rather risk security then to find and confront the problem of who was taking my state-issued time card.

For the most part during my twenty-eight years, it always seemed that the bullshit always trumped security. Take for example the 2003 Elmira Correctional Facility escape. The same dep walked in the prison one hot July morning right past a white sheet hanging in a corner that was visible to the human eye, but the dep failed to see the long white sheets tied together for a robe that hung from the top of the building, to close to the ground. Yes, the top security member of the administration failed to detect what was right in front of his nose, but just as I said, a lot of people would walk around with their heads down. I don't know if it was shame or pure guilt. The dep was one of those who walked around with his head down a lot. Imagine you're the highest-ranking security staff and you fail to see a white makeshift robe made of bedsheets against a red stone exterior of a building that's hanging a good three stories down the building and you walk right by it. Yup, I would dare say you have some answering to do. The rope was placed there by the two escaped inmates now on the run. The robe wasn't noticed by anyone until it was around the time the 7–3 shift officers started to arrive and some well-observant officer spotted it and alerted the watch commander, which was after the time the dep had arrived.

After the watch commander was notified, a facility count was called, and the inmates who had just been counted were recounted, and to the surprise of those in the block where the two inmates locked, they were short by two on the count. Yep, they were gone—the two inmates had done a Houdini act. Well, actually, it was the old hole in the ceiling act. They had managed to make a hole in the ceiling and made their way to the rooftop, where they went down the white makeshift rope that was undetected by the dep of security.

I was working in the mess hall when the sergeant informed the staff that all the inmates were going back to their cells and the facility was being placed on lockdown. At first, there was no explanation, but we soon found out we had two escapees. After locking the inmates in and returning to the food service as requested by the sergeant to help with the preparation of the feed-up meals for the now locked-down inmates. After getting job assignments from the sergeant and as I attempted to do my job, the burned-out ex-weight lifter had one of his raging out-of-control episodes directed at me. He started threatening and verbally harassing me keeping me from being able to do what the sergeant had requested. The sergeant lifted the area to go upfront to help with the now state of emergency. No sooner than when the sergeant lifted this out-of-control, childish man started, just as a kid would do. He also had other members of his posse such as the bucktooth rabbit, and the others under his thumb also joined in. The civilians were intimidated by his cowardly show of emotions, so they would hide in the office to avoid the out-of-control, raging coward.

Now to remind you, we had two escapees on the run and if harassing me was at the top of your priority list, I would dare say you're in the wrong profession. This man's priorities and his mental state were both in question. His rage directed at me was solely in retaliation of me filing charges against those that were harassing me, including him.

I offered to go into the small broom closet to settle his dispute that he had conjured up. I was going to shut him up, which he refused. Even though the offer was made and refused by him, he still insisted on threatening me. Even though I offered to meet him off state property to settle the dispute or disputes that he conjured up, he also refused to do it. I would dare say this man was trying to get me to assault him at work so I could lose my job. He was being allowed to do this the administration as well as the security and civilian staff had all witnessed at one time or another this man harass or threaten me, but they would either choose to lie and be part of the harassment or denied the truth by saying they didn't see or hear what just happened in front of them with the exception of one officer, an older Caucasian officer who also worked in the food service area. He himself had been subjected to harassment by the raging out-of-control coward and his posse of followers. They would harass this man because he associated with me at work. They would tell him, "Go kiss Brown on his big, fat lips" or "Why don't you go to corn roll school with your brother Brown?" When he was questioned about the harassment that he had witnessed that I was being subjected to, he corroborated my version of the events. After he did that, he put himself in direct fire of those out to harass me. I had and have much respect for this man. He is a standup type of guy—truthful, righteous, and unafraid. I was the only black officer on the shift fighting for my rights, but this man was going against his own for what was right.

My family and friends would support me and keep me uplifted during my epic battle. They would say that they were praying and tell me what I was doing by standing up against discrimination and injustice was the right thing to do. They would also tell me what I was doing would directly affect those coming behind me. But still with all that said to me, the real standup guy was this man. He was going against everything, including his race, a true standup guy. During the time I had the pleasure of working alongside this man, we were able to learn a lot about each other. We were both very security minded. While working in the food service area, he would keep a daily log of everything. The log would include names, places, and times, along with information about events as they unfolded during the course of the day. I kept a daily diary in which I would document all the harassment I was being subjected to. Officer Q would document everything. For example, if you were working with him and you had to leave the area to use the bathroom, he would document what time you left and what time you returned. As a matter of fact, there was a young officer who was under investigation for a foiled escape attempt. The officer's whereabouts was being brought into question, and this officer's job was on the line. When they started questioning others, it was learned that Officer Q had documented the young officers movement due to the fact he was working in the area it and the time and whereabouts of the officer being where he said he was supposed to be was corroborated by the daily log that Officer Q was keeping, helping to clear the young officer of any wrongdoing.

I and Officer Q were made out to look like bad guys in the food service area for just doing our jobs. Others would hang out off their post. Most of the time the officers that were supposed to be in the mess halls watching the inmates would be found grouped up at the kitchen desk post, so you would have three or four officers just hanging out, and I and Officer Q would be on our jobs in the area watching the inmates. The area sergeant would see what was going on but would do nothing or say nothing to those not doing their job. When it came to the rules, these guys had none. These officers seemed to be put in place to hang out and cause havoc. They would give the inmates unauthorized items. They would also allow them to take from the facility food supply for sale to the inmates throughout the jail. For example, the inmates were frisked when they entered and left the food service area, and the rule was that the inmates were allowed four to six slices of bread and two pieces of fruit. The officers working in the mess hall were responsible for doing the frisk. As the inmates entered and exited for the day, I would watch as the inmates exiting were frisked or checked by the rogue officers along with the sergeant but allowed to pass by without unauthorized items being taken from them by those frisking. I and Officer Q would take any items that weren't allowed over the allotted amount authorized. The inmates would complain about me and Officer Q doing our job. They would say, "You guys are the only ones that do this shit," meaning taking the unauthorized items, which would be anything from bags of raw chicken, pounds of sugar, bags of rice, and other stuff.

Speaking about bags of rice, I remember stopping an officer in G block from helping an inmate steal a garbage bag full of rice. The bag was so heavy the inmate was dragging it along. A lot of the staff was dealing with the inmates in some form or fashion, whether it was bringing in some form of contraband or turning their heads the other way for a pack of smokes or something else. The rogue officers would assist the inmates in stealing. The doors to the storage rooms would be locked, but still the inmates would end up with all kinds of state food from the storage rooms. When they weren't letting them steal, they were bringing food and other unauthorized items in for them. The sergeants were ineffective in controlling the rouge officers. They themselves were placed under their thumb, those giving control to the rouge officers who seemed to be in control. Even though the sergeant was well aware of what was happening, they would do nothing. When it came to jobs in the area, I and Officer Q would seem to be the only two that were there for care, custody, and control. The others were just there. If you are working in a prison and think your job is to harass other employees and to be a co-conspirator with the inmates, you're working in the wrong place.

You would think, But now wait—if the administration and officials in Albany know what is going on and it's reported to them and they do nothing, what does that make them? Well, let's see—rogue officers being allowed to run free and do as they wish, breaking laws and departmental rules and regulations and nothing is done? It almost sounds like we lock are criminals and law breakers in a criminal enterprise that we call prison. There were officers that were no better than the inmates when it came to criminality; they just hadn't gotten caught. The white officers were protected by the union and the wickedness that ruled the day; those in high positions were making the decisions. I always said that a blind man could see what was being done to me, but no one, not a supervisor, no one in the administration, no one in the union, no one in Albany could see I was being harassed and retaliated against for filing charges for discrimination. They all knew about and allowed for the harassment to happen, and they themselves were all willing participants. The higher-ups in Albany didn't care about what was happening. It's scary to even know that a large governmental state agency would conspire with others to discriminate and retaliate against a state employee, but that was the truth. This was the classic David versus Goliath. It wasn't me versus those that had discriminated against me, which would have been a fair fight! But no, they made it me against the whole Department of Corrections and Nyscoba and the arbitration system that was used as a retaliatory tool to harass, intimidate me, and ultimately fire me through the arbitration system. I was truly working in a hostile working environment. There were officers doing any and everything they pleased—breaking laws and rules and never being disciplined or given a NOD.

There was one officer who was working one of the entrances where the vehicles enter the facility for deliveries and state transportation, also known as the truck trap. It was a highly secured area as the vehicles enter and exit they are inspected and are to be thoroughly checked. Well, one of the state buses arrived for either drop-off or pickup or in most cases both, and this officer greeted the state bus with a warm hello and then asked the question to all on board, "Who wants to see my pierced dick?" It was reported he then displayed his pierced penis coved with blood from the fresh piercing job he had just performed. Just before the state bus's arrival, he was reported to the administration by someone on board the bus, and he received no NOD (notice of disciplinary) for his action. Occasionally, they would lock an officer out, usually for assault on an inmate, but most times, it would never be to the level of a NOD, it would be through the administration, and if they were locked out without pay, as I had been many times, they wouldn't have to worry about that. Either the members or the union along with the staff would take up a collection to pay the locked-out officer's salary. Staff, it seemed, truly never had to truly worry about being charged with assaulting an inmate because the state would then be acknowledging they had a problem, and in the state eyes or their position, a problem cost the state money. My fellow officers had no problem lying on me, supervisors had no problem running with that lie, and worse yet, one at the largest state governmental agencies, the New York State Department of Correction had no problem helping my harassers by filing charges on me just on the word of those harassing me without doing an investigation. The state's employee relation board was ultimately in control of filing NODs (notice of discipline). Speaking of investigations, what a joke that the department had an IG (inspector general) unit, which employed Department of Corrections employees. Most or all were correctional officers. The other officers called them the Rat Squad, dirty rats, and other names they would come up with. The department was truly policing itself. It answered to no one. The department would send members of the IG investigation team in all the time after an inmate had been physically assaulted by staff. The investigation would go like this—the IG office would send a team of investigators into the facility. They would get dirty stares and glares from the moment they entered into the facility. Some of those out-of-control individuals would even call them rats right to their face, and they would complain to the administration, but the officers were never punished. The phones throughout the jail would begin to ring off the hook to announce their arrival as the rat squad made their way through the facility. They would question both inmates and staff to obtain information into an investigation into one thing or another. An inmate could look like he was hit in the face by a two by four by a group of officers, and no one would be charged. The so-called rat squad would come, and it seemed that their job was to just cover up what they could to lessen the state's liability into any misconduct by staff and also trying to avoid any legal liability because it is truly all about the money. The so-called rat squad would attempt to silence the inmates with fear of some form of retaliation. If the inmates were trying to file charges on staff, it seemed that the rat squad was only investigating the state's liability. They were more like insurance adjusters trying to find a way to wiggle out from under their responsibility if at all possible. Yes, over my twenty-eight years, I had many inmates tell me of their interaction with the IG unit, a.k.a. the rat squad, after they had been involved in an incident of one form or another. The inmates version is never believed because anyone that works in the department of corrections knows that all kinds of things happen, and many chose to turn their heads or lie or play the "go along to get along" game, like Martin Luther King Jr.

said, "Two of the most dangerous things are conscientious stupidity and sincere ignorance," and my harassers seemed to suffer from both. Also, when it came to the inmates' vision of an incident, most of the time, those doing the investigation know that it was usually a really high probability that the inmate was telling the truth. I would know best because the rat squad also attempted to discredit me and chose not to believe me when it came to the relentless harassment inflicted upon me by my fellow officers and the department for me reporting outright racism, which seemed to be deeply rooted not just at the Elmira Correctional Facility but also deeply rooted in the department itself. During my twenty-eight years, I would wonder why those who chose to do the wrong thing would fear the IG's office and take such a defensive stance against them when they were truly working with them. I think that there were those who thought they were truly above the law and answered to no one for their out-of-control behavior, and those in high places supported them, so even requiring them to be subjected to an investigation into an accusation an inmate made was asking too much of them remember they answer to no one.

As I continued working in the mess hall or food service area, the group of rogue officers continued to harass me, along with others they had recruited to the "We Hate Officer Brown" hate group. There were officers I had a good working relationship with that were persuaded by my harassers not to talk to me. They wouldn't talk to them. If they talked to me. It was scary because the majority of the staff acted as if they had a childlike mentality one of a high schooler. I witnessed grown adults act more like kids than adults and unable to stand on their own and would let others decide for them whom they talked to and whom they didn't. It wasn't just the lower echelon; it was those higher up in the administration who acted the same way.

I remember being the only African American on the day shift until that day ended when another local black officer transferred into the facility. We had grown up in the same neighborhood in Elmira, and our family knew each other well. After he had been at the facility a few days, we ran into each other and we talked. He asked me what was going on around here and informed me that the white officers told him not to talk to me. He assured me he told them he would talk to whom he wanted to, and he informed them he had known me a long time. I then gave the other black officer a brief rundown of what I was being subjected to. He wasn't shocked at what I had told him. He was well aware what was going on. The Department of Corrections doesn't hide what they do; they cover up what they do. Those that were harassing me were so hell bent on it they tried to convince a black officer to help them harass me by telling him not to talk to me because they weren't. We talked for a while and laughed. It was a relief having another black officer on the shift with me after being the only one. It was also nice having another officer that I could confide in. Having another minority didn't stop the harassment or help me because he wasn't working around me, and they would make sure that didn't happen. I would have staff harassing me verbally, and when I put them in their place, they along with others would all run to the area sergeant and tell a twisted version of what may or may not had transpired if he the sergeant himself wasn't there harassing me. It was obvious I had two choices: keep my job and wait for my day in court or walk away and quit my job. I chose to stay and fight; quitting would only give them what they want. They wanted me gone.

While still working in the mess hall, my day would start with me being harassed. After I punched in and went to line up, the sergeant would be standing just feet away as I would be mocked or belittled by my fellow officers. They would be allowed to say and do whatever they pleased, and if I responded or complained about my treatment, I would be written up and brought up on some form of charges. I know my fight for my rights would again have to be a nonviolent protest. My fellow officers were aware of my past experience with racism in the Department of Correctional Services, but they still choose to discriminate against me and test my tolerance. They were well aware that I had sued the department in the past, and some of those officers that had been named in that previous suit were now working at the Elmira correctional facility. They were now out to get me at any cost. I now not only had the inmates to contend with but now the staff as well. I was ostracized by my fellow officers. In jail, there are only two colors, they say—blue and green, at least that is what they tell you in the academy at Elmira. They made it perfectly clear that it was blue, green, and brown, and the line was drawn in the sand. One would truly have to wonder if they discriminated against me and openly harassed me, a correctional officer. What the hell were they doing to the inmates? Answer: any and everything they wanted. You had groups of rogue guards that were protected by the union and ex rogue guards who were promoted to high positions within the department who turned their heads the other way, or they themselves would orchestrate the coverup to protect the coward guards who would abuse the inmates. The abuse would come in many forms. I had seen inmates physically, verbally, and emotionally abused by these rogue guards. If the inmates complained about their treatment, it would only get worse. The harasser would recruit other staff members to assist in the harassment. This would include not only officers but civilian staff as well. For example, the inmate's councilor, teacher, or vocational instructor. They would all be on board, and the harasser or rogue guard would do this with just a phone call to these individuals, asking them to put the inmate on the burn, meaning don't help the inmate with anything, and to write him up for anything they could come up with. Also, the inmates packaged his meals. His recreation time, which included phone time, his visitation, and his movement would all be altered by a phone call. They would also lie on the inmates at the drop of a hat, writing them up, and then testify at the inmates' tier hearing, a hearing held after an inmate receives a misbehavior report for breaking a rule. It was always a joke that when correctional staff testifies, it's not testimony, it's lie-mony because a guard knows it's his word against a convicted felon and no one really cares what happens to the inmate in question. Now don't get it wrong—there are many inmates that break the rules, but at the same time, there are as many staff members who do the same behind those walls.

While still working in the mess hall, I remember this one particular guard that worked the 3–11 shift that relieved me from my post in mess hall number 4. He was one of those officers that was allowed by the state to live in Pennsylvania and employed in New

York state. He was also a washed-up weight lifter who was recruited by the others to harass me. He would come in the mess hall to relieve me and would attempt to threaten me to try to get me to put my hands on him so I'd be fired. Some of these guys were sure punks, all talk. He was told to see me away from work, which he refused to do. One day, when he came in running his coward mouth, I stopped his rant with "Hey, I'm only going to tell you once! Don't have any more of that inmate commissary creatine up in the officer's locker again." He then hurried over to the officer's locker in the mess hall to see if it was still there. This guard was openly trading with an inmate. He would buy a muscle magazine, and the inmate would get a bottle of creatine from the commissary, and they would trade. The officer would then place it in a locker that is used by the officer that is on duty in the area, those making the officer in the area at the time solely responsible for whatever was in it. I had warned him to stop, so about two or three weeks later, I was working in the area and opened the locker to place my things in it, and there it was— another bottle of creatine, which I dumped down the drain. When the big, stupid coward arrived to relieve me and started spouting off at the mouth, I informed him his creatine had to be dumped down the drain. Once again, he scurried over to the locker to check its content. He opened the locker and looked inside and slammed it shut. He began yelling. I then remained him I had warned him about having his unauthorized contraband in the officer's locker. He then continued yelling as he scurried to the back of the food service area, where the sergeant and the other officers were gathered. Even though the area supervisors knew of the incident of the rogue guard having unauthorized exchanges with the inmates, he was never disciplined from day one. A good officer knows if you bring an inmate something, you bring him anything, so to avoid that you only give them what they have coming from the state of New York, what the department has authorized.

You had many officers like this loudmouth rogue officer. He lived in an area in PA where it is 97 percent white and worked in a prison that is 90 percent minority. You had many officers like this in the upstate rural areas. They worked in the prisons and were raised and lived only around their own, so they knew little to nothing about other ethnic groups with the exception of what they had seen on TV or in the news. Then you put them to work in a state prison that is predominantly black and Hispanic. The outcome is not good. These men and women usually have no communication skills, understanding, or knowledge of any other race or culture with the exception of their own.

Wait a minute. Stop the press. On October 6, 2018, after leaving my sister's sixtieth birthday celebration at a local restaurant, my wife and I were riding down one of the main roads that is attached to a large shopping area. As we were riding down the road, a white male came speeding by beeping his horn emphatically and yelling out the window, "Fuck you, motherfucker!" while sticking his middle finger up in the air at us out the window. As we drove along, I was startled and taken aback and left wondering, What did I do? As we continued down the road, we were approaching the red light, and turning left. The ragging, out-of-control white male in the pickup also got the light. As I attempted to drive in the turning lane, I was cut off by the male in the pickup truck, who then yelled out the window, "That is you! You fucking nigger!" he continued yelling. "Fucking nigger!" It was clear he didn't want his identity revealed by blocking me from turning left, which would have had me on his driver's side. As I turned left, he cut in front of me. I was now in back of him, at which time a photo of his license plate was taken and me and my wife continued on and I called the police. I waited outside the store as my wife went in. Once the county sheriff deputy arrived, I explained to him what had transpired. I told him about the raging, out-of-control white racist male who had just accosted me and my wife as we rode down the road. After I described in detail what had happened, the deputy asked me when he caught up to the individual if I wanted to press charges against him. I paused for a moment and responded with I would hate for someone to go to jail for that, so I suggested that maybe I could talk to them and find out what he was thinking and why he felt that way. The deputy said he would see what he could do and that he would be in touch.

A few days later, the deputy did call our home, and I spoke to him regarding the ragging racist, out-of-control white man in the gray pickup. The deputy informed me that he had gotten in touch with the man and spoke to him, and he was giving a different version of the incident when I and the deputy had spoken. On the day of the incident, I had alluded to the fact that from the side of the man's face, it looked like a guy I had worked with at the Elmira Correctional Facility, so as the deputy spoke, I asked him this guy's name, and I said the name. The deputy got quiet for a moment. He then responded with "Yes, that's his name."

I said boldly, "Oh, hell no. I want to press charges. This guy was harassing me at work when I worked at the Elmira Correctional Facility." The deputy then informed me when I could meet with him to do just that, press charges. A couple of days later, I along with my wife met with the deputy and pressed charges. Now this is the same guy who was harassing me for throwing out the inmate property that he had traded the inmate for, the same one who would come into the mess hall searching me out to harass me every day. He along with the other officers who had been recruited by their handler, the burned-out ragging, washed-up weight lifter who had also intimidated the area supervisors and would do what the ragging guard told them to do or would face problems in the area created by no other than the ragging guard and his merry band of rouge officers, who had a network of inmates who stood ready to cause chaos when called upon to do so and would be paid off with food out of the facility food supply or some other form of payment for their loyalty to the rouge guards that they stood ready to serve.

Days after filing charges against the ragging, out-of-control racist, he was formally served. He then filled false charges against me because anything other than the way I and my wife described the blatant, ragging, racist, verbal assault we were subjected to would be an outright lie. This wouldn't be the first time that he and the other rogue guards had lied to cover up their wrongdoing. Remember, their testimony was laughed at as many have admitted to lying while being questioned under oath about one thing or another and it was often joked about as being lie-mony. My goodness was this racist, ragging, rogue guard conjured up by just writing about his wrongdoing. It sure felt like this guy was infatuated with me. I had been retired for around a year and eight months, and he still insisted on harassing me. This sick coward racist needs mental help. See, this is one of the things that is covered up in the department. You have many staff members who them self-suffer from mental illness that was on full display. Each and every day inside these facilities, these individuals such as this guy are mentally unstable, unable to properly communicate, rationalize, and comprehend right from wrong themselves and they are in trusted with the care, custody, and control of the incarcerated citizens of New York State. Now let's not get it wrong—you have many more dedicated men and women in the department that are mentally sane and have a rational state of mind, but you have many staff members who don't have this state of mind, just like this guy who was unstable and unfit for duty, but the facility administration, the union, and the employees all turn their heads, close their eyes, and cover their ears to all the wrong, even if it means jeopardizing their own integrity. The last time I checked, wrong is wrong and right is right—I don't care who you are. I have seen employees who would lie for one another and cover up misdeeds for one another. You see, the department takes the stand that all law enforcement agencies take—they have a thin, blue gutless line that they expect not to be crossed. That line has nothing to do with looking out for one another and keeping each other safe. It is there to protect wrongdoers. When one of them gets out of control and does something to break the same laws they have been sworn to protect, they assume they can hold every man and woman accountable to their thin blue line. The line is a tool that the corrupt lawbreakers in uniform use to control the masses and keep good people from being just that—good—and having some type of integrity. A lot of staff couldn't care less about what is going on around them, just as long as they receive a paycheck every two weeks, and they keep coming. They will lie, cheat, and steal if necessary. If you lie for others to cover up wrong doing and don't report wrongdoing, you have zero integrity. What you have is loyalty to wrongdoing and corruption. My loyalty was to the Department of Corrections, not to the union and its members.

They didn't sign my check, and I am that type that doesn't care what the hell you think about me doing the right thing, and that posed a direct threat to all who chose to break the rules and harass me, just as those who chose to do the wrong thing and are corrupt have a line drawn in the sand. So do good people who have integrity and stand for what is right. We also have a line. It seems that having integrity in the Department of Corrections is taboo as a correctional officer or even a civilian worker in a prison when those rogue officers decide to go off script and assault inmates or verbally abuse an inmate or staff member and others are eyewitness to it. They become deaf, blind, and dumb to the incident, protecting those rogue officers in fear of retribution if they were to come forward with the truth. They, the mass majority of prison workers, are put under a shadow of fear and intimidation by their peers who shun and harass them for speaking out. The administration also participates by turning a blind eye and deaf ear to that harassment, so in essence, they themselves are condoning and participating in the behavior of those who administrate the injustice to the just. The department heads in Albany who are supposed to know all that goes on are misinformed, lied to, and manipulated by the administration, and the sad thing about it is they just play along. So let's see—you have retribution, intimidation, participation, and manipulation, which all adds up to corruption. That's why a lot of employee reference the department as the Department of Corruption. Now see yourself as the only black officer around, and one of those rogue, out-of-control guards decides they are going to say or do something to not only make you feel uncomfortable but also is outright discriminatory and racist, and you check their cowardly racist ass. That's when they start lying and covering stuff up and trying to make you look like the bad guy for fighting back against the abuse and their wrongdoing.

I had this psycho guard who was stone cold out of his mind and everyone knew it. When he would enter the facility and traveled through the gated front entrance, he wouldn't use his hands like a normal person. He would literally kick the gates with his foot, causing the gate to swing back fast. No supervisor or any other higher up addressed him even though it posed a direct danger to others traveling through the gate. This same nut had a position in the rear kitchen area of the food service area where the trash and loading dock were located. There was a small office for the officer where the cleaning supplies and other items were kept like a toolbox and other items. One morning, I walked to the back to get supplies for the mess hall area. I was working when I stepped in the back. I noticed there were more than the allowed number of inmates hanging out in the rear kitchen area. I immediately asked the inmates who was assigned to the area and who wasn't. The inmates who weren't assigned left the area. I then asked the inmates that were assigned to the area where the officer in charge was. They then pointed up toward the celling, saying "Upstairs." I then looked around to find the door leading to the outside open and the office door wide open. Not only were the doors left unsecure, but in the office on the desk was the tool box wide open. Inside the tool box were approximately three or four screwdrivers, wrenches, and pliers. If my memory holds me, also inside the box was a checklist of the contents of the box. I stood there and thought for a moment and thought about this being me in this situation, and this man had damn near the same time as me. As a matter of fact, I believe he had a year more than me.

I then looked down into the box and saw the ten-inch long screwdriver and thought about the damage it could cause in the hands of an inmate, so I chose to make it a learning session for this veteran guard. I took the large ten-inch screwdriver and hid it. I then secured all the unsecured doors and returned to my area. I placed the screwdriver in a secure locker and went and found the spineless supervisor and spoke to him regarding what I had observed in the rear kitchen. I then suggested that he have the officer in the rear kitchen area inventory the tool box to ensure everything is there. I laughed because even though the sergeant may have had bad feelings toward me. He knew it made good sense to check it out. A short time later, the sergeant went in the back and asked the guard to inventory the tool box to ensure that everything was in there. I observed him ask and I even witnessed the guard get the tool box out and look in it.

A short while later, the sergeant came into the mess hall where I was at and said, "Hey, Brown." He inventoried the box. Everything was there.

As the sergeant turned to walk away, I stopped him and said, "Hey, Sarge, you might want him to re-inventory that box. He missed this ten-inch screwdriver," which I pulled from behind my back. The sergeant's eyes popped wide open with surprise and astonishment. I think the sergeant was surprised I had it and astonished that that crazy guard lied to him. I just laughed after the sergeant left, thinking a supervisor with no spine who allows those under him to lie to him and not having enough guts to write this nut up. The guard I wasn't laughing at, he was scary to work around, knowing he had little to no security sense. For the sergeant it wasn't just about not having a spine; it was the culture at the Elmira Correctional Facility. The almost all-white supervisor staff never disciplined there all most all-white subordinates. Now let's see—this guard was allowed to leave an area unattended with multiple inmates in an isolated area, doors unsecure, and a tool box full of potential weapons sitting on a desk, and me, a correctional officer, not a supervisor, had to check him for his lapse in security. Most but not all white shirts at the Elmira Correctional Facility were worthless. They choose to buddy up with those that they supervised, those rendering their ability to supervise fruitless. What the state has is a correctional officer in a white shirt that the state is paying more money for them being there. It was unheard of for a correctional sergeant or lieutenant to write up a correctional officer for anything. The supervisory staff allowed fighting among staff, allowed staff to report to duty drunk, allowed staff to be off their post on and off facility grounds. They help their underlings cover up misdeeds such as assault on inmates. They help facilitate inmate abuse within the inmate disciplinary system by locking inmates up unjustifiably and by falsifying reports and other critical paperwork. This is all acceptable, but the one thing that isn't allowed or acceptable and will not be tolerated whatsoever is a black correctional officer. Notifying the state and outside agencies of their discriminatory practices and harassment that is happening is not tolerated whatsoever not by the supervisors not by the staff and administration both at the facility and in Albany, and not by the union that represent the almost all white workforce. This is considered taboo, forbidden, prohibited, not allowed, so after reporting those harassing me, the supervisory staff, the sergeants, and the lieutenants joined the rouge guards and others on a campaign to harass and discredit me with the hopes of getting me fired. The sergeant in the food service area had spoken to me one day about a complaint I had made, and he seemed more interested in protecting those that were harassing me than doing what's right, so I had told him prior to filing this charges to tell my harassers to back off. I then asked him also how it was that these guys got to beat the shit out of each other at the drop of a hat fight each other over minor disputes, but if I were to latch a hold of one of these guys harassing me, I'd get written up and fired. He had no explanation, so I offered him one. It was because I was black. I then sternly told the sergeant if I couldn't fight back physically, I would come out swinging with a pen and notify the department's affirmative action.

The sergeant's response was "You better not."

My response was "Watch me."

Days later, I filed a formal complaint with the department's affirmative action. After doing so, the harassment was stepped up by the bloodthirsty staff that demanded no more or less than my job at any and all cost for doing so. For me, I was put on heightened alert ready for any and everything that the out-of-control staff would try to subject me to. You see, I had always known that the majority of the almost all-white staff didn't have respect for one another, so respecting me wasn't going to happen. They showed their disrespect for one another in a number of ways. You had staff members who called themselves friends of one another and would go behind each other's backs and sleep with one another's wives and girlfriends, cut each other's throats for overtime and job assignments, put each other down behind each other's back, steal from one another, and I'm to think they have any respect for me really? One would be totally naïve to think they did. So knowing all this, I knew they would try any and everything to try to fulfill their mission of trying to have me fired. They had declared war against me, and they fired the first shots. The war was lopsided. I can hardly call one against hundreds fair, but as we know, all is fair in love and war. I knew I was going to have to be up to the task if I wanted to survive. The rascally charged staff were set on getting me fired, and I was set on seeing my retirement, so the war was on for justice. I literally had to strap on a backpack and care for it wherever I went in fear that any bag I brought into the facility left unattended by me would have definitely been tampered with, so for the remainder of my career, I was subjected to never being able to safely leave anything of mine unattended. I know how foul and disgusting and hateful some staff were. The thought of them putting some form of contraband or doing something to the food items in my bag—trust me when I say this—it would have been careless to think otherwise.

After filing an official complaint about the outright discriminatory practices and racial harassment that plagued the Elmira Correctional Facility, I proceeded with caution and skepticism of all that went on while on duty. Remember, I had crossed the blue line. It was now me against the whole department of correction. It was truly David versus Goliath, as I was ostracized and shunned by my fellow officers.

I continued to perform my duties as a correctional officer at the Elmira Correctional Facility. It wasn't hard for me because I only did my job, which was care, custody, and control, and I performed my job to the T, or to the letter, and I was always on my game and ever so mindful of those that were out to get me. Like I had said, there were good officers that didn't condone the way I was being treated because of the color of my skin, but they themselves wouldn't step forward to tell the truth when one of the out-of-control guards had a fit of rage. Again, there is a difference between an officer and a guard. An officer within the department performs his duty as described by the department's rules and regulations and polices and procedure put in place at the facility. A guard is a person that preforms his job using his personal feelings animosity, hate, and uneducated perceived notions of others as a guide to perform their duties as a correctional officer. Attach this to their personal agenda and it brings nothing but chaos, confusion, corruption, and abuse to the Department

Of Corrections. Within the system, there are many unprofessional, unethical, immoral guards with zero integrity, and at the Elmira Correctional Facility, there are many *guards* who wear blue shirts and the white shirts of the supervisory staff. It was controlled by those who had a guard-type mentality. It seemed to be the mind-set of many of the staff members at the facility and their loyalty was to one another and to the injustice and discord they promoted and forced upon the inmates and staff that they chose to harass and abuse. As I continued to be harassed by those who chose to do so, there was nowhere I could turn for help. The staff and the administration at the facility and the departments higher-ups in Albany, along with the union which represented me as well as the racist guards who were harassing me, choose to turn their backs on me as well. So while being subjected to the harassment, I had nowhere to turn. If it wasn't for my love for God and the love and support of my family and friends, I truly wouldn't have survived the eleven-plus years of relentless harassment and abuse that my employer allowed me to be subjected to. I personally have never seen so many men and women who allowed others to think for them and allow cowards and liars to rob them of their integrity and humanity just for the sake of being called friends. I witnessed good officers be turned into guards by peer pressure from other guards who would demand their loyalty if they wanted to work at the Elmira Correctional Facility. It was made obvious and perfectly clear where my loyalty was, and it was in the following order: God, family, and my employer, not to an out-of-control racist guard who is set on administrating justice as he or she feels fit and is abusing the system in any and every way they can, and then they lie and somehow try to justify the injustice they unleash upon others. I could and never would have let a man or women make me choose my integrity over friendship. Those that choose to be loyal friends to the out-of-control guards were truly making deals with the devil, and even they weren't truly loyal to each other. When push came to shove, they would turn on each other when it came to self-preservation. It wasn't just the inmates at the facility I had to attend to; I also had the staff. I can honestly say I felt the staff posed more of a threat to me than the inmates. There were inmates that the rogue guards would use to harass me.

I remember an incident in the mess hall where a white inmate who was working in the mess hall I was on duty in was observed earlier by me having a conversation with the out-of-control washed-up weight lifter who was working the kitchen desk area. The conversation looked more like the inmate was receiving orders or instructions on what to do. That's really what a correctional officer is supposed to do—give inmates guidance, direction, and orders to help keep the inmates from getting into trouble when they are dealings with some issue they may be having. The rogue guards never offered sound, reasonable advice; they offered only chaos, confusion, and discord as a solution to any problem. After observing the exchange between the inmate and the rogue guard earlier in the morning, when the morning chow began to be served, the inmate in the back who had taken direction from the rough guard was spotted by me giving one of the inmates going down the serving line double portions of food, which was not allowed per the facility's food service area policy, nor was it tolerated by me. It was wrong for one inmate to be treated differently and given more than the rest when others would also like to receive double portions but were denied. Hell, they were just as hungry as the inmate getting the double portions.

After I witnessed the rule violation, which the inmate had previously been counseled about by myself and other staff as well, the inmate was ordered off the serving line by me, at which time the inmate screamed bloody murder. He began accusing me of harassing him. He then started pacing back forth behind the enclosed serving counter. He then yelled out, "I'm going to stab your black ass." It was obvious that the inmate's behavior was a deliberate act.

After the inmate threated to stab me, I immediately notified the area sergeant. When the sergeant arrived, I explained to him in detail what had transpired with the inmate making a threat to stab me. I then told the sergeant I wanted the inmate removed from the mess hall for threating to stab me. The sergeant then took the inmate just outside of the mess hall area into the hallway where I could observe the two of them having a conversation. Now remember, I'm a correctional officer and this is an inmate who just threatened to stab me. Moments later, the sergeant was let back into the mess hall area with the inmate following close behind. The sergeant was refusing to have the inmate escorted back to the block and locked up for threatening me. I was totally shocked, floored by the sergeant's decision to bring the inmate back into my work area after he had threatened to stab me. I again explained to the sergeant that the inmate had just threatened to stab me, and his reply was, "The inmate said he didn't say that. And he also said he isn't going to stab you."

Meanwhile, as I was expressing my concern for my health and safety that was falling on the sergeant's deaf ears the inmate had walked back down to the serving line I had just ordered him off of and continued serving food. It was obvious that the sergeant didn't give a damn about me or my family because ultimately, we were here to keep each other safe and see that we all went home to our families safely, which didn't seem to matter to him. He also took the word of an inmate over mine.

When the sergeant turned and walked out of the mess hall, leaving my immediate threat alongside me for the remainder of the day, I could hardly believe the sergeant didn't do the right thing and lock the inmate up for the outright threat to stab me. If that would have been one of the white staff members being threatened to be stabbed by an inmate, all hell would have broken lose. The inmate would have been beaten from an inch of his life and thrown in the SHU unit until he healed up. All I was requesting was the inmate be removed from the area. This took place early in the morning, so for the remainder of the day, I was forced to have my back to the wall with my immediate threat in front of me, trying not to take my eyes off him.

A few days later, the inmate was moved to another mess hall to work. I also witnessed the inmate hanging out with the leader of the rough guards that worked in the mess hall, hamming it up at the guard's desk area like they were long-lost friends. There was no doubt that this racist, out-of-control, raging guard had put the inmate up to the task of threatening me. It was very disturbing to know even the supervisor was part of this very serious incident.

There was one guard who worked in the area that was controlled by the head racist guard in the kitchen that ran one of the mess halls. He would come into work and do whatever he felt like doing. He was about 5'9" and medium built. He wore his state ball cap pulled way down on his head. He looked like a mess every day. He was allowed to come into work smelling like alcohol. He was also a heavy gambler who not only had a thrust for alcohol but he also thrust for the horses, ponies, and trotters. He was out of control. As we worked in the food service area during the same shift, I and another officer noticed that he took a fine liking to the inmates that were openly gay. Any inmate that came to the food service area that fit that category, he would try to make it a point to get the inmate working in his area. You would openly see his horseplay with the inmates of his liking.

One afternoon, I had to go into the mess hall where he was working. As I walked into the mess hall, I observed one of the white openly gay inmates sitting at one of the mess hall tables along with this guard, who was having his lunch, which consisted of chicken wings. I observed the guard who was just finishing his meal with a chicken bone in his mouth take it out and toss it back into the Styrofoam tray that was piled with the remains of the bones from the chicken meat he had eaten off of them. As he discarded what appeared to be the last chicken bone, he pushed the tray over across the table to the gay inmate that sat across him. The inmate opened the tray and stared to devour the chicken bones that the officer had so kindly offered him. He placed one of the chicken bones in his mouth. The inmate started sucking the leftover sauce off the succulent bones and nibbled the remainder of the meat off the bones. Neither the guard or the inmate acknowledged or observed my presents as I stood watching in plain sight. The guard was smiling at the inmate as he went to town on his garbage.

After I had observed enough to turn my stomach inside out from watching another man eat from the mouth of another (it looked more like a sex act than just eating wings) I spoke up from behind the counter where I had stood in plain sight. When they observed me, both the guard and inmate were taken by surprise. Both turned their heads quickly in my direction; they had both been oblivious to my presence as they enjoyed each other's company while on their hot wing lunch date. I and other concerned staff members had observed this type of unprofessional and unethical behavior from this guard with his special relationship with this inmate and others, but the sergeants and other supervisory staff that were aware of what was going on would turn their heads and act as if nothing was happening.

I wonder if it is sincere ignorance or conscientious stupidity when you see what is happing right in front of your face and you refuse to acknowledge reality as truth and you as a supervisor choose to take the position to do nothing. You have effectively made yourself useless. There were many useless supervisors who worked at the Elmira Correctional Facility. There were supervisors who would go above and beyond their duty to do their job in a professional manner, but they were few and far in-between. The majority were controlled by their guard friends who would harbor ill feelings and animosity toward them. If the supervisor would dare cross a guard and question the way that guard performed his duty or take the side against a guard that had broken a rule or law inside the facility, this same guard who was allowed to have unprofessional and unethical contact with this inmate would also harass me at the direct order of the head guard that controlled him and the other guards in the food service area.

On one Saturday morning, after the inmates in the mess hall were finished with the morning chow run and the area was cleaned up, the inmates were permitted to go to rec. There was a recreation area in the food service area located in the rear of the mess hall. The officers and guards who worked the mess halls were required to be in the rec area to observe the inmates during their the rec period. Now may I remind you the chicken wing inmate-dating officer not only had a thirst for gay inmates but he also thrust for, remember, the horses, trotters, or ponies. Now let me remind you it was Saturday morning. The inmates were in the designated area for their recreation period in the rec area. There were showers, a TV, at one time there were phones that were later taken out, and then on the outside were weights for lifting and a full court basketball area.

On this particular Saturday, I was positioned inside, observing the inmates as they utilized the recreational area. Some were watching TV and others were showering, and some mingled and played cards or chess. Inmates were watching *Soul Train* on the TV when in came the X-rated wing-eating guard, who picked up the remote and turned from what the inmates were watching to a horse race. The inmates, who were primarily black and brown, went crazy. They started yelling and screaming about their program being interrupted. The guard at first just stood there smiling as they all screamed in his direction. As a correctional officer, even though I sat right there witnessing this out of control guard disrespecting the inmates, I had no choice but to protect this idiot from being assaulted or worse. I tried to first defuse the problem by reasoning with the guard by explaining the inmates were quietly watching the TV. That didn't move him, so then I explained to him that the TV was for the inmates watching and the state wasn't paying me or him to watch TV. That's when he lost it, and I now became his problem. He became loud with me. The sergeant and others reported to the area after the inmates became louder along with the out-of-control guard. The sergeant and the other guards quickly sided with their crony until the inmates all spoke up and quickly shut down the guard's bullshit and put fault on the guard for turning the TV to his desired program while they choose to watch something else. The sergeant motioned to the out-of-control guard to come with him, and they both walked away practically hand in hand, leaving the area. The sergeant never asked me or questioned me about the guard's dangerous and foolish act that would have gotten me, along with other staff members, hurt all over his deep desire to watch horse racing. They, the out-of-control guards, were allowed to do anything they wanted. If the inmates would have done anything, I'm sure they would have covered it up and made it look like it was my fault.

Soon after this incident with the X-rated wing-eating, dangerous, foolish guard, he then doubled down on the harassment he was trying to subject me to. Soon after, I was in the kitchen food service area, using the employees' bathroom, which was located in the kitchen area. As I went to the bathroom, I had to pass though the kitchen and pass the head racist, out-of-control guard. As I stood relieving myself in the bathroom, someone started banging on the door loudly. I yelled out twice, "I'm in here!"

My warning to the person on the other side of the door went unreceived or not comprehended. As I was just finishing up, the door flew open, and in stepped the X-rated wing-eating, dangerous, foolish guard, who was up to some more shenanigans. As I fastened my pants, I turned and asked him if he had heard me yell out, at which time he then started speaking to me like he and other out-of-control guards talked to inmates, very reckless at the mouth. I then went to exit the door he was blocking, and I assured him he wanted to move out my way, which he did. He continued to yell and make a scene until others were alerted, including the sergeant who had conveniently posted himself in the office close to the bathroom. (On other days usually, you could not find the sergeant. He would be off hiding, ducking his responsibilities.) The sergeant quickly intervened as I exited the bathroom area, followed by the out-of-control guard who was yelling in my direction as I was trying to get away from him. Even though I wasn't the one yelling, the sergeant yelled out for me to stop. The sergeant then ordered me into the office.

Once inside the office, before the door was even shut and before even asking what was going on, he laid into me with a threat to write me up. The office was located straight down from the head racist guard's post. He stood staring toward the office with a wide smile on his face. The office had a large front glass window and a glass door window, which made it easy to see in a large portion of the office with a unobstructed view. The head racist guard stood staring as the sergeant put on his performance. It was clear that it was all a setup by the rough guards and the corrupt supervisor. They stood there ready to spring their trap as soon as I used the bathroom and had to pass by the idiot working the desk. Once I did, he summoned the hot wing-loving guard with a phone call, and he came to the bathroom door to harass me, and the sergeant just happened to be on his post on this day waiting for the trap to be sprung.

A few days following this incident, while I was on duty, I was ordered to report to the dep of security's office up front. I was relieved from my post by a guard that seemed to be well aware of why he was relieving me by the smart "Good luck with that" statement he made as I departed my post in the mess hall. As I made my way up front, it seemed that all on the route knew where I was heading, and you could tell by the dead silence and the blank stares thrown my way as I passed by. Once I arrived at the dep's office, I was promptly ordered into the office area and informed by the dep that I was being written up and given a NOD for the incident with the same guard who was allowed to have lunch dates with inmates, which amounted to dereliction of duty, turning a TV to his desired programming which in cited conditions in the facility could have gotten staff and inmates hurt. He was allowed to comes to work smelling of alcohol most days. He was allowed to harass me at the direction of those who have chosen to harass me, and this was just a month's worth of this guard's shenanigans. There was much more.

As the dep of security looked at me with hate in his eyes and malice in his heart and proceeded to inform me that I was being written up, he then began to accuse me of being the instigator in the incident with the out-of-control wing-loving guard. I sat listening to the false charges that I was being set up with. The dep seemed to be in his glory as he too had his opportunity to harass me. It seemed that they all wanted a shot at me. I sat quietly listening as the dep made himself feel good by exhorting his power over me. I thought to myself that this must make him feel good—to have power over somebody in the jail—because he surely didn't have power over the almost all-white workforce. They seemed not to care about him or anything he had to say, which was obvious by the staff's out-of-control actions and behavior on a daily basis. I felt a deep need to give the dep a reality check after he finished accusing me with false allegations and lies that he felt so comfortably charging me with after his rant. I spoke and asked the dep if he really believed that version of the incident that makes him believe I was the instigator. I reminded him I was the one using the bathroom that the out-of-control guard barged in on. I was the one trying to walk away as he was yelling at me. I was the one that he and the administration had turned their backs on that gave these out-of-control staff members the okay to harass me. I was the one that tried to avoid contact with the racist, out-of-control staff, and most of all, the dep wasn't there himself to witness the incident, so he was going solely on the word of my harassers.

Well, upon speaking to him, he wasn't engaged with me at all. He started acting like he didn't have time to hear anything I had to say. It almost reminded me of a kid plugging his ears and saying over and over, "I can't hear you, I can't hear you."

I ended my conversation with "Can I go back to my post now?" and the dep dispensed of me sending me out of his office back to my post with the same wide devilish smile the racist head guard had given me when he was looking in on me and the sergeant the day of the incident as the sergeant performed for him. This is what these cowards would do. They would try their hardest to find a way to have some form of conflict with me, and then they would get together and lie about me, and the administration would assist by disciplining me. Albany would then back the administration by allowing the employee relations board to file charges on me over and over again. The union would turn their back as they would allow the almost all-white workforce at the Elmira Correctional Facility to violate my civil and constitutional rights even though both the department and union in their own omission in their mission statements and their polices and declaration both stated that they didn't discriminate against the people they hired and the people they represented. I can tell you firsthand that is one of the biggest lies ever told. The union and the department are and have been morally bankrupt for a long time. They sadly take the position of what can and can't be proven against them no matter what the situation, and the people at the top in the department and those running the union have a guard-type mentality, not one of an officer, and most have worked in some of the worst prisons in the state where they have themselves been questioned for some of the questionable things they have done.

What would one expect? Well, this is what I received as I tried to navigate the system to find some kind of relief, coverups, lies, manipulation, abuse of power and authority, harassment, and discrimination, and this was from the top to the bottom. So yes, I would call that morally bankrupt and full of corruption—a department and system that is practically beyond repair because of the systematic abuse that seems to be more than just a system allowed to run amok. It's deeper—it's a system that has evolved into a cultural system that has fostered hate, discrimination, retaliation, and abuse wrapped in a blanket of corruption.

Most of the prisons are located in rural upstate New York towns that are usually isolated in an area that is primarily white. These jails are filled with black and brown people as inmates and staffed with an almost all-white workforce that has been culturally conditioned throughout the years by others that have worked in these prisons. They have harbored hate and discrimination, and they refuse to change.

Take Attica Prison for example. The guards and staff there still harbor ill feelings toward the inmates over the Attica riot. It's been said some of the staff at Attica act as if the riot were yesterday and not 1971, some forty-eight years ago. I never worked at Attica, but I did work with some guards—and I mean guards—that worked at Elmira that had been transferred in from Attica as supervisors such as sergeants and above. Their attitudes were, let's see, the epitome of the word *guard*.

Remember, there's a difference between a correctional officer and a guard. A correctional officer does his or her job with integrity and uses the department's rules and regulations along with the facility's policies and procedures as a guideline to perform his or her job. A guard is just the opposite. They couldn't care less about rules and regulations. They are driven by a cultural conditioning that they willfully or forcibly adopted though peer pressure as their ideology. Many staff members have relatives that have either friends or family that have either worked at these facilities or are still currently working there.

As I waited for the arbitration hearing on the false charges that the union and state allowed to be brought against me, the racist, out-of-control guard who seemed to be in control of the other guards in the kitchen area would taunt me with threats about the outcome of my upcoming hearing. He would make direct and indirect statements to me like "Yep, they're going to fire his ass" or "We are finally going to get rid of him" or his outright omission, "Yep, we got his ass," which solidified the fact that they were out to get me. The truly telling statement of this racist was when he yelled out, "Hey, your lynching is coming!" referring to the arbitration hearing as a lynching. His statements would be made in front of others who would hear him make the statements but would deny the truth, some in fear of repercussions or in compliance with the plan to get rid of me at the Elmira correctional facility. My harassers would harass me and would have no problem finding a guard or a civilian staff member to back up their false accusations against me. The harassment that the head racist guard subjected me to would sometimes take place in the presence of supervisory staff, who would also not hear or see anything that the racist guard was doing.

Approximately a week or so before the arbitration hearing or, as the racist guard called it, my lynching, the racist guard that had been allowed to harass me at will and was unchecked by the supervisory staff or the administration for doing so upped the ante by going all in on me. One early morning, as I walked to the back of the kitchen to a side door that led outside, I stood in front of the door, which was an automatic push-button roll-up door. At the side of the door was a large chain that hung on the side that was used to lock the door. The chain was hanging loose and not locked back as it was supposed to be. Whoever had used the door last had left the chain unsecured. As I stood in front of the door, someone ran behind me and attempted to place the large quarter-inch steel chain around my neck as I stood with my back to them. As my assailant attempted to wrap the large chain around my neck, I was quick enough to place my hands in between my neck and the chain, peeling it from around my neck. Once I was able to free myself, I turned to find this racist piece of shit still clutching the cold steel quarter-inch chain in his hands. As he attempted to back away from me, I grabbed a hold of his dirty state-issued jacket by the lapel area and pulled him close to me. I put my face close to him. I saw two of the civilian cooks looking out the large side window, watching it all. I then pushed him back away from me. I told the racist guard I would beat his ass if he ever put his hands on me again, and he was lucky he had witnesses that were watching that would lie for his ass.

He then said, "I was only showing you how they are going to lynch you." If there was ever a day I was going to put my hands on one of these coward-ass guards, this was it. I was so mad I could hardly believe that this racist guard felt comfortable enough to wrap a steel chain around a black man's neck and call it a lynching.

After I had calmed down a bit, I went to the area supervisor and told him what had happened. The supervisor, the sergeant, couldn't have cared less, so I then went up front to the dep of security and informed him one of his guards had just wrapped a steel chain around my neck. The dep also couldn't have cared less. I then wrote a letter to Albany to the head of the department, and you guessed it—they also couldn't have cared less. That's right—a state agency that allows racial harassment to exist on state property, a mock lynching of a black employee, and they couldn't care less. Who knew that lynching was still legal in the United States of America? Truly, if you don't know, there is no anti-lynching law in the United States of America as of this date, 2018. Can you believe it? There is no law that says lynching is illegal. I don't know if the racist ass guard knew this or not, but he sure felt comfortable about what he had done and seemed unconcerned about any repercussions for his racist action. None of my harassers were ever disciplined for what they did to me—only I, the victim of their racial assaults and harassment, was disciplined for reporting what they did.

One would really have to wonder if they were doing me an employee like this, what were they doing to the inmates? The atmosphere and the tone set was one of a slave and master mentality that the guards subjected all to that aren't of their race. The state of New York and the Department of Corrections have allowed these upstate prisons to be run and controlled by the almost always all-white workforce that has in some of these prisons been hand selected. Many of the civil staff are family members or close friends of some higher-ups who practically handed them the job. The security staff is hand selected by using fear and intimidation to control correctional officers into playing along to get along, and if you fail the test, you'll be subjected to harassment and shunned to the point you would be forced to leave, which I have seen. While all of this is going on, the ones at the top look the other way. They have allowed over the years for a culture of hate, division, and separation to exist and white privilege to prevail as the norm. The union also takes this stand, protecting only those that have this privilege.

When I went to the arbitration hearing or my "lynching," I was the only black as usual. The judge was white, the state's attorney was white, my attorney was white, and my accusers and the witnesses against me were all white. While it looked like the angry mob was all gathered and in place, the only thing missing was the rope. During the hearing, each of the witnesses assembled took their turns lying to and misleading the arbitrator/judge as expected. This wasn't my first arbitration hearing, and I was damn sure it wouldn't be my last. The judge seemed to already have made his decision. The hearing was the classic dog and pony show. All the details had been worked out and decided on before I went to the hearing. At the end, I was given additional days of suspension, losing both money and time and another false accusation added to my personal file.

You know, a wise man once told me, "The more they rub you the wrong way, the shinier you get." Shine I did. I refused to be intimidated by a bunch of punk cowards. These cowards would use any and every one they could use to harass me. I was being harassed at work and home by local law enforcement. The writeups continued to come my way at work. It seemed that they had declared an all-out assault on me and my job. I continued to work in the kitchen. As I did, I continued to be harassed. The stress of coming to work and never knowing if I was going to have a job to support my family from day today started to take a toll on my health.

I had a local doctor here in Elmira whom I saw so I made an appointment to be seen. During my appointment with my doctor, I expressed to him the stress I was being subjected to. This was my regular treating physician, whom I had seen many times. I had remembered during prior visits having small talk with the doctor before the harassment. He started asking me if I know different guards that worked at the Elmira Correctional Facility, calling them by name while speaking to the doctor regarding my stress symptoms and what I was being subjected to at work. He seemed unwilling to believe what I was saying, and he refused to file worker compensation papers for my stress-related condition caused by work. He basically shooed me out of his office and sent me on my way, never treating me for my stress-related injury.

A couple of weeks later, after doing some investigating into the doctor and his known associates on the hill, the Elmira Correctional Facility, I found that the doctor spent time hunting with some of the guards at the facility, so it was now obvious to why the doctor refused to do his job. After that last appointment with the guard-hunting doctor, I never went back to his office on Madison Avenue in Elmira. Again, imagine a doctor more concerned about his hunting buddies than your health. I was literally forced to leave New York state and go over into Pennsylvania to seek treatment. During my visit with the doctor in Pennsylvania, I again expressed to him what I was being subjected to at work and the stress symptoms I was having. The only difference with this doctor was he cared for me and treated me for stress, and he didn't pick his hunting buddies over his patients. It was scary knowing you had someone like the hunting doctor, whom you had entrusted with your life, to have no integrity, and he would seem to have no loyalty or respect for his patients or to the oath he took—you know, the Hippocratic oath. He seemed to have it confused with the hunting buddy oath.

You know the old saying, "Everything works out for the best." Well, in this case it did. I couldn't have asked for a better doctor than the one I found in Pennsylvania, a true shining star, a professional, the true epitome of what a doctor is supposed to be. My old hunting doctor could have used some training from this professional doctor. What the doctor in Elmira was doing was helping to stop me from filing a worker's compensation claim for my stress-induced injuries by refusing to do his job of giving me a fear and professional evaluation of my injuries. Instead, he based his evaluation on his personal feelings, which must have been filled with animosity, and his undying loyalty to his hunting buddies. He in no way should be called a doctor—a quack, yes.

Let's recap—I have the guards at the Elmira Correctional Facility, the administration at the Elmira correctional facility, and the local police harassing me, Albany allowing the harassment, and I have a doctor who is refusing to treat my health issues. Oh, I left out no attorney in the area interested in helping me seek justice. I felt like a fly in a spider web—oh, what a wicked web they weave. I always said a blind man could see what they were doing to me. After filing multiple claims for workers' compensation for stress, they continued to harass me by writing me up and locking me out of the prison. They seemed to use the holidays a lot of the time when they would decide to lock me out or suspend me without pay or they would do some foul coward move and right before my scheduled vacation they would pull something to have some form of confrontation with me. It got to the point I would bang in (call in) right before my vacation, so I would be unavailable to harass and lie on. Their intent and timing became obvious. I would try to avoid the troublemakers or, as the inmates would say, I tried to stay sucker-free. That wouldn't stop them from still trying to have me fired. I truly had to watch my every step because around every corner was danger or a trap ready to be sprung. It seemed my fellow employees were a bigger threat to me than the inmate population. It was truly a sad reality knowing that, but the truth was if a riot would have jumped off, it wouldn't have been the inmates I feared; it would have been the staff I had to fend off. It seemed that the almost all-white workforce hated me as much as they hated the inmates that they swore to pervade care, custody, and control to. It seemed that the only thing that would satisfy the thirsty mob was me being fired.

The guards acted more like a mob or gang than professional peace officers. As they continued harassing me, I continued going to my new doctor, who would treat my stress-related issues. This in return would cause me to file multiple worker compensation claims for stress-related injuries, which the administration didn't want me to do. That is why he, the Hunting Dr., was basically refusing to treat me after the claims had been filed. I had to find a worker's compensation attorney. I searched the Yellow Pages and contacted a couple of attorneys in Elmira, New York, and made appointments to see each one of them to discuss my stress-related claims. After meeting with each of the two attorneys from two separate law firms and informing them of my work situation of being racially harassed at the Elmira Correctional facility, they both promptly turned me down and shooed me off. I then looked up a couple of other law firms and called and made appointments, and they too shooed me off. This went on through six of the local law firms, who all refused to represent me against the Elmira Correctional Facility. It almost seemed like they were trying to protect them by blocking me from receiving fair representation for my stress claim. I found it odd that these same attorneys through their own admission to me, admitted to representing many of the guards at the Elmira Correctional Facility, so what made me and my case any different? The only difference I could think of was I was black, and I was claiming stress for being racially harassed. I could hardly see why that would preclude me from being represented by a licensed New York state attorney who had sworn an oath to practice law in a fair and ethical manner. I'm also certain some were in that oath. It says something about integrity.

Living in a community that has no black attorneys has its pitfalls because it almost seems that those in power in small towns control and use those around them to protect and shield them from justice, I didn't give up on my search for an attorney to represent me, I was soon blessed to find not only an attorney but a good soul of man who was soft spoken and had the patience of a saint, and may I add, one of his biggest attributes was he had integrity. When I first meet him to discuss my case and I told him about the racially harassment and retaliation, he didn't give me some lame excuse for why he couldn't do his job and fairly represent me. Instead, he told me my rights and how he could represent me. My worker's compensation case was turned into a long, drawn-out battle that lasted years. I remember the time and attendance lieutenant at the prison who was in charge of keeping track of the correctional officers' time on the books told me.

One day, while I was dropping off some paperwork regarding my worker's compensation case, he closely examined it and said boldly, "You'll never receive compensation for this."

I then responded back to him in a stern and faithful tone, "Yes, I will. Watch." My comment and reassurance of my statement took him by surprise by the way he pushed away from the desk. As I walked away, leaving him with the stone-cold stupid look on his face, after that, every time he would see me or if I had to hand in paperwork to him regarding my worker's compensation case, he would stare me down with contempt on his face. My compensation attorney had previously warned me it was going to be a long-fought battle for justice against the state for compensation for work-induced stress, but he assured me we would get there and we would be victorious.

The battle for justice raged on. I believe the worker's compensation case lasted well over three-and-a-half years with many hearings in front of the compensation judge. Some of those who were harassing me were subjected to appear at some of those hearings. One of those was the chicken wing eating guard, who had to appear a number of times. He would swear to tell the truth but would lie to cover up his misdeeds when questioned over and over. As time went on over more than three-and-a-half years and the state's refusal to acknowledge my stress case as work-related, I myself began to grow weary and very skeptical of the whole compensation system. Part of the reason was, as I went through my case, I would watch as other employees would file claims for compensation for one reason or another and would be well compensated for whatever their problem was, and most would receive quick results. Hell, even the false fraudulent claims for compensation would be honored and accepted by both the Department of Corrections as well as the compensation board.

Many staff would file claims for injuries that they had received while off duty and would hobble, limp, or drag themselves in and promptly make a worker's compensation claim for their injury with none the wiser. There was the guard who reportedly, by his own admission, slammed his own hand in a window to receive worker's comp, which he did, and was paid well for his false insurance claim. Or how about the racist troll who wrote on both my time card and my locker? He was allowed during the month of June when his children were too young to be alone during the summer months because he and his wife both worked. He would have a claim for some form of injury that would put him off for the whole summer, compliments of the New York state compensation board. He did that for years until the kids were old enough to be left alone. Or how about the drunk, out-of-control guard who had received multiple DUIs and was going to be locked out without pay? He was ordered to report to the dep's office, which was ironic because the dep had a drinking problem. After the guard with the multiple DUI's arrived at the Dep's office, he was informed what was happening and he was notified that he was being suspended. He kindly asked the dep if he could step outside and have a smoke, to which the dep agreed. The guard walked out of the office found a nice spot on the floor, laid down. Saying that he hurt his back and that he couldn't move and wasn't going to get up until an ambulance came.

Now this guard killed two birds with one stone. The administration was unable to lock him out without pay because he had hurt his back and was now on worker's compensation with a back injury. He was allowed to avoid discipline and file a fraudulent claim for worker's compensation. A lot of the compensation fraud would happen in the summer months and hunting season. Both were prime time for a fall or spill. I myself had received directions by comp pros on how to defraud the compensation system when I broke my big toe. After a large item had fallen onto my foot, some of the comp pro guards suggested to me if I really wanted to get paid for my broken great toe, I should have them amputate it and I would be sure to get a large pay day for the loss of my digit. I found the idea to be absolutely insane, highly questionable, and very fraudulent. How could a reasonable human being possibly find it reasonable or sensible to have a digit cut from their body unnecessarily in the hope of receiving cash for it? I really wondered about some of those nuts because that was such a crazy idea.

Or how about the time I popped my Achilles tendon during a pickup game after work at the prison? When times were better and I wasn't being harassed, almost all the guards present suggested to me I should hobble into work the next morning and report that I had fallen down the stairs and hurt myself. To avoid using my sick time and or vacation time while I recovered from my injury, it didn't surprise me to hear that so many of these guys would opt to defraud the system rather than do the right thing, which I did by remaining home. I called in and reported the injury and when and where it happened just the way it happened while playing basketball after work. And by being truthful, it all worked out, and it wasn't reported as a false worker's comp claim, I was able to work light duty to avoid using all my sick time and vacation. I did, however, have to use my time but not all of it. One injury was being used so much they had a name for it. They called a shoulder injury a F-150 injury because of the amount of money that was paid out after the claim and settlement a shoulder injury was enough to buy a new F-150 after the first few cases were a success, and others observed this and saw how easy it was to get a shoulder injury accepted though worker's compensation, and get paid for it. It soon became the injury of choice. It was almost like the California gold rush. Everyone rushed to stake their claim on a F-150. During peak compensation time, summer/hunting season, when a red dot which is an emergency call for help was called usual for a fight amongst the inmates. The guards looked like the Keystone Cops running to the emergency situation, literally running each other over to be the first to arrive so they could have a fall, spill or bump that could be claimed as worker's compensation. This would place them off of work. The compensation system was much abused. I believe it's a money grab and used to avoid using one's time that has been accumulated on the books for vacation and sick time. None of this would be possible without a good doctor, who might even be a friend, and a unethical attorney with no integrity, who are willing participants.

Now from my personal experience, I don't think they have to look far or shake too many trees to find those in the Elmira area that are more than willing to help these guards navigate the compensation system with proven results. Back to my compensation case that has taken three-and-a-half years, I asked the question why. The answer was obvious. It was a claim basically for stress-related injuries for discrimination and retaliation, and the state didn't want to conceive or acknowledge my case as compensation as a work-related injury, so as time passed, over those three-and-a-half years, I would sit and watch and listen as the judge, the state attorneys, and representatives along with my attorney would go back and forth over my claim and my attorney would leave the hearing once again without answers hiring. After hiring, it would seem we were no closer to victory than when we had entered the hiring. The soft-spoken but very effective attorney would tell me to hang in there and would inform me we were getting closer. As we departed each of the many hearings, well, the day came when a hearing on my case took a turn that I do not think the state attorney or the representative seen coming during a hearing. The chicken wing-eating guard was being questioned about an incident I had reported in writing as harassment, and the judge asked him if he could tell him what happened. The racist idiot guard looked at the judge and requested to see a paper he had written in response to an incident by saying, "Can I see my to-from?" which was the memo he had written. The judge denied his request by asking the racist chicken wing-eating guard to describe the incident in question. He again denied the judge's request by asking to see the to-from he had submitted to the administration at the Elmira Correctional facility regarding the incident, and once again, the judge denied his request. The fourth and last request to see his to-from before answering the judge's questions sent the judges into a frenzy. He yelled, "Just answer the questions," then the judge said in a stern and authoritative voice, looking at the state representative who looked stunned like a deer in headlights from the judge's reaction.

The judge then rendered his ruling by saying, "He refuses to answer my questions. This has gone on way too long. I rule in Mr. Brown's favor." The judge then ordered the state to accept my claim of stress and ordered the state to reimburse me any money or time I had lost due to stress-related illness. The state representative for the department who was fighting tooth and nail to stop my claim looked defeated and stunned over the judge's decision. The idiot guard sat looking confused, defeated, exposed and humiliated until the judge sent him on his way by telling him he was free to go.

After the hearing, the judge apologized for the delay in my case and thanked me for my patience and wished me good luck. As he dismissed me and my attorney, I noticed while leaving the state representative was huddled in a corner on the phone. Now I wasn't privy to the conversation, but it looked like he was checking in with someone with the results of the hearing, and by his expression, it wasn't good. I and my attorney both walked away, smiling as winners do. I would have never received worker's compensation if weren't for the soft-spoken, diligent, and persistent attorney who helped me get it. I know there was no other attorney in Elmira, New York, who would have fought for me like he did, proving to me there are attorneys with integrity who are willing to help those in need. Those other attorneys from other area law offices that I was shooed out of were more set on helping the Elmira Correctional Facility conceal their discriminatory practices, and God forbid they are ever exposed for what they really are. I think many may have been willing participants; however, some may be none the wiser and are being duped and bamboozled into thinking otherwise. As far as my lawsuit against the Elmira correctional facility for discrimination and retaliation was concerned, the compensation win had just given it more credibility and momentum. So after the hearing, my attorney and the worker's compensation board settled on my lost wages and time, which were added up and calculated into an award amount. The final paperwork was mailed to my attorney, and I was then directed to hand in a copy of the paper to the personal office at work, which meant to the same lieutenant who worked the time and attendance office who had told me when I first filed for compensation that I would never be compensated for my stress claim—yep, that same one. I now had the pleasure of handing him the paperwork that would force him to put all the time back on the books I had lost due to being out of work for stress-related issues. I have to say it gave me pleasure to hand him that sheet of paper. He quickly took from my hand, and again, thoroughly inspected, it was only like four lines of writing and numbers instructing the facility to restore my time loss and the amount. The way the lieutenant was looking at it, you would have thought it was written in hieroglyphics or his stupid, racist ass could not read and comprehend. As I stood waiting for him to read the document and for the information to travel to his brain so he could understand what he was being directed to do, I stood with a winning smile plastered on my face. After, I guessed it had registered to the lieutenant when he looked up with a look of hate and contempt all over his face. He then said, "I got it." I then walked out and away from the now hot-under-the-collar worthless lieutenant. The refusal of the compensation game was over now. As they harassed me and I reported to my doctor and he deemed if it was job-related, I was now covered under New York state worker's compensation for the harassment I was being subjected to.

I remember following my compensation victory, the harassment slowed down, the kitchen quieted down for a short period. The chicken wing-eating guard seemed to be on the outs with his racist leader and his cronies after they had learn he had choked and couldn't remember the scripted lie he had told because he wasn't allowed to read from his scripted memo he had submitted to the administration—yes, the same memo they used to file a NOD against me. It is hard to remember a lie, but it is easy to remember the truth. The way the chicken wing-eating guard couldn't remember what he had written because it was a stone-cold lie. That's why he couldn't answer the questions without reading from his script that he begged the judge for. After the others learned of his failure, he was kicked out of the Correctional Officer Brown hater club and sidelined.

Wait a minute, once again, I have to stop the press. On November 8, 2018, I went in front of the judge at the Horseheads New York town court in regards to the harassment compliant I had filed against the racist, out-of-control, washed-up weightlifting guard who called me a "motherfucking nigger." Several times after he had successfully tracked me and my wife down by following us in his car and then violated our civil rights by subjecting us to what amounts to a hate crime by screaming at us over and over, "Motherfucking nigger." He made sure to drive his point home by yelling it over and over; he looked and sound like a man possessed. My wife and I showed up promptly at court at the designated time, and to my dismay, so did the animal. It was a cold mid-November night, and the animal needed no coat to keep him warm.

When my wife saw what this man looked like, she immediately said to me, "He looks half-crazy and looks like an animal. The only thing missing was his leash to keep him under control. I do know for a fact that bears and wolverines have a naturally thick winter coat. The nutty guard must've had one too. His wife accompanied him, and she was bundled up in her winter coat, as was everyone else who entered the court. His face sported a grimace of a look. When he spotted me, he looked as if I had done something wrong. I thought to myself, *This big dumb, racist, raging animal must think in his twisted narrow mind what he did was acceptable behavior.* See, the thing is, it is acceptable behavior at the Elmira Correctional Facility. And now we were going to find out if it was acceptable in public.

As court started, the judge had about six or seven people who were already in custody who were accompanied by local law enforcement that the judge got out the way first. As I listened to the judge administer justice, he seemed to be fair, swift, and respectful to all who stood in front of him. As I sat waiting, the animal tried to stare at me my wife my sister as we waited for my turn in front of the judge. After the judge finished with the people who were brought in by law enforcement and the court was clear of them, he continued to call a couple of other people before he called the animal. When the racist out-of-control animal of a guard was called, the judge seemed to be taken back by his actions and sternly informed him of his charges and options and allowed him to leave under his own recognizance. After the judge finished with him, he quickly returned to his seat next to his wife and closely examined the paperwork, which the judge handed him, charging him with harassment. The judge then called a woman to stand before him.

As I continued to wait my turn, the racist guard also decided he would wait. Just as the judge was in the middle of speaking to the women he had in front of him, the racist beast was eased out of the courtroom by his wife. My sister went outside to ensure that he didn't vandalize my vehicle as I waited. This is something that these out-of-control guards are known for—beating up cars. After the judge finished with the women, he paused for a brief moment and then called me to stand in front of him to be charged with the false instrument that had placed me here in the moment. The judge read the brief charge and then also informed me of my options. The only thing he didn't do was to say he released me on my own recognizance as he had done to the racist beast. The false charges were brought by the racist beast after I brought charges on him for what I saw as stalking, harassment, and a hate crime for following me and my wife and seeking us out for the purpose of racially harassing us by yelling "That is you, you motherfucking nigger," which he repeated over and over while he had his racist fit of rage while he cut us off as we waited for the red light to change to green. My complaint that I reported to the Chemung county sheriff's department was deemed harassment in the second degree. The complaint that the racist filed was a false instrument made up of delusional lies and deception to cover up for his misdeeds, which seems to be a characteristic treat of the Elmira Correctional Facility.

Guards seem to hold dear to the ideology of lying at any cost to protect themselves and others like them from being brought to justice for their unethical, inhuman, and violations of the law and somehow feel justify for doing so, and they are helped by those at the top in the department, and the judicial system that seem to voluntarily help cover up the wrongdoing with lies and manipulation and backed by a union who has been able to buy the respect and loyalty of legislators with whom they had built a relationship through lobbying judges and lawyers to whom they have cozied up to, which have all helped to reinforce the cultural environment that triumphs the day in the Department of Corrections a system that is corruption to the core, I will however remain optimistic about the judicial system and continue to seek justice for the injustice that those in the New York State Department of Corrections and its employees continuously subject me to. Back to the continuation of the twenty-five years of hell I was subjected to after getting my compensation for the undue stress I was being subjected to, and the judge ruling in my favor didn't stop the racist guards and the administration from harassing me. Remember, this was a war to them I was an invader on their hollow grounds and I had to go at any cost. They had regrouped and soon continued their discriminatory assault on me, bringing out their full arsenal of hate and racism.

In June of 2006, my dear beloved mother passed away, who was loved and cherished by her family and friends as any normal human being would be. I was more than heartbroken losing my mother. As adults, we know that death is inevitable, and as we live, we will watch as many family and friends pass away. The one death that is hard to deal with is the death of your mother. I believe because of the maternal connection and the love that a mother gives makes it hard to say goodbye. My mother had struggled with health issues for many years, and I helped her as she did, doing whatever I could to help make her life a little easier. Losing my mother, I had lost my biggest cheerleader. A mother, you know, is the one that gives you unconditional love, the one that is there no matter what goes wrong. Yes, losing one's mother is the biggest and nastiest pills to swallow as we live life. I had to take bereavement time off from work. No one from the jail reached out with condolences. The union which I thought I was a part of and I paid dues to offered no condolences, no card, and sent no flowers. After returning to work, this one slope racist sergeant who was part of the head racist guard's army came up to me and said, "Hey, sorry about your loss," in a nonchalant manner, with no feeling. You know, when someone is legitimately concerned about you and when they aren't. I had to bite my tongue to keep from cussing his racist ass out. Sympathy from a racist did nothing for me. There were a few guys whom I knew were good guys who were just under distress from the racist guards who offered their heartwarming sympathy, whom I thanked my first day back. There were more inmates who showed me sympathy and offered their condolences than the staff I worked with at the Elmira Correctional Facility.

During my first day back, I was working in one of the mess halls, doing my job as usual, and as usual, the sergeant and the racist head guard, who was working the desk area, were all grouped up with others at the desk, plotting and planning. There were four mess halls, and I was the only officer required to be at his post. The sergeant on duty would hang out with the racist guard and his crew at the desk area, where they would all gather. The sergeant allowed them to be off their posts as they all gathered, leaving the mess halls unsecured with inmates in them. Approximately a hour after the desk meeting with the racist head guard and his crew, I had to walk into the kitchen area to go to the back to get supplies for the mess hall. While

I was walking back through the kitchen with the supplies I had gotten as I walked past the kitchen desk where the racist guard stood, he picked up the phone as if someone had called him even though the phone hadn't rung. As I passed by, he yelled out the chicken wing–eating guard's first name and said, "Has anyone seen my mother? Oh, that's right—she is dead," and started laughing hysterically in my direction. That day was almost the day I lost it. As I ran upon him to knock his ass out, he stuck his face out and said, "Hit me." That's when reality hit me. This peace of shit was going to be the sacrificial lamb offered up as a sacrifice for my job. I got close to him and told him I would knock his punk ass out cold if he ever disrespected my mother again. There were two civilian cooks who had stood right there and witnessed the whole thing but when questioned became deaf, dumb, and blind.

The next day, I was called up front at the dep's office and locked out the facility. The racist guard, after the confrontation in the kitchen, where he had laughed at the death of my mother and his stupid racist ass didn't get the reaction he had wished for, had gone into the employees' bathroom, and emerged with a tiny scratch on the tip of his noise, which he boldly claimed was suffered at no other than my hands during the confrontation he initiated. The small cut or scratch was dead center of his nose. I was immediately locked out of the prison and arrested and booked at the New York State Police barracks in Horseheads, New York, a few miles outside of Elmira. I was finger-printed, mug shot, and booked on assault charges two weeks after the death of my mother. I was allowed to return to work while waiting for my court date to answer to the outright lie that the head racist guard was allowed to make, and those in charge seemed to be more than willing to assist him in doing. It was clearly an outright lie and now not only was I heartbroken and grieving the loss of my mother but I also had to fight a false charge of assault.

But once again, I was blessed. Another good soul of a man, a lawyer who worked for the advocate group for the Chemung County Public Defender's Office, who was honest, fair and had integrity. After speaking with him, he assured me that he would help me to seek justice against the false accusations that had been bestowed upon me. After returning to work, while waiting for my court date, I was subjected to ridicule and humiliation by my peers and the administration. The racist guard would make it his business to inform all he came in contact with that the small cut on his nose was caused by me whenever in my presence by announcing, "Brown cut my nose." And then he and whomever he was speaking to would laugh. One of the cooks who was an eyewitness to the incident confided in me and told me he had observed the out-of-control guard go into the employees' bathroom and he had emerged with a small key-like scratch on the tip of his nose, and he was laughing about it as he showed the others in the area before filling his false accusations against me. I guess the old saying is true: they will kick a man when he is down. It felt like they were doing me just like they do when the out-of-control animals beat and stomp on inmates when they feel the need. Only difference was they were stomping on my mind, hoping I would eventually lose it, by subjecting me to continuous harassment and retaliation for me reporting their discriminatory practices.

As I waited for the trial date, I met with my attorney, who continued to offer me sound legal advice. I have to say sound legal advice because just as any advice, legal or otherwise, it's not always sound advice. I trusted his legal knowledge and advice, and knowing he had always been known in the community as a warrior for justice for all. So moving forward, I and my family knew we were in good hands as the racist head guards' false claim worked its way through the justice system in Chemung, county city of Elmira court system, which had proven itself biased to the degree of siding with law enforcement members in the area whether they were right or wrong. Losing the case would mean my admitted dismissal from the department. Remember, these charges I was facing were a collaborative effort of the racist head guard and those in power in the Department of Corrections who were allowing me to continually be harassed and outside law enforcement agencies who helped willingly or were duped or inclined to participate in using the justice system as a tool to harass, intimidate, and discriminate against me to help get rid of me in the Department of Corrections. My family, church family, friends, and associates were all outraged at the treatment I was receiving from the New York State Department of Corrections and its employees and the local law enforcement's inaction or patriation.

No one was surprised in the black community in Elmira, New York. The black community had always been this way. As Joe Madison, the Black Eagle, puts it, "We as a society are culturally conditioned to believe that white is superior and black is inferior." And the manifestation of that conditioning is that black people are undervalued, underestimated, and marginalized that is obvious by the treatment that I received by the Department of Corrections and its employees along with the justice system, who have all collaborated together to bring injustice. Being a black correctional officer fighting a system that has stacked the deck so high it seems to be untouchable, I found the justice system seemed to work differently for blacks and minorities. It seemed that Old Lady Justice, who is supposed to be blindfolded is no doubt peeking from under that blindfold to see whom she is serving.

As the case against me worked its way through the justice system, I thought justice for all we would see. I continued to come to work and putting up with the constant harassment by the guards, who seemed to be emboldened by the prospect of me losing my job over the false accusations levied against me. I remained prayed up, and hopefully, I would prevail as the trial date neared. I continued to keep in close contact with my attorney in Elmira, who was handling my case and keeping my attorney, who was located in New York City, handling my discrimination case against the department in the loop as it progressed. A day or so before the official trial date, I was notified that there would be no trial, and the case against me was thrown out. That's right—the charges I was booked on like a common thug at the New York State Police barracks in Horseheads, NY, where I was fingerprinted and had a mug shot taken for the vicious assault on the white racist guard who had received that small laceration on the tip of his nose that he placed there was thrown out of court.

It's truly a scary thing when a racist is shown. Special privileges by the court system and law enforcement allow them to use the justice system as tool to harass and intimidate those whom they choose and they are given carte blanche and assistance by those entrusted with administrating justice. Yes, we should all be concerned and as a black man, scared to death. Immediately following the false assault case being thrown out, the state decided to hit me and my attorney with their sudden need to hold a discovery hearing regarding my federal law suit for discrimination and retaliation.

Now remember all of this took place immediately after the passing of my mother. You talk about a bunch of coward racist bastard that have zero empathy for me, and the truly sad part was this was coming from the top of the department, not from the low echelon. Yes, that was proof positive I was being harassed by Albany itself for exercising my civil and constitutional rights. Now the department will say and put out communication to its employees and even to the public that they don't tolerate discrimination, but as soon as someone such as myself complains about discrimination, I am subjected to harassment by those who are discriminating and retaliating against me as well as those at the top for reporting the discrimination to them. So I wish the state and the department would both quit lying. You help encourage what goes on inside of the New York state prison system. Some of the head people that make decisions in Albany that hold top positions within the department are ex-superintendents of correctional facilities that ran like crap or were riddled with corruption, mayhem, and had very questionable practices that consist of violations of basic human rights. Those are the types that are leading the department and are allowed to make crucial decisions in running the department. They are usually awarded these jobs for their loyalty to one another through the old boys' network, and this is after they have retired from their superintendent's post.

So after waiting damn near eight years for the state to move on my case in federal court, someone at the top felt it would be a good time after the passing of my mother to have a discovery hearing, which me and my attorney obliged them with prior to the days leading up to the two-day scheduled discovery hearing. My attorney informed me of what was going to take place and what we expected to gain from the hearing.

During the hearing, the state lawyer was a woman in her thirties who represented the state. One of the first things during the discovery hearing was both sides exchanged documents that they planned on using in court. The state handed over a small stack of papers to my attorney, which consisted of about ten sheets of papers that my attorney quickly thumbed through. He then looked up and asked the state lawyer if that was it, and she responded with a yes. My attorney then reached down into the large black bag that was on wheels and pulled out a pile of papers that was the equivalent of a rim and a half of paper and let it hit the table, which we all sat around. The first stack went *boom* on to the table. The next stack went *boom*, and the third and final stack went *boom*. He then pushed the three large stacks of supporting documents across the desk at the state attorney, who asked quickly in a panicked voice, "What is that?" as she pushed back away from the table in her rolling chair.

My attorney responded by saying, "They are supporting documents." She was truly taken back and overwhelmed by the amount of documents that were offered to support my case. As I watched the exchange, I was celebrating inside, knowing the end was near. I would soon have my day in court. There was no way that the lawyer for the state could have been told the truth about anything about this case by these racist guards and the administration, evident by her reaction to the document swap.

I remember the first guard questioned was the chicken wing-eating guard, who had failed miserably in the compensation hearing that I had won. When he arrived, he looked to be under the influence of something. He was sweating and looked unraveled. He looked much like a man that wanted to be anywhere but here. He tried to poise himself, but the look on his face told the whole story. Whenever a guard would be questioned by outside sources, he is prepped by the union NYSCOBA or by one of its attorneys that they have on their payroll that has sworn allegiance to the union and not to the fundamental thumb of the law that they have sworn an oath to but instead have chosen to represent and help shield those who should be brought to justice, those helping to keep the perpetual cycle of abuse that is allowed to go unchecked in the Department of Corrections, the union NYSCOBA. Its deep pockets use the dues it collects from its members to buy lawyers as well as politicians to help achieve their goals. Rather than seek a new contract or discipline an officer, the union wants what it paid for—loyalty to them and their agenda, those that have chosen to help them no matter if its right or wrong, and so many are willing to sell their soul to the devil to enrich themselves even if it means lying, stealing, and cheating to do their part.

The state lawyers are no different. They work to cover up and shield the department, helping to stop the onslaught of lawsuits that the many inmates file. The department and the union, along with those who help to cover up the wrong doing in the department. They would like the public to think that the majority of the inmate lawsuits are frivolous, but that is a lie. The state is well aware of the complaints the inmates have and what is coved up. Hell, they called my lawsuit frivolous, and I know my complaint was valid. The state favors to settle many of the lawsuits it faces rather than go to court and fight, because ultimately they know they will lose. The systematic abuse and coverup is so persuasive. I have seen or heard of cases where inmates look like they have been hit by a Mac truck and would blame it on the classic line, "He fell down the stairs." Yep, that's right—that classic lie still works today. The state doesn't seem concerned with guards and staff violating state and federal laws. It's almost like a double-edged sword because the department, it seems, would have an obligation to the tax-paying public to safeguard and spend our tax dollars wisely in an effort to save the taxpayers' money, but instead it chooses to pay off the many lawsuits that are brought on by the staff inside these prisons who refuse to do their jobs or freely administrate their own form of justice at their discretion, and staff being allowed to go unchecked, and the state would rather spend an exorbitant amount of money than to check the staff with disciplinary charges if their name isn't Curtis Brown being disciplined with false allegation it would seem.

During the discovery hearing with the chicken wing-eating guard who was questioned by my attorney regarding the harassment and relation with regards to my federal lawsuit he was being accused of, once again, he folded under pressure. He couldn't remember what he had written or accused me of in memos that he had written to the Elmira Correctional Facility administration that my attorney was now seeking answers to. He was either outright lying or giving evasive answers to my attorney and the state lawyer as well as to the stenographer, who carefully documented his every answer. The lying guard was trapped in his own snare.

As the noon hour approached, both sides agreed to a break until after lunch. As we broke, I noticed the lawyer for the state looked at the lying chicken wing-eating guard with disappointment and shame. As he got up to leave, I and my attorney remained in the room as the state lawyer and the stenographer left. We could see out the window as the lying guard quickly got in his car to leave and my attorney turned to me and said, "Hey do you think he will be back after lunch?" and we both laughed.

I thought for a moment and I responded with, "He has to come back, right?"

And then my attorney said, "Yes, if he doesn't, we will send the marshals to round him up." Once again, we laughed. I thought about the federal marshals going to the lying guard's favorite watering hole, which everyone said was the local strip club, and retrieving him. Now that would be funny.

As I exited the building, the state attorney was outside on the phone with someone having what appeared to be a serious conversation, just like the state compensation lawyer had when the compensation judge ruled in my favor. It was to the utmost importance to watch everything going on around me. That way I could take the temperature so I could judge for myself to see who we were dealing with. And by what I could see, the state was losing. Once again, the chicken wing–eating guard was a gold mine of helpful information in proving my case in showing a pattern of systematic racism, discrimination, and harassment, which was prevalent at the Elmira Correctional Facility.

After the lunch break and the discovery hearing was started back up, the lying guard was the last to arrive. I would imagine he was in no hurry to return. When he came back, he tried to hide the nervousness that was written on his face when he had arrived in the morning, but it was so obvious. There was no hiding it. When they had prepped him for his testimony, they should've given him a black mourner's veil to hide behind because his look told it all—priceless.

During the continuing questioning, he continued to be a great help. He was a treasure trove of lies. I think someone forgot to tell him this was all going to be used in the pending federal court trial. After my attorney finished with questioning him, he was sent on his way, and he couldn't leave fast enough. Next up was the retired lieutenant who had made the statement at the funeral home directed at me: "Hey, I didn't know they let niggers in here." He came in and sat down with the "I don't care" attitude and seemed to be at ease being questioned, but he had underestimated my young attorney. He was playing at the top of his game and was as thirsty for justice as I was during questioning. Questions are usually asked to you in different forms. A good attorney will catch you if you're lying or trying to be deceptive. And the lieutenant was proven to be very deceptive during his questioning. You can imagine that during the lieutenant's long career at the Elmira CF, he had testified in other court proceedings. There were many staff members during the lieutenant's career that had been part of a well-known case called *Santiago vs. Myles* in which the Elmira Correctional Facility was found guilty of discriminate against the black and Hispanic inmates at Elmira in housing and job placement, as well as other discriminatory practices. The administration and employees were being allowed to subject the black and brown inmates to whatever they deemed fit, not using a far and logical means of thinking to achieve a standard that would have been acceptable and fair to all.

After the facility was found guilty, the court ordered and mandated that the facility have mandatory cultural training for all staff members, security and nonsecurity personnel, it was at the time the only facility ordered to do so. Also, it was placed under the watchful eye of the federal court system, which would be monitoring their decision-making in jobs, programs, and housing for the inmates, and the stats would be closely monitored. The case was in 1991. I started working at Elmira in 1996, and I remember all the staff did was complain about being under *Santiago vs. Myles*. You would hear security staff, members of the administration, and civilians all complaining about having to change their discriminatory ways. It seemed to bring out more animosity and hate in those who had it out for the inmates. The loss in court was taken to heart by many; you could tell by the way they did their jobs. I guess the racists don't like to lose at their own game, on their home field. They truly took the loss to heart. During questioning of the lieutenant, he was asked about his knowledge regarding the notorious case *Santiago vs. Myles*, and he immediately got amnesia and tried to deny even ever knowing about the case, even though it directly affected the way the lieutenant did his job. After I, my attorney, and the state lawyer all looked at him with astonishment and disbelief, he retained his memory or, shall I say, he came to his damn senses and admitted he knew about and he was aware of the case and its direct impact on the facility. That was a chalk mark for me because the lieutenant had directly lied during his testimony. Remember, this was being archived by the stenographer for the upcoming federal court trial. The lieutenant must have forgotten where he was at, when my attorney continued questioning him. After he dropped the golden nugget in our lap, he was asked about calling me a nigger, which he seemed to think was no big deal. My attorney asked him, "Have you ever called any other black or African American correctional officer a nigger?"

And the stupid dumb racist said, "Yes."

My attorney then said, "Can you remember who it was?"

As I waited intensely for his answer, he said my uncle's name. Yes, you heard me right—the man said he called my uncle, who was retired, a nigger when they worked together. To say I was floored would put it quite mildly, because I know my uncle, and he would not let this lying racist bastard disrespect him. I thought to myself, *I can't wait to get out of here today because my uncle would love to hear this.* When the lieutenant made his outlandish remark or answer to the question, you could tell he didn't believe the shit himself. Yes, these liars were getting snared in their own traps; they were telling on themselves, and this was only a discovery hearing. I couldn't wait until the big show, the federal court trial or, as I would say, my day in court, where all of this was going to be used at trial.

After finishing with the lying, retired, racist lieutenant, he too was sent on his way. This same lieutenant had two boys who worked at the Elmira Correctional Facility. Also, one was let go after he pulled some compensation scam. The other was a do-nothing, worthless sergeant who just came to work to hang out with his buddies and was clueless. I used to laugh inside when he would see me. He would try to give me the evil eye or the killer one look for reporting his racist father, who was named as a defendant in my federal lawsuit. Many of the coward guards would look at me with hate and animosity. I would just laugh. Most were cowards unless they were in numbers. These same guards, when I saw them alone in a corridor or walkway, they would pass by with their heads down, not giving that tough guy look anymore.

After finishing up with the discovery hearing and it was finished, the state lawyer and my attorney had a brief conversation with the state lawyer telling my attorney that he would be hearing from her. Later, I and my attorney talked about the outcome of the discovery hearing, and my attorney said he felt it went well for us, and there was a lot of information gained from the hearing. We later parted ways—me going home and he heading back to New York City. After I returned to work the next day, I was met with double the glares and double the stares from all who felt slighted by my audacity to seek justice for the injustice I was receiving, The harassment continued under the watchful eye of the administration and union NYSCOBA.

Immediately following the discovery hearing, I was walking down the flats or corridor area when the chicken wing eating guard, who had fallen short of his expectations to lie and cover up his wrongdoing walked past me. As he approached, he sounded like he was bringing mucous up from his throat and acted as if he was going to spit it on me. He curled up his thin chapped lips and formed them in the ready to spit position. As I walked past, that's when I warned him, "If you spit on me, I'm going to knock every damn tooth out of your head that you have," and then finished with "Try me." Damn isn't that what whites did to black protesters in the South during the civil rights era? They spit on us, they kicked us, they put dogs on us, they hit us with high-pressure hoses, all in an effort to silence us into submission to their racist ways. You can trust one thing—if this racist guard would've hurled his mouth full of spit and hate at me, I would have surely knocked all of his damn racist ass teeth out of his head.

You can trust that. I reported the incident to the superintendent and assured him that the first one of his employees that spit upon me was getting knocked the hell out. He became argumentative and tried to tell me that he didn't think anyone would do that, and he doubted if anyone had tried covering up for the out-of-control staff.

As I awaited my day in court as time went by and as Officer Q would often put it, the wheels of justice grind slow but they grind fine. Sooner or later, the state would have to stop delaying justice and stop impeding on my constitutional rights and allow those who have chosen to discriminate against me be bought forth to face their accuser, and it seemed my harassers were well aware of this as they attempted to step up the harassment I was receiving. I continued to come to work and do my job, and I continued to get falsely written up and suspend for whatever lie they had chosen. I was still the only correctional officer being written up at the Elmira Correctional Facility and suspended without pay. Ironically, there were police officers who would be placed on administrational leave with pay after killing someone. I remember an incident where the sergeant and the racist head guard placed a known homosexual in the mess hall I was in charge of to work. He came into the area and thought he was going to receive preferential treatment, until I assured him he would be treated like all the rest of the inmates who work in the mess hall. I would observe the inmate in long, lengthy conversations with the head racist guard at the kitchen desk and with the chicken wing-eating guard, who was known to take a liking to the homosexual inmates in the facility he worked in the mess hall where I worked for around two weeks.

One day, when I was working the scullery area connected to that mess hall, the homosexual inmate got into a fight with another inmate who seemed to be doing more wrestling with one another then closed hand fighting. As I responded to the fight, so did the officer who had stepped away from his post but returned just as I was going to break up the fight. As the two inmates grabbed hold of each other, they were separated by the guard who was working in the mess hall. As I approached, the homosexual's shirt was soaked in blood and looked odd, seeing that the two inmates had done more wrestling than fist throwing. The next thing that was odd was the scumbag guard made sure to grab the inmate from the front were the blood was at, and he made sure to press the front of his body into the homosexual inmate where this large accumulation of blood was at, on the inmate's white mess hall work shirt. The two inmates then acted as if they were still trying to get at each other as I held the other inmate back with little to no effort, while the scumbag guard continued to bear hug the bloody known homosexual inmate.

After the two had been separated, there were no cuts or stab wounds to either inmate, yet there was enough blood for a murder scene. The bloody lying guard then ran to the sergeant and accused me of not helping to break up the fight because I had no blood on me and his blue shirt appeared to be a bloody mess. I was quickly written up and suspended. Now may I remind you neither inmate had a cut or stab wound on him, but there was enough blood for a murder scene. It had all been staged; the blood was fake blood. There was no correctional officer in his right damn mind going to grab a blood-soaked inmate from the front to contaminate himself with blood over a fistfight. Really, the scumbag guard was stupid, but he wasn't that dumb, although he was the same stupid guard who had an inmate crawl inside the large industrial dishwasher to clean it out and then turned the hot, scalding water on the inmate, sending him to the hospital and court. Yep, this was also the same dumb ass who had a delivery truck back up at his command to rip down the roll-up door. He forgot to put all the way up. May I add that was a pretty expensive door that had been ripped from the frame. He was a frail-looking man that weighed about 160 pounds soaked wet in his uniform and always had a cigarette hanging from his mouth and a cup of coffee in his hand. The blood was fake. They had their pet inmates use fake blood for the stunt. How else can you explain the blood? The inmates had no cuts no stab wounds, not even a bloody lip or nose, so where did the blood come from? There was truly nothing they would not do to rid me of their prison. I have to say *theirs* because remember, they think they own the place.

After the new false allegations I was charged with, I was once again given a N.O.D seeking my dismissal from state service. Each time I was written up, the state Department of Corrections along with the public employee relations board as well as the union would have knowledge regarding the suspension, none would raise the question of suspicion of the black officer being the only one being disciplined at the Elmira Correctional Facility. Let me remind you there were approximately 460 security staff and only 5 were African Americans. The percentage is 0.01086, and the common denominator was a federal lawsuit. That is why the facility along with our own state government in collaboration with NYSCOBA formed what seemed to be a hit squad against me for standing up for my civil and constitutional rights. From each suspension, I lost more and more money and time accumulated on the books. I and my wife were blessed to have good sense with our money and saved, so each time they suspended me, we could draw the equivalent of my biweekly paycheck from our savings before even becoming a correctional officer. We both worked and saved for a rainy day.

After becoming a correctional officer, my uncle who was a correctional officer, the one the lieutenant had referenced as being one of his racial victims, he had warned me in advance of taking the job. He said, "Whatever you do, make sure you put some money up for a lawyer."

My response was, "Why? We have a union."

My uncle looked at me with a serious look and said, "Listen to me, that damn union doesn't give a shit about your black ass. They throw us to the wolves, but they protect the white officers. Do not forget that."

So immediately after finishing my probationary year, I and my wife started putting money aside for just that, an attorney, which proved to be wise and sound advice from my uncle, and it was also spot on. Now when one of the white officers were suspended without pay for one of the things they got locked out for, which was DWI or DUI, they would take up a collection from both the staff and the union to ensure he or she could provide for their family. Most of the staff were literally hand to mouth when it came to their financing. As one staff member put it one day, "You have to remember you are working with some that are the working poor." One would wonder how can one struggle so much when you have a good job, paying a decent living wage in upstate New York. The answer is poor or no financial education, poor judgment, along with bad decisions, which makes for a recipe for financial disaster, which many seem to suffer from. Many also seemed to be affected by one of the 3Ds: divorce, drinking, and drugs, which also affected many, and let's not leave out the big *G*, gambling, which was out of control at the Elmira Correctional Facility. Many staff members would bring their life problems to work and unleash their frustration out on the inmates and staff to relieve their pain, which many have brought on themselves by willingly or unwillingly allowing themselves to fall victim to the madness. This didn't just affect the lower echelon; these same things went all the way to the top of the department to the decision makers.

While I was working in the mess hall, there was a guard who was from a small town outside of Elmira, New York. Its population was 99.9 percent white. He was ex-military. He seemed to mind his business and do his job even when it came to communicating with me. We would talk and even sometimes laugh. The working relationship was good until one day he came in and looked upset, frazzled, and stunned. I remember keeping my distance as this guard seemed to be trying to work out whatever he was going through. As the day went on, he struck up a conversation with me. We were about the same age. As he talked, I could see there was something bothering him, so I asked him if he was all right because he wasn't acting like himself, and that's when he hit me with the Jerry Springer response, "My best friend took my wife and kids."

I then hit him with the Dr. Phil response: "Wait a minute. You do know that guy was never your best friend, let alone your friend. He was your worst nightmare." After, I consoled him more than the rest would have done for him. The others would have just laughed in his face and teased him about his wife's decision to leave him for what this man still referred to as his best friend. Well, while this guard was going through his divorce, I now became a target of harassment for him. He also joined up with the racist head guard in the kitchen, and he too would make me the fault of his marriage being destroyed by his best friend. His attitude changed. He no longer would do his job. He would take his frustration out on the inmates, refusing them even what they were legitimately entitled to. He would be allowed to come to work and sit reading large five-inch thick novels when he was required to watch over the inmates. He became a mess and a problem. If I would have to put an estimate on the percentage on the number of divorced guards, I would have to say it was in the high 65 percentile or maybe more. With divorce came child support, alimony, and a dividing of property, and sometimes, that included pensions and 401s or in the state employees' case, our deferred compensation plan. All would be up for grabs as the two sides split. It would also seem even baby car seats.

One guard, his wife left him high and dry and left the kids with him with no car seat. He couldn't afford to purchase the car seat, so he attempted to steal it from a local department store where he was apprehended for theft. When that happened, I thought the thin blue line of corrections had no compassion or love for one another because if it did, its members would have made sure their so-called brother had a car seat and not a theft charge, so many would be left with half of their salary half of any savings and some would even have their pension cut in half. The employees who were going through this would be an absolute mess, making all around them suffer as well. All you would hear is the constant complaining about their ex-wives, taking them to the cleaners. Their coping mechanism would be one the other two D's, drinking or drugs. Some of these guards would show their frustrations in front of low-ranking and high-ranking supervisory staff who would turn their heads the other way to ignore the problem that the guard had or was becoming as they vent their frustrations out on both staff and inmates. The guard in the mess hall was no exception to this. This was a prime example, although it didn't seem to take him long to recover, because soon everyone was teasing him about his love affair with the dep of security's niece. She was not employed at the facility. He had, early on, fallen head over heels for her in a very short time so much, so he allowed her to purchase a car with the title in her name and the payment in his, and a short while after, she dumped him, leaving him to foot the bill for her car. Everyone laughed at him and teased him, and they asked, "Can you buy me a car please?"

I thought to myself, *This man is either naïve or clueless about love.* In many of these divorces, it seemed the kids were the ones that suffered the most by listening to and watching the staff going through it. The guard in the mess hall who said his best friend had taken his wife was beyond out of control after losing his wife to his friend and buying a car for someone who wanted nothing to do with him. He would harass me to no end because of his frustration and hate. I even wondered if his best friend was black because I had nothing to do with his problems, but he made me his sounding board with his verbal harassment and his refusal to work together. He was also in the Army Reserves. I really don't know how because if he was any indication to what our ready army was, we were all in trouble. He was one of the laziest guards I had ever worked with during my twenty-eight years of service. Later on, during my career, his mouth continued to spiral out of control with me as well as others.

There was this one guard—he was short and stockily built. This same loudmouth whose best friend had taken his wife had supposedly disrespected Shorty's significant other, and Shorty was having none of that, so on the gallery area in one of the smaller blocks, there is a pass through to the other blocks. Shorty put plain Shout Your Mouth into action. Shorty was working the midnight shift. Big Mouth worked the day shift along with myself. I wasn't present, but the same story was told over and over all day after the altercation by staff and inmates who were in eye and earshot, and it was told like this: Big Mouth was cutting though the block to get to his post in G Block—hey, the same block I was working. As Big Mouth cut through the block, Shorty was lying in wait out of sight. As Big Mouth approached, Shorty jumped out in front of him and confronted the loud mouth about disrespecting him and his significant other. There was a question asked and a fist thrown. Shorty was probably a whole five inches shorter than Loud Mouth, but Shorty was in good shape, evident by the ass whipping he put on the loudmouth Dolly Do Right looking guard who was reportedly slammed to the floor by the much smaller officer and hit upside the head with a barrage of furious punches aimed to Shout His Mouth. One officer who was an eyewitness said he ran into the block where he was working to avoid being questioned about the assault or fight.

After they were pulled apart, it was obvious that Loud Mouth had lost by the condition he was in when he had arrived at G Block—his clothing messier than normal, a dazed look in his eyes, but the truly telling sign was the two-inch knot or hematoma on his forehead that seemed to keep growing. He looked as if he needed a good corner man to patch him up. The hematoma seemed to need immediate attention. The sergeant, the immediate supervisor in the area, was more than aware of what had just transpired. He saw him, and he took part in hiding the loud mouth guard in the basement area of the cell block to shield him from others seeing him and questioning him about the two-inch speed knot that grew like a beautiful budding flower filmed in time lapse to show its rapped growth from bud to beauty that now adorned the loud mouth's forehead. He was allowed to hide out in the basement area for the entire 7–3 tour with no questions asked. Also, neither one of the guards were ever disciplined for anything, even though they had a knockout, drag-out fistfight in front of staff and inmates. They, the white officers and guards, seemed to be shielded from any and all wrongdoing with the help of an implicit administration and a union that goes out of their way to shield and cover up the wrongdoing of its members by any means necessary.

After receiving that ass whipping, the loudmouth guard did shut his mouth for a short while, but he was soon back at it again, offering his ass up for another whipping. The facility food service area and the kitchen/mess halls were being ran amok with the facility food service area budget remaining to be stretched to its limits. A lot of the problem was the staff that was stealing both food and paper supplies.

The bucktooth rabbit, the racist guard's go-to man, was getting married again for the second or third time, and he and his wife-to-be were planning the wedding of their dream. Their caterer and venue weren't hard to find. The caterer was ELM-CF, a very well-known establishment that has been around since 1876 and has served millions of tasty meals. Their venue was a building on top of a hill overlooking the city of Elmira. It was truly a wedding fit for royalty, a true fairytale wedding. Okay, the truth was the bucktooth rabbit used the Elmira Correctional Facility's food service area as a private food service establishment to cater his wedding. He got the head civilian in charge of the food service area at the prison to order roast beef for the special occasion, and then the rest was other food in the facility food supply to feed the inmates. All the food used to supply the dream wedding was out of the state-budgeted money to feed incarcerated inmates and was cooked and prepared at the prison. Just down the road was the wedding venue, the facility clubhouse used for training and union meeting. They also have their yearly steak bake/clam bake/Klan bake sponsored by NYSCOBA. The majority of black officers referred to their yearly gathering as such, the Klan bake, where the white officers gathered and did what the majority of them did best—drink and gamble, and in the past, many of the black officers I had spoken to who had gone to the Klan bake felt disrespected by racially charged comments or very questionable behavior, and it was a union-sponsored event. We would kid around and ask each other, "Hey, you going to the Klan bake?" and the response would be an overwhelming "Hell, no."

The bucktooth rabbit and his guests dined on the prison cuisine as they celebrated their new union at the clubhouse. The wedding took place on a weekend, and that following Monday, the stories and rumors started to fly all over the facility, how the bucktooth rabbit was refusing to pay the civilian cook for the state food. He had supplied to the bride and groom and their guests at the dream wedding. I myself had personally seen and heard the two of them in the kitchen arguing about the money owed the civilian cook for the state food he had supplied him. All the civilian staff in the kitchen, as well as the security staff and inmates, were all aware of what had transpired with the two and had knowledge of the dispute over money for the catering service rendered. Many of the civilian and security staff in the kitchen had been invited to attend the wedding without even inquiring into the bucktooth rabbit's dream wedding. Every one of the civilians that attended came to me and laughed about what they had witnessed at the wedding. One cook who went had a photo of the bride and groom. He came to me and said, "Here Brown, I took this just for you." He pulled a photo out of his pocket. He then said, "Man, that is one hard-looking woman." It was his comment, not mine, but when I looked at the photo, the bride looked like the head racist guard dressed in drag. I laughed and asked if it was indeed him. The cook laughed and assured me it was the bucktooth rabbit's new bride. I laughed at the comment also. Others came to me, telling me about the wedding and how it was a joke or the reddest redneck wedding they had ever attended. Some even talked about the food they had dined on and how it was stolen out of the facility food supply. Some of the staff seemed to be depended on the facility to feed them and were worse and more costly to the state financials than the inmates we were trying to stop from stealing. Food was literally going out of every door. Even though the supervisors and administration were all the while aware of the theft of state property, little was done to stop the staff from taking what they wanted. The bucktooth rabbit and the food service manager were at odds for months about the money he refused to pay for the stolen food until the next big questionable event happened to draw attention. Elsewhere, we would always say that working in the prison was like working in a continuous twenty-four-hour soap opera. There was always something going on. If it wasn't the inmates, it was the out-of-control staff being allowed to run wild inside the prison.

Soon after the stolen wedding food fiasco, the chicken wing-eating guard had tragedy hit his family. There were members of the facility that took up a collection for him and his family. The head racist guard even comforted him and seemed to show him compassion unlike he did when he harassed me about my deceased mother. After the collection was taken up for the chicken eating guard for him and his family, shortly after, it was handed over to him. The racist head guard got wind of what the money collected was used for by the chicken wing-eating guard. It was said that the money was used for his favorite pastime, which was well-known to be gambling and not for the relief of his family. The racist guard now was on a relentless campaign to harass his once-trusted ally who had helped him harass me. I sat back and watched as sparks flew as the racist guard harassed and tormented the chicken wing-eating guard into submission. Once again, he was out of the inner circle of the racist head guard. He was shunned, harassed, and humiliated for spending the money collected to satisfy his gambling addiction. The head racist guard would report to work approximately one hour before the rest of us in the food service area because he worked the desk area, and that job had different hours than others in the food service area. I would also work that job. During his days off, he would come in and cause chaos and confusion. It was told by some of the civilian cooks he would come in and flip over large steel prep tables and toss and throw things around in what would appear to be a fit of rage. He would draw and write on walls, lockers, and anything else he chose to leave his hateful mark on. The chicken wing guard arrived at his post in the mess hall one early morning to find large money signs, $, marked in black marker all over the mess hall on doors, lockers, walls, and cabinets in protest of him spending the collected funds for his family on his gambling habit.

After his tragic event, the racist head guard and one civilian cook along with a few inmates who were brought down to set up and prep the morning meal were in the area. Everyone in the area knew the racist guard was responsible for the money signs all over the mess hall, but the immediate supervisor nor the administration never held him responsible for the destruction of state property the chicken wing guard seemed to never recover from the life-changing event nor the harassment he received for spending the money collected. His habits seemed to get worse. His skin started to get these red splotches all over his face. His teeth started to get real brown, almost rotten-looking, and those who dared to get close to him said his breath smelled something terrible. It looked like he was being eaten by something. Even though his appearance and his demeanor were alarming to the average person, no supervisor or representative from the union stepped in to help him. He looked worse than some of the inmates that come into the prison off the street that were in society struggling.

On March 10, 2008, I was home sick off of work for the day, when I received a call from the watch commander ordering me to report to work to see the superintendent. Once there, I was directed into the superintendent's office and told I was terminated from my state employment. I was fired. I remember this date well because March 10 is me and my wife's wedding anniversary, and they know this too, but this is what the state department of corrections and facility administration did. They would harass and torment me and my family on holidays and special occasions. They only needed to look into my personal file to get birthdates and our anniversary date. I remember this day well because my wife drove me to the Elmira correctional facility to find out what was going on. Once there, the superintendent informed me that I was terminated from my job. As he told me, I could see the pleasure he was having notifying me that I was fired. After he said I was terminated, he waited patiently for my reaction. He seemed to be bracing himself for the negative reaction to come. I denied him the pleasure of seeing what he waited so patiently for his perceived perception of what a black man was supposed to do when he was terminated. Unjustifiable. His perceived perception was destroyed with me laying my badge and ID on his desk, and I then made the bold and defiant statement, "I'll be back," and I then walked out of his office, truly unsure if I would be back.

As my wife waited patiently in the car, I got in the car on one of our happiest days of the year, the day we celebrate our wedding anniversary, and I had to tell her I had just been fired. She looked at me in disbelief of what I had just told her, and I then said it again. I was terminated or fired. My federal lawsuit was still on the table awaiting trial, so after arriving home and gathering ourselves, we went into self-preservation or survival mode. I notified my attorney and let him know what was happening, and he assured me I would be back to work. My attorney immediately filed paperwork to do just that, to get my job back. That was allowed to be taken unjustifiably by the state. Now remind you, I'm a member of NYSCOBA, the correctional officers' union, who made no objection to my firing. So it's safe to say the state department of correctional services and NYSCOBA were working together. It took many months for my appeal to the state Supreme Court to render their decision on my case of unlawful termination, but as they say, the wheels of justice turn slow, but they grind fine. So be it.

After months of waiting, a decision was rendered in my favor, and yes, I was unjustifiably terminated by the state of New York. The state was ordered to reinstate me and to pay me back for lost money and time. After returning to work and giving my harassers another set back and loss by me being reinstated, I now knew the state didn't have a leg to stand on when my federal case was brought forward in court. I remember returning to work my first day after my reinstatement. From the moment I stepped into the facility, I received stares of hate and contempt. No one I passed said "Welcome back." I then had to first report to the superintendent's office to retrieve my badge and ID. Once there, I was given my badge and ID from the same self-serving racists who demanded it in the first place. As the superintendent curled his tiny thin lips up to speak, I sat waiting intensely to hear an explanation for the unlawful termination, which I never received. What I did receive was some made-up mumbo jumbo about it being me and my attorney's fault. After he said that and was unwilling to speak to me with common sense. Everything else that came out his mouth sounded like the old Charlie Brown cartoon when the teacher is speaking, "##**###**" mumbo jumbo. Even though the court said it was unlawful, this idiot wanted me to believe me, and my attorney fired me. After he finished, he didn't say "Welcome back." He said "Good luck," which was taken as a direct threat that more of the same was coming my way. After retrieving what should have never been taken in the first place, I was informed to report to my post. As I walked through the prison, guards in passing would walk by with their heads down, offering no eye contact or acknowledgment. It seemed that they had been tipped off that I was on my way, and some seemed to be unhappy about my return. As I passed, they would make grouting sounds of "He is back" or "There he goes," as they would stare at me with pure hate and contempt. These guys really felt that they had the right to pick and choose who was going to work at the Elmira Correctional Facility. I had a family that was counting on me to provide for them just as many of them had, but you see, they had been allowed over the years to have a false sense of privilege. Many seemed to think that it was their right and not a privilege to work at the Elmira correctional facility, some over years of family nepotism and some for other reasons like years of being allowed to go unchecked regarding their out-of-control behavior, whether it was directed at inmates or staff by anyone in power that can demand change, so for anyone to go against the system or the out-of-control guards that were allowed to run amok was an enemy. Yes, getting my job back was good for me and a bad thing for those trying to rid me of their facility.

I remember my first day back trying to get acclimated back to my duties. The inmates started to come up to me and welcome me back, and almost every one of them had a story to tell about the guards running around the facility, bad-mouthing me when I was gone as they celebrated what was thought to be my demise. But yes, just like the Phoenix, I rose again, and as promised, like the Terminator, I was back. Yes, it was a true victory. The agony of defeat was written all over the faces of my harassers as they shot stares and glares my way. It was funny because I wasn't intimidated by the weak cowards. Hell, it would take four or five of them to beat up a handcuffed inmate, so no, I wasn't intimidated at all. The inmates over the years had come up with many names for when someone would steer them down with hate on their face. They called it ice grilling, the murder one look, or my favorite of all time, face fighting. That's when the person you're trying to intimidate with the tough-guy look gives it back and you look like you're face fighting, trying to make each other scared of each other with a look when the weak guards would snarl there face up. I called it the ice cream look and laughed.

As I continued to work in the mess hall, the day came when the one person who worked alongside me and had my back announced that he was retiring. Q had enough of the day in and day out struggle of working in the prison, and it had taken its toll. He too would be harassed and tormented for speaking out against the racist guards. He was like an advocate on my behalf reporting and supporting some of the claims I had made about the harassment I was receiving. Yes, they, my harassers, were glad to see him go for me. When Q retired, it left me more vulnerable to attack by these out-of-control racists. Soon after Q retired, that's when the heat in the mess hall was turned way up. They had a little skinny sergeant that couldn't have weighed more than 140 pounds. His hair was very, very greasy. He would come into work with his hands dirty with grease and dirt caked up under his nails. He smelled of dirt. His greasy hair and his small-framed body with his large feet made him look like a dirty duck. That's the name the inmates gave him when they were caught making comments about him. He would support the racist head guard in his bid to get me fired. He would turn his back as the racist guard would verbally harass me and denied any wrongdoing that had taken place in his presence.

Before my federal lawsuit was brought to trial, I was written up and then taken out of the mess hall. My job that I had bid on through my union rights was allowed to be taken by the administration, and no objection was raised by the union. I paid dues too with no objection. If that had been done to one of the white officers, they would have shut the jail down in protest. I was then placed on a job in the service unit or guidance unit that an officer had bid off of. It was where the civilian councilors and other civilians worked, including the facility chaplains. There was a Protestant chaplain, a Catholic chaplain, a Muslim imam, and a Jewish rabbi that all occupied the rear of the guidance unit. The officer's desk was located at the front door of the unit, and the door was controlled by the officer at the front desk. With the push of a button, the door was opened, and when shut, it automatically relocked. The area was air conditioned for the civilians' comfort. Also on the unit was the inmate grievance office, where the inmates filed any complaints they had. There was a separate officer who was in charge of the grievance office, also known as the IGRC office, which stands for the "inmate grievance resolution committee." This office was located just across from the officer's desk at the front door. In the grievance office was an officer, the head civilian, and four inmates, two who were elected, and two clerks. In the rear were the clergy. There was also an officer to oversee that area. In the front, where I was posted, you had the IGRC office and all the counselors and the secretaries. My job on the unit was to run the front door to assure no inmate entered without a valid pass or call out to see someone on the unit. I was also responsible for calling the inmates in and out of the waiting area to see their councilors. I was also required to make rounds to assure the area was safe and secure.

Upon first arriving on the unit to work, all the councilors were white—male and female—and were almost evenly divided. There were approximately anywhere from ten to twelve councilors and two senior councilors to oversee them. There was also a sergeant who worked the area who was responsible for the guidance unit and had other responsibilities throughout the prison, so his time was spent in between them. After being forced off my job in the kitchen by the administration, I worked in the guidance unit for a number of weeks. The administration refused to put me back on my bid job. I decided to bid the guidance unit job full time. When the bid came down, I won the bid, and the job was now mine.

This job also required me to take a group of inmates to chow from G block, and also I had to work G-7 gallery on the weekends, so on a normal weekday, I would report to G block following lineup and make a round on 7 gallery to ensure that all the inmates on the gallery were accounted for and to prepare the gallery for the morning chow. The guards who worked G-block along with the knuckle head sergeant all seemed to have a love for gambling and cooking, which seemed to be more important than security itself. The card game would be played in full view of the inmates and staff right at the desk of the A officers, which was located as soon as you walked in the block. There, every officer in the block with the exception of myself would gather around to wager or bid their money on the next hand of cards dealt by the dealer. As they all posted themselves around the crowded desk, fighting for a place to sit to have a chance at the next jackpot, the area sergeant would join in or go lock himself in his office to nap. I was assigned to 7 Gallery, so that is where I would go. There was a small office area on the landing area of each floor, but they would be seldom used because the officers in charge of those galleries would be downstairs playing cards or eating from the makeshift kitchen that had been allowed to be built in the basement area of G block, where the correctional officer or, in his case, guard was allowed to spend four or more hours out of his eight-hour shift preparing meals for anyone who wanted to purchase one. Even the facility watch commander would buy meals from the G block kitchen, allowing the guard to neglect his duties as a correctional officer. Instead of care, custody, and control of the inmates, he was in charge of helping to secure the inmates and do what he was hired to do. This clown was allowed to cook. It remained me of the Old West. He was like the old chuckwagon cook. Yes, this guard who was being paid a good salary to be a correctional officer was allowed to shift his job title to part-time cook. It was a full-scale operation. I would watch in the morning when this guard was allowed to bring into the facility bag after bag of groceries to prepare his meals for sale. When I first started working the service unit job with part of my duties requiring me to work also in G block 7 gallery, this same guard, as part of his duties on Sundays, was to open up the Protestant chapel, which was located in the basement of the facility gymnasium. My duty on Sunday during church service was to remain in the block on 7 gallery, where I was assigned. These were assignments that had been placed on these jobs though planning and staffing and union input.

After being locked out for being assaulted, after three weeks or so, I was allowed to return to work. After returning to work, my job assignment in G block had been changed to accommodate the guard/cook. I was now responsible on Sunday mornings to open up the Protestant chapel while the cook remained in the block preparing breakfast and lunch for all in the facility that purchased a meal. No sergeant, lieutenant, ranking officer, or the administration objected to the change to accommodate the guard. How was he allowed to come to work and sell dinner plates instead of doing his correctional job, which was care, custody, and control of the inmates at the prison? The whole facility knew what he was doing, but no one objected to the outlandish dereliction of duty that this guard was allowed to display. I would often wonder if the governor of the state was aware that he had hired a short-order cook and not a correctional officer who was being paid seventy thousand dollars plus overtime and benefits to sell dinner plates to the staff. What a scam! Also, they would have a few inmates they trusted to be allowed in the restricted basement area to clean and wash up the mess and also help themselves to the leftovers as a reward. Neither he nor any supervisor was ever written up for the dereliction of duty. He was allowed to do day after day, year after year.

When I spoke to the dep of security regarding my job duties being changed, he seemed to not give a damn. He himself knew the guard was being allowed to neglect his official duties. While having to work in G block was the worst part of my new bid, the rest of the job outweighed the negatives of working in G block. Each day, I worked in G block. I would get the key for the office area located on 7–8 gallery where I would post myself. All the other staff would gather at the main desk area located on the bottom floor, where there would be anywhere from six to seven officers hanging out together playing cards and usually up to some kind of shenanigans with all neglecting their official duties. You would think that the area sergeant wouldn't permit this, but you see, the area sergeant would be playing cards with them. Some of the staff members had made comments to the higher-ups about the card playing in the facility. I once myself told the dep they needed to charge at the front door for entry to the casino.

G block wasn't the only block doing what they were doing; it was happening throughout the whole prison under the watchful eye of the administration, all of whom were aware of the persistent problem plaguing the facility. The card playing and refusal to do their jobs over a card game would result in programs not running on time and the inmates not being let out of their cells in a timely manner, whether it was for a visit or a facility callout. Even the loudmouth union reps would take part in the daily facility card games that were a violation on state property under the employees' manual to the best of my knowledge. Over my many years working at the Elmira CF, no employee was ever disciplined over it. Hell, you have to remember the supervisions were also playing cards in G block and throughout the facility.

The officers and guards were required to do what was called the bar and hammer check that was brought on by the escape from

Dannemorea/Clinton, where the inmates had been trusted just like the ones who cleaned up the mess in the cook's makeshift basement kitchen in the restricted area of G block. The bar and hammer check was when you would have to physically go into every cell on the gallery with a rubber mallet to check the integrity of the inside of each cell, checking the windows and bars to make sure the occupant hadn't messed with its integrity like losing or cutting at the metal. You were also looking for holes in the walls or ceilings of the cell as well. The only officer or guard to do the bar and hammer check in G block on a Saturday morning would be me, Officer Brown.

As I would make my way down the thirty-eight cells on 7 gallery in G block, the inmates would yell out, "Brown, you're the only one that does this shit." The officer who worked 8 gallery would do the cell check because he would have to open each cell for me from the lock box, which controlled the opening and closing of the cells. As I went down 7 gallery, I would then do the same for him. He seemed to be the only one other than myself who came to work. The others, including the block sergeant, would be downstairs at the main desk area playing cards and eating breakfast meals they had purchased from the makeshift basement kitchen prepared by the guard/short-order cook.

There was a sheet that you had to sign saying you had performed the cell inspection that was forged by all those who were just hanging out refusing to do their jobs. The sheets were then all handed into the watch commander, who was usually the highest-ranking security staff on duty during the weekend. The area sergeant knew they had been forged. It was an all-too-common practice, forging paperwork. the fire and safety reports that were supposed to be handed in daily were also forged or not even documented, and when an audit of the fire and safety office would be conducted, they would back date paperwork to reflect the paperwork being up to date and in compliance to hide the fact that the staff weren't doing their job.

As I would be posted on the 7–8 gallery landing in the office area, the guards that were all hanging around the desk area would have the nerve to call me up on the phone and ask me to let out an inmate on the next level down 5–6 gallery. Or if the regular 8 gallery officer was off, the guard who was filling in would also be downstairs requesting me to do their job by letting an inmate out of his cell for a callout or visit while they remained downstairs playing cards and eating or just slumped back in a chair. I guess ordering the inmates around like slaves wasn't enough for some. They also seemed to think that me being the only African American officer around, I would be required to submit to their slave mentality. I quickly put them in check with my defiance and rejection to their request for me to do their job. The conversation would go like this. The phone would ring. I would answer, "Officer Brown, 7–8 gallery."

The caller would say, "Hey, Brownie, this is [the caller would give his name]. Could you let cell number "20 on 5-gallery out for a callout?"

And this would be my response to the caller on the other end: "What did you say?" knowing exactly what he had said. I would just be daring the lazy idiot guard to repeat his foolish request, and when he did, my quick and swift response would be, "You better get up off your lazy ass and come do your own job the state is paying you for," and I would hang the phone up on them.

The guard who was the A man or first officer in the block was also running the G block casino would sometimes call back and plead his case for the lazy guard and try to justify me doing a guard's job while he hung out at the desk with him playing cards or eating and relaxing. He would say it's helping out in the block. His foolish misconception of Officer Brown doing anyone's job was soon realized when he too was put in his place with a stern refusal from me. These requests were made when I first started working G block. After a few unsuccessful tries by the lazy guards to get me to perform their duties, they came to what common sense they had and stopped asking, and when the phone would ring, it would only be for a request to let inmates out on 7 or 8 gallery, the gallery I was in charge of. A lot of the time the sergeant himself would be right there when this idiot called as he too would be at the desk area all in on a hand of cards. I always said if they spent as much time doing their job and with as much dedication as they had with harassing me and playing cards at the Elmira Correctional Facility, the place would have been the most secure place on the planet Earth.

There was one guard that the area sergeant took a liking to. The sergeant, when he was an officer, was one of the laziest guards in the facility. He spoke with a heavy lisp that was mimicked by many of the staff members as well as the inmates. Prior to him being promoted to stupid-visor, he weighed about a hundred and twenty pounds more. He used to have a full-sized submarine sandwich that was enough for a regular size family of three and then would sit and nap it off. It was funny when he lost all the weight from the gastro surgery he had. He then started trying to do his job. He took a liking to one of the young officers who didn't have much time on the job. His father retired as a correctional officer from Elmira so he thought he had his time and his father's time because he was allowed to roam around the facility with no questions asked. Whenever the sergeant had an inmate in the block he was looking to get rid of or was unable to get the goods on, he would send this guard into search the inmate's cell, and to their amazement, the guard would emerge with shank after shank in hand, quickly proclaiming he had found it in the cell. What made it so obvious was sometimes, the inmates cell would have already had been searched and no contraband found, but as soon as the sergeant had his pet guard search the cell—bingo. To the best of my knowledge, this guard didn't and doesn't possess x-ray vision and doesn't have supernatural frisk powers, so one would really have to wonder. This is and was a practice that has gone on for years. The inmates have no chance in hell of ever beating the charge because the guards word is always believed over them even though there are some guards that are worse than the inmates. We have been entrusted with their care, custody, and control. The inmates are always on the losing end. I myself cannot say I witnessed this personally because if I had, I would have reported it even though I know it would have been covered up, but from the mouth of other staff that also suspected the same was going on with the sergeant and the rogue guard, it would be hard for me to believe it wasn't just from working around them.

I myself have never set an inmate up. If an inmate was doing something, I would sit back, watch, and wait, and sooner or later, they will indict themselves, and then I would write them up. I played no games. During the weekend in the block, the inmates on 7 gallery would request to shower in the shower located at the front of the gallery, which I could and did allow. There was a white inmate that was on 7 galley that never showered when he was at rec in the recreational areas. The gymnasium/fieldhouse/outside yard—all these areas had showers for the inmates to use, but the inmate refused to shower. He was thinly built and scruffy-looking with a unkept beard. His clothing was dirty and soiled. His cell that was located toward the rear of the gallery was a mess. The cell smelled of body odor and cigarettes. The cell floor was black from dirt. His state-issued sheets were soiled. His mattress was also heavily soiled with dirt. The walls and ceiling in the cell were even dirty. He always reeked of a heavy, musky body odor.

I was working on the gallery for a short while. One Saturday morning, while doing the razor exchange, where the inmates were allowed to exchange one state-shaving razor for another and the officer examines it to ensure it hasn't been tampered with or altered from its original purpose of shaving and wasn't broken into a weapon and you would check to ensure it was still in the inmate's possession, as I made my way down the gallery of thirty-eight cells to do the razor exchange, I could smell the stench emanating from the dirty cell that the inmate occupied from five cells away. When I got to his cell, I stood back from the cell and proclaimed, "Today is the day that you're cleaning up." I ordered the inmate to sweep and mop his cell, which he promptly refused with an "I'm not doing shit." Fuck this place—the inmate was a mental hygiene inmate, meaning he was receiving treatment for some form of mental illness. After his refusal, it now became my mission to persuade him otherwise. While I stood in front of the smelly cell, the inmate went on a tirade about him not caring about his appearance and he didn't care what his state cell looked like and his hate for the sergeant in charge of the block.

As the inmate shouted in my direction, I kept in mind his supposed crime. Many of the guards and staff had said he had killed his mother and others he was living with before coming to jail for just that. After he calmed down from what appeared to be a mental breakdown from my request to clean up his cell and himself, I told him, "The porter is going to get you the cleaning supplies so you can clean the cell up." I then walked away. A short while later, I returned with the porter and cleaning supplies, which I directed the inmate to leave in front of the cell. I then went down to the front of the cell block to open the inmate's cell so he could retrieve the items so he could clean. I opened the cell door, and the inmate quickly shut the cell door. I then reopened it, and again, he quickly shut it. This went on three or more times until I closed and locked the box that controls the cells and I quickly made my way down the gallery toward his cell. The small mirrors poked out from the cell doors so they could see what was going on. The inmates used their small handheld mirrors to see up and down the gallery by poking them out in either direction to get a line of sight, which was prohibited. As I walked, I ordered the inmates to get off the gates with their mirrors. When I reached my destination, I now stood smack dab in front of the inmate refusing to clean his cell, trying to get this inmate to comply with what was first a request and was seeming to be more difficult than I thought. I stood there again and listened to him go into a psychotic rant on why he wasn't going to comply with my request. After he finished, I told the inmate the hard and undeniable truth about himself and the cell he occupied and what was allowed. Prior to me working the gallery, it was no longer going to fly as being acceptable.

The stern statement seemed to get his attention because when I walked away to reopen the cell, he retrieved the cleaning supplies and started cleaning the bad-smelling cell. As he cleaned, I went down to ensure he was making a good effort to do just that. The cell smelled so bad I could see it was going to take a lot of effort to get rid of the stench. After he finished with the cleaning of the cell, I then informed him he needed to shower, to which he also refused until I informed him I was going to lock him in the shower at the front of the gallery, which he accepted. What I found unacceptable was the sergeant and others in the block were allowing the inmate to live in the condition he was in without confronting him and making him correct this.

I took great pride in doing my job. Any area where I worked had to be clean and polished. That was part of what we were—care, custody, and control of the inmate population. Many of the staff members had long forgotten about their true or main purpose or function in these prisons and have opted to ignore or neglect their true duty.

G block had one of the union officials who worked in the block that had a loud mouth and was literally one of the biggest cowards in the jail. One morning, he was working in F block, which was part of his bid. The story tells it—and it was from multiple sources, some eyewitnesses—like this: He was running the main desk area in the block when he started ranting and raving about something and started screaming at this other psycho guard who had multiple family members who worked at the prison. It was early in the morning, and both must have forgotten to take their meds because the union idiot screamed in the direction of the other idiot, and it was said he slapped the shit out of the union idiot, who stood stunned after being slapped, and he made zero effort to return the slap. They said what he did was sit his ass down and shut the hell up for the remainder of the day. The whole jail was aware of the assault, but as I said, the white officers could fight among themselves but I had better not ever raise a hand to one of them. The union loudmouth idiot could have struck that other idiot back, but he was too scared to protect himself but was one of the facility loudmouths—what a coward.

G-block was run amok on the 3–11 shift. You had staff that were giving inmates pots and pans so the inmates could cook for them. The staff were also bringing in groceries for the inmates so they could prepare that delectable meal for consumption. At one point they even had a staff member that was allowing a large number of inmates to run around the block when they were supposed to be locked in their cells. The only inmates that were allowed out were the porters that were supposed to be locked on the gallery, but this guard would allow inmates to roam free in the block. He too had inmates preparing food for him, and he would also tax the inmates by requiring them to pay him commissary items when they went to the store such as ice cream and junk food items, the items that made up the bulk of what was sold in the commissary. The rogue guard would demand his cut for the special favors or services he had rendered to the inmates.

This guard was also one of many—and I mean many—who had opted to have some form of gastro surgery to lose the weight he had gained. There were so many of these guys getting the surgery. I remember being locked out for one of the many false charges that I was brought up on and returning to work, and upon leaving through the crowded gated area packed with staff, I heard a familiar voice, but I didn't see the very heavy guard that it should have been coming from. I quickly scanned the area where we all waited to be let out. As I looked around, I spotted the almost familiar face that had been shrunken down to half of its size. I was stunned by the massive weight loss. The man was literally half the size he was the last time I had seen him, approximately six months ago, when I had been suspended. But yes, when he opened his mouth to speak, it was indeed him. So many of the guards would just sit around all day at work and eat, and then they would go home to finish by eating even more and topping it off with a few or more cold beers. They would then find themselves in a oh-so-familiar place. So many had fallen victim to obesity in the department. Some of the staff would seem to grow right in front of you. There were guys whose stomachs stuck out so far they looked like they were twelve months pregnant. Some couldn't even look down to find their own zippers on their trousers if they tried.

It wasn't just male guards—it was also the females. There was one female officer about five feet tall and very overweight. She could put food away like a hungry lumberjack. One officer said he had witnessed her eating her dinner meal on the 3–11 shift. She had KFC for dinner. Her gravy for her meal was in a plastic water bottle she drank from while she dined on her chicken and mashed potatoes and biscuits. It was later confirmed by others verifying this as true—the gravy for her meal was in a sixteen-ounce water bottle she turned into a turn-up gravy bowl.

Many of these same guards wouldn't bring lunch. They would order out large meals from the area restaurants that delivered to the facility. The regular lack of exercise and unhealthy eating seemed to plague the staff.

On G block, at one point, the movement and control seemed to place a large number of gays or homosexual inmates in the block. There was one on 7 gallery, and he had no program so he would stay in his cell during program hours. It was told to me by the loudmouth union rep that when I would leave off the gallery to my assigned area, which was the service unit, the idiot guard whose family had been taken by his best friend (his words, not mine) would be in charge of letting inmates out for call outs and was also in charge of the porters on the gallery, which was anywhere from one or two inmates, to clean the gallery. When all the inmates were gone to programs out of the block, this guard was sneaking upstairs to where the openly gay inmate was at and open his cell up and leave the gate open so other inmates could access the unsecured gallery and spend time with the inmate. The loudmouth union rep said he had observed the guard who unlocked the gate standing in front of the cell watching what the gays were doing in the unlocked cell together, and it's more than safe to say if the loudmouth guard had divulged that information to me, others working the block, including the supervisor, were well aware of the despicable dereliction of duty that the rouge guard was allowed to display.

While on my post in the service unit, the IGRC officer was very chatty with the inmates that worked in the IGRC office. The state computer that he used was filled with personal photos that he would display. Opening up a window into his personal life so the inmates could look in was and is forbidden. He had twenty-seven or more years on the job, so he was well aware of the departmental rules and regulations, which prohibits fraternizing with the inmates, but still he did as much. I would be an earshot away and hear the personal conversation he would have with the inmates and hear the personal information spill from his mouth, opening his life up like an open book for all to read. He was the first of the three grievance officers who held the job during the time I worked in the service unit. There were also a number of sergeants who supervised the area while I worked this post. The area also went through a few officers who worked in the rear of the unit where the chaplains' offices were located.

When I first started working the post, I was still waiting for a trial date for my federal lawsuit that the state was delaying. It had been eleven years since the case had been filed, and the state was doing everything it could to avoid justice. There was no doubt the state was seeking to delay my day in court-justice delayed is justice denied. The very state government that was and is supposed to be for the people of the state was only working for some and helping to cover up and protect those who had chosen to violate my state and federal constitutional rights, and it seemed they have no problem doing it. My many complaints of discrimination that were sent up and down the chain of command in the department and to those in power in our state government and to the agencies that had been put in place to protect the citizens of New York state—all were denying me my rights. The Elmira correctional facility had even been subjected to diverse cultural training for all its employees, but even that didn't stop or deter the racist guards and other employees from practicing open racism in the form of hate speech aimed at all that weren't their kind. Once a year, all employees were subjected to attend diverse cultural training that was mandatory for all except for me. After the filing of a federal lawsuit I was no longer allowed to attend the training for years even though the training was mandatory for all employees and was mandated from the lawsuit that had been lost in federal court for violating the inmates' civil rights and other violations and inscrutable practices the staff and administration were allowed to do.

The training was a waste of taxpayers' money from the few training courses I was allowed to attend. The guards were the same ones that violated others' rights and had no respect for anyone that wasn't their kind. They would sit there complaining about having to listen to someone tell them not to discriminate against others. Some of the comments in the training I heard were "I don't know why we have to do this?", "F—— this bull——" or "Man, I don't care about this," as they would sit and thumb through the newspaper or converse with the other nonengaged racists whom the training lesson had been designed for.

Some of the guards who were allowed to be training officers were also strongly opposed advocates of the diverse cultural training, and some would start his training class off with, "Hey, I know no one wants to be here, including me, but we have to do this" and some would follow with, "Don't worry, we're going to take lots of breaks." To say the training was subpar would be an understatement. The training was a waste of taxpayers' money and a waste of time. Even though the training was mandated by the court and the department was ordered to have the facility comply with the order so the department wasn't in contempt of court for refusing the order, no one at the top in the department seemed to care how or what information was disseminated to its employees. The Department of Correctional Services would like you, me, and the justice system to think that the diverse cultural training lesson was putting those that violated the rights of others on notice and they would be held liable for doing so, which was far from the truth. What I do know I was subjected to retaliation for reporting the outright discrimination. Some of the same forms of discrimination outlined in the diverse cultural training class that all employees at the Elmira correctional facility were mandated to have, it was all just a smoke screen to make it appear that the facility was doing the right thing and was in compliance with the court.

Months after starting my job in the service unit, while at home one evening after dinnertime, the phone rang. I answered it, and it was my attorney calling, He told me he had some news regarding my case. He then went on to say, "The state wants to settle your case out of court." He then went on to say that they had offered me an amount of money, which I turned down.

I said to my attorney, "No way I'm taking that amount of money for over eleven years of relentless discrimination, harassment, and retaliation." I then went on to say I would take my chances in a court of law. Thank God my attorney agreed and said he would set up a meeting with the state lawyer to try to negotiate a better settlement offer.

A week later, I received another call from my attorney with a settlement offer that was comparable to what would or could have been won in a trial. I accepted it, and after the state wrote up the paperwork and I signed it, my eleven-year federal lawsuit regarding discrimination at the Elmira Correctional Facility was over. It was settled out of court. That's what the state does when they have no justification or legal argument to justify the actions of their racist, out-of-control staff. Many of the lawsuits brought against the state are settled out of court to hide and shield those who are allowed to violate the civil rights of others. It is an astronomical amount of money that the state spends to quiet those who have been violated, and the worst part is New York State taxpayers' money is being used to settle the many lawsuits that are brought against a corrupt and racist system. The amount of money paid out is staggering. It's almost incomprehensible to believe that the state would allow an agency of their own to be run with such recklessness without making those in charge responsible for their actions.

After the settlement was finalized, I was required to go to New Jersey to my attorney's office to sign the settlement agreement. The lawsuit had taken so long the young, ambitious attorney Marc Garber had progressed though his career from starting out on his own in a small Manhattan office to now working at a large prestigious law firm in New Jersey. So one early fall morning in 2009, my wife and I traveled to New Jersey and met with my attorney, who had now become a friend after knowing each other the many years it had taken with the long, drawn-out federal lawsuit. I signed a number of documents, agreeing to the terms of the settlement. My attorney then introduced me to two very important people, an investment banker and an accountant. There was no big check placed in my hand. The money was later transferred into our account via a wire transfer. The large amount of money brought no immediate jubilation or satisfaction from the many years of constant discrimination and harassment. What I did feel was let down and empty, never having had my day in court to expose the racist guards who are allowed to work in these state facility with carte blanche to act and do as they wanted with total immunity and secrecy and never being exposed for what they really are and what they really do. Yes, the state would rather pay me an exorbitant amount of money then have the Elmira Correctional Facility exposed to the public for what it really is. It felt just like the state used a wad of money as a gag to silence me and avoid responsibility for the discriminatory practice, thus empowering those who choose to practice and engage in discrimination and keeping these predominantly white run correctional facilities exclusive to just them.

After the settlement was complete, I made it my purpose to go to work with a nonreactional attitude—meaning I didn't go into work with the "Ha ha, I won" attitude. I didn't make a victory lap around the prison. I did none of that. What I did was I went to work the same way I had been coming. I didn't seek out those who had been named in the lawsuit to rub in my large out-of-court settlement, which was supposed to be confidential. I told no one at work of the state's desire to pay me off rather than face litigation in a court of law. I didn't say or do anything to bring to light that the state had settled the lawsuit. Instead, I waited to see if they would react to the news, which I didn't have to wait long.

Weeks after the settlement, I started hearing from staff members, asking me questions about my federal lawsuit, which they hadn't done in the past. I even had some staff that had been so emboldened they came right out and asked, "Hey, how much did you get?"

All the inquiries into my case were usually met with my response to the inquiring minds, "Go check with the superintendent, he should be able to tell you." It was obvious the administration and the union had revealed to the staff at the Elmira Correctional Facility that my case had been settled out of court because I had never told the staff as much. I now had the racist staff that were harassing me mad that I had been paid for their discrimination. I had staff glaring at me not only with hate and contempt but now with jealousy and wonder, wondering just how much of the ten million dollars that the lawsuit requested I had actually gotten. The inquiring minds were dying to know.

Also, soon after, one of the inmates that worked in the IGRC office, a.k.a. the inmate grievance office, had a callout to the inmates' law library where the inmates do their legal work such as researching cases to appeal their own convections and charges. After returning to the service unit from his callout, I opened the door to let him back on the unit. He immediately said, "Hey, Brown, guess what was in the law digest? (a legal reference of case law)"

I then unknowingly said, "What?"

He then said, "Your case."

I was shocked to hear this, but I then thought it was a federal lawsuit. He then went on to say all the inmates in the law library were reading about the case. That's when the inmates started to make open comments about what they had read regarding the settled lawsuit. I could be standing there among other staff members as a group of inmates pass by the inmates would greet me with a "Hey, what's up, Officer Brown?" And then as they continued walking, they would make side bar conversation with the other inmates. They would say, "Brown sued their asses" or "Man, brown sued them racist bastards" or "Man, Brown got a lot of money." I would observe the reactions from the guards and officers who were around to catch the unsolicited comments regarding my case.

For a while, the harassment stopped right after the large hush money payment, but it seemed my victory was just a minor setback to the bloodthirsty racist guards as I worked the service unit job. One of my duties was to escort G block 7 gallery to chow in the morning and afternoon to the mess hall. G-block ate chow in mess hall 1. It held approximately three hundred inmates when full, which thank God it never was, the reason being the inmates were usually rushed in, served their meal, and rushed out. So as a large group would enter, a group would be preparing to exit the mess hall. You would never have a larger than desired group gathered. When chow was being run, the inmates would enter the mess hall though the right or left side front door area and follow the outer wall to the front of the mess hall where the serving lines were located. What door the block entered depended on the block's designated setting area. The large blocks were kept separated from one another, meaning in mess hall 1, G block was the only large block that used that mess hall along with the smaller blocks on the side of the prison where G block was located and the other two mess halls were run. The same large blocks were also kept separated at recreation. This was done so the mass number of inmates could never fully communicate with each other, thus limiting their ability to plot some diabolical plan to protest, take over, or cause mass chaos.

This wasn't just at Elmira—all of the state's prisons are run this way. This is one of the sensible things that has been done for years. Once you, the officer, enter the mess hall, you are required to go to the service line to hand out spoons to the side of the serving line where your group of inmates are being served. You would usually greet each other, and the guard or officer would offer a plastic glove from the gloves placed by the spoon bucket were the spoons were located, but as I would approach, the officer or guard would walk away from the line to avoid handing me a glove or a civil greeting. It was usually received with a chuckle by the few guards that were in the mess hall as they watched for a reaction. I would just shake my head and pick up the pack of gloves and do my job.

After another group of inmates entered the mess hall in the same serving line, the guard would relieve you. After you were relieved, you were supposed to find a spot in the mess hall to stand to observe the inmates as they ate chow. I would take up a position in the middle of the mess hall on the wall area, smack dab in the middle of the mess hall. That was where I stood each and every day. I was required to be there. I stood alone, keeping a close visual on the entire mess hall. The middle of the mess hall was the best location for observation of the area. The others in the mess hall, including the supervisor, would stand in the mess hall entertaining each other with idle conversation and horse play. It would usually be some half-wit sergeant standing at the front of the mess hall along with a gathering of ass-kissing guards smoothing the sergeant's ego as he would stand there taking in the attention. Other guards would be in conversation with one another, oblivious to what was going on as they talked, looking directly at one another, counting each other's cavities in one another's mouth. I used to stand there thinking, you don't need to stare at a man as he is talking or watch his lips move; you can hear him with your ears. I can't say everyone that worked in the mess hall was like that, but most were. you had other officers who were just as vigilant as myself, but the majority weren't along with most of the supervisors.

Back in the early days of my career, the supervisors wouldn't have tolerated such a lack of security in the area they were supervising. As a matter of fact, I can remember the older staff when I started off didn't tolerate an officer cuddling up with a supervisor. I witnessed firsthand back in my early career an officer attempting to have a playful conversation in the mess hall with a supervisor, and an old timer walked up to him and the sergeant and said boldly and loudly, "Hey, why don't you get off the Sergeants d——k and get your ass over there and watch my back while were in here?" And the guard scurried off and stood in a spot away from the sergeant where he could observe the mess hall and his fellow officers' backs, as requested by his more senior fellow officer. Now most of the staff operate with the "I don't care" type of attitude about everything, even what they were hired to do. Some would refuse to do what was required of them even if the refusal may get someone hurt. Some cared less, and some cared more.

While working in the service unit with the civilian counselors whose jobs were to counsel the inmates, some seemed to be more in need of counseling themselves than the inmates they counseled. Some would fly off at the mouth and disrespect any and everyone around them to include staff and inmates. There was one who, like many of the employees at the Elmira Correctional Facility, had family members who worked at the prison and did as she pleased. She would torment the staff with false accusations whenever her inability to perform her job was called into question. I myself was on the receiving end of a few of her what seemed to be emotional breakdowns.

One day, while making rounds on the unit, I walked past to find her sitting in her office behind her desk with the lights off and multiple candles burning, wrapped in a blanket. Seeing her in this state, which was so out of place for a prison setting, I immediately asked her if she was all right. Her response was she was waiting for an inmate that had written a grievance about her complaining about her harassing him. When he was called to her office for counseling, in the inmate's grievance or complaint, the inmate had mentioned she acted like she was crazy, so she said she was giving the inmate she waited for in the dark crazy. She would yell at her immediate supervisor. She would verbally abuse the inmates in the presence of others. For instance, she would fly off the handle in her office that was located in different areas of the service unit at different times. One time, her office was the furthest away from my desk area on the unit, but you could hear her yelling and screaming at inmates she was counseling for some reason or another. Most of the inmates would wisely get up and walk or run out of her office to avoid getting trapped off for no reason of their own.

For years, I was writing the IG's office informing them of the harassment I was being subjected to. I called and I wrote letters to no avail, but the moment the out-of-control counselor lied about me and falsely accused me of harassment, they were there in a flash. I remember she accused me one week, and the next week, I was ordered to report up front to be questioned by IG.

It was mid-morning on the day I was questioned. I walked into the office that the IG officer was using as an interrogation office. The investigator greeted me as I entered, "Hello, Officer Brown. My name is…" And he said he was with the office of the inspector general. I then sat in the chair he had ready, and the first thing he did was offer me a doughnut from the half-eaten box that sat on the desk.

I looked at the investigator like he had lost his rabbit-ass mind. I then said, "No, I don't want a doughnut," and I followed it with "I know one thing—I better not be in here for that that crazy-ass counselor." And I said her name.

The investigator confirmed that was why I was there.

I then said, "She has a problem with everyone, but you call me up here because she is starting shit, right?" I then followed it up with, "As soon as I walk out of this office, I'm calling my attorney, and then we can sit down and talk." The interrogation was quickly shut down by the investigator and I was free to go.

Days later, the troublemaking counselor was banished from the service unit and relocated to Shop 5, which houses the print shop with office above on the top floor. One of her brothers was also a guard who worked the shop, so she should have felt right at home.

Her brother was a story in himself. He too had major personal problems. He too would run throughout the prison like he owned the place. He was one of those guard's that kissed the supervisors' butts to get close. The notorious 5 Shop was also the shop where a horrific assault took place against a female counselor perpetrated by an inmate. I was not there, but by all accounts, the assault took place in the counselor's office where the inmate viciously assaulted the female counselor. The area where these offices are located in the shop is a hallway with the officer's desk located just outside of the offices that line the hallway. The officer's desk isn't around the corner—it isn't hidden. It's smack dab in the hallway. It was said that when the guard wandered upon the assault, some of the furniture in the room was tipped over and the inmate was on top of his victim. The would-be assailant then escaped the guard who stood in the same room. It was said the inmate ran out of the office and exited the shop. He was then apprehended in the mental hygiene unit, known as MHU, by other staff. His capture was questionable because it was said some of the guards didn't feel others handled the business like some would have liked them to.

The inmate was known to me from working in the food service area. He worked in the mess hall that I was in charge of. He was also...are you ready for this? The inmate was one of the racist guard's pet inmates that he would use to harass me with false grievances and chaos. The inmate would refuse to cooperate for me in doing his duties as a mess hall worker, and for doing so, I would write the inmate up for different rule violations, and even though the racist guard that worked the kitchen desk area wouldn't be present as a witness to the inmate's rule violation, he would be allowed to come to the inmates aid and solicit the area supervisors and others to prevent the inmate from being disciplined. As I have said, some employees refused to do their jobs the right way even if that refusal may get someone hurt. Some let their feelings and emotions trump their duty and responsibility to the Department of Corrections.

There were many guards like the racist head guard in the kitchen, but the scarier and more daunting fact was some of the supervisory personnel at the top of the prison system have the same mentality as the racist nutcase in the kitchen. After the crazy counselor moved her office to the shop 5 area, all the other counselors, including the senior counselors, were exhilarated. Being rid of the loudmouth, troublemaking, crazy counselor brought a smile to all of their faces. But one, her clone who was just as crazy and backed up her bullshit, was not happy that her crazy handler was not going to be with her on the unit. There would be no more of their ten daily cigarette breaks. Neither one had each other to lie for them. The two of them would do whatever they wanted. They couldn't even be supervised by the senior counselors, who themselves were also questionable about the way they did their jobs. If the overall counseling department had to truly be rated without manipulation, it would receive a failing grade.

It seemed that just as the guards were protected by NYSCOBA, so were the almost all-white civilian staff. They have protection by the two unions that represented them and also shielded them from being held responsible for their unprofessional and unethical behavior. The administration would also shield them. The tall, oblong-shaped counselor would tell lies to the staff just for the sake of conversation. She like 65–70 percent of all the employees at the prison, went through her divorce from her husband, who was said to be the one seeking the divorce. During that time, I witnessed this woman lose what mind she had left. Just as many other staff members were allowed to do, she would come to work and unload her problems on staff and inmates. She would have open outbursts of extreme anger at any and everyone she felt she could use to release her anger. Even though the prison had what was called EAP, which was the employee assistance program, to assist those with problems like this, it seemed that few or none used it for this. I had heard officers tell stories of guards running to the EAP when questions of drug abuse had come to light or a guard was in trouble.

During my time working in the service unit, there were two black counselors who came to Elmira to work. The first was an older heavy-set black woman from the western New York area who came as a senior counselor. When she arrived, I thought to myself, *This should be interesting. The all-white staff have a black supervisor.* She was met with discord and animosity by many of the counselors.

There was one in particular—his office was located close to the door and the officer's desk where I was located. I watched as this man had a hissy fit over the black female counselor getting the job over him as he too had put his hat in the ring for the position, which was canvassed statewide, meaning all counselors in the state could apply for the open position at the Elmira Correctional Facility. The older white male counselor actually felt let down by the department for not being chosen for the position. I would hear him complaining to all his comrades about being overlooked for the position prior to the black female senior counselor coming to the facility. The now disgruntled white male counselor seemed to think he was privileged and had the right to have the senior counselor's position now also looked at me, the only other black person on the unit, as a threat and problem because he was mad and salty about not being given what he thought was rightfully his. That was the thing—many of the staff had that mentality of being privileged, leaving them with false and delusional thoughts of grander and white privilege, which the now disgruntled counselor seemed to suffer from.

I watched as the new black female boss attempted to embrace her new position. As she slowly tried to take charge, she was met with negativity and discord that awaited her around each and every corner. I would watch as some of the counselors would group up in numbers in the disgruntled, white-privileged counselor's office, where they strategized to rid the unit of the unwanted black female senior counselor. As I sat at the officers desk, taking in the disgruntled discord that was unfolding on the service unit all around me over the hearing of the black female senior counselor, I thought, Damn, all of the counselors were white, and the inmates that they served were a majority of black and brown inmates. The all-white counselors—not all, but it seemed to be the majority—felt that the black counselor had no place at the Elmira Correctional Facility. Now if that isn't the epitome of white privilege and exclusion, then what is? The black female counselor didn't have to put up with the discord for long; she was transferred back closer to her home in the western New York area, where she would be welcomed and wanted.

The Elmira Correctional Facility was so exclusive that out of all the civilian clerks that input date and filed paperwork, they were all white with the exception of one black female. The administration was all white, the maintenance department was all white, and the hospital or infirmary was majority white with the exception of a couple of minorities spaced out in different areas. If one was on the outside looking in, one would think that it was a private prison and not state-run because it was being allowed to exclude minority by nepotism, harassment, and outright discriminatory practices that they at the top turned their heads to those creating a workforce that felt privileged and empowered. Now if there were a large private company that did what is being allowed at this all-white correctional facility in upstate new York, excluding minorities and openly practicing discrimination, our New York state attorney general would have a foot deep in their ass and would be seeking justice for those New Yorkers who suffered from that company's discriminatory practice, but it would seem that the state's own entity, the New York state prison system, was not subjected to the same federal and state discrimination laws that the other business and companies in New York are subject to and expected to obey or face fines and or sanctions by the state of New York.

After the exodus of the black female counselor came a black male counselor who was from a city around an hour from Elmira, New York. When he arrived after the black female counselor, he too was met with controversy and discord. he would come to me on many occasions complaining about other counselors unwilling to help him navigate the ins and outs of the Elmira Correctional Facility's inmate counseling program. Even a few of the senior counselors were roadblocks to his success and were unwilling to help and support him, so he was left to figure it out himself and to fend for himself. He didn't last long. In less than a year, he was gone. I never did find out what happened to him. He was just gone.

Some of the counselors were more of a hindrance to the inmates that they were there to serve. Some would purposely go out of their way to stop or block inmates from obtaining certain programs to fulfill their parole requirements. I would observe and overhear conversations from counselors speaking about inmates they had ill feelings toward, saying that they were not going to help them and would refuse to do the simplest of tasks to help an inmate to obtain what he needed to ready himself for parole.

Some of the counselors were an outright mess and were clueless to what professionalism meant. There was one—we'll call him Rudolf the Red-Nosed Reindeer. He once worked in the service unit, but he too had been sent to another area for his lack of effort in doing his job and his too playful attitude. He would still come to the service unit on a daily basis to retrieve paperwork. He would enter the area through the door and would yell at the top of his lungs, "EAD!" He would then yell out, "Eat a dick!" The area was filled with women, and no supervisor ever confronted him about his outright disrespectful behavior. Now what job can a man go to and yell such absurdities and disrespect in front of female staff and not be disciplined? The only place I know is on New York state property, where it seems the employees aren't subjected to the same state human right laws as private companies in the state. It was and is a free for all for the almost all-white staff in these upstate prisons, who have free rein to do as they want and say what they want and fear no retribution for their more than questionable behavior. He too had a father who worked at the facility that had more than a few years on the job as a correctional officer, but he suffered like so many other guards with divorce, making it financially impossible to retire comfortably because if they were to retire, their ex-wives were waiting to collect their half of the pension. So he, like so many, were forced to keep working well past the twenty-five years needed to retire with full benefits.

There was one poor soul who worked one of the wall towers who had a staggering forty-plus years on the job and had openly stated, "I will die in this tower before my ex-wife collects a dime of my pension." These guards were some of the most miserable people to be around. I called them "the left behinds" because all the people they had started their career with were long gone. Rudolph the Red-Nosed Counselor and his father were also soon joined by their son and brother, who was also given a counselor's job at the Elmira Correctional Facility. Now there were three—talk about nepotism.

Just like some of the security staff, you also had civilian staff that would come to work either intoxicated or high on an illegal substance, but they too would be overlooked by their supervisors who chose to look the other way. The supervisors knew who they were just as I did. I do know what high or intoxicated looks like, just as others do. A lot of the time, more time was spent on playing grab ass and horse play than doing counselor's work, even though the position of counselor required a college degree. I could hardly see where it was necessary by the way many of the counselors performed their jobs. The majority were unengaged or detached from what their jobs were. From what I witnessed and observed a person could easily be showed the job and told what was needed to fulfill the position and they could be just as effective or more effective from the lackluster effort I observed put further by the counselors on the service unit at the Elmira Correctional Facility. I observed some of the counselors work with officers to derail or help hinder an inmate from qualifying for a program like the family reunion program or a nonviolence program. The inmate may need to satisfy his parole needs or a job-type program that might pay a little more.

There were many things a counselor could do to be a hindrance. Some of the counselors would openly say what their intent would be to mess with the inmate because they or some other staff member had ill will toward the inmate. Some of the counselors would also subject you to undesirable and unsolicited information about inmates and their crimes, which would come in the form of information that they would pass on to all staff within an earshot. For example, there would be an inmate in the counselor's office, and when the inmate would leave, some of the counselors would say, "I hate that piece of shit." They would then go on to tell the inmate's heinous crime, which usually involved a child and would naturally make everyone uneasy. I didn't make it a habit like a lot of staff did by going to counselors to obtain information about an inmate's crime, which was readily available upon request. There were a few of the counselors that had a professional demeanor and did their jobs to the best of their ability, while the other counselors ran around the unit with the animal house, college frat house mentality. Those few who had chosen to do their jobs were seeking promotions and seemed to steer clear of the bullshit going on.

There was one office where the counseling staff would all gather for long periods shooting the breeze and horse playing even though work and other tasks needed to be done. The supervisors would sometimes request for them to stay out of the party office, but the request would seemingly fall on deaf ears because the party would continue. I guess they thought, *Ain't no party like a service unit party.* One of the out-of-control counselors would come and go as he pleased. He was even on a first-name basis with the superintendent. He would say as much when the superintendent was on rounds by calling him by his first name. He would easily be tardy to work three out of the five days of a work week, absent two or three times a month. He seemed to fear no punishment for his lackluster effort or his disregard for his duty and responsibilities. Man, you talk about privilege—he truly had white privilege.

A couple of the counselors were ex-correctional officers who had switched jobs in the department. One of the two counselors was on the money. He seemed to be career-driven and was looking for advancement. After going from correctional officer to counselor, he seemed to be well-fit for the job.

Then there was a younger female who had also transitioned from a correctional officer to counselor who seemed to have a hard time embracing her new title. She no longer wore a correctional officer's uniform. She wore regular clothing to work. She would try to be a correctional officer without the uniform. As a correctional officer, she had a bad experience in an outside hospital trip. It was with a young knuckleheaded officer who was one of the facility babies whose father had retired from the facility, so he like many of the other facility babies would have three or five years on the job, but when they added their father's twenty-five or thirty years to it, they though they knew it all. No one could tell them any different. When the female counselor was a correctional officer, these two were out on an outside hospital trip with an inmate, and she had the state-issued .38 on her side when the knuckleheaded guard left the female officer alone in a room at the hospital with the inmate. It was reported that the inmate lunged at the female correctional officer and tried to take the revolver off her side. It was said upon his return to the room, he opened the door to find the female officer in a fierce struggle with the inmate over the weapon. They were ultimately able to subdue the inmate and keep the gun out of his hands. If the young knuckle-headed guard had been supervised correctly and held responsible for his other blunders and mishaps, for other things he was doing wrong, he may have made a better security-minded decision and the almost tragic situation could have been avoided, It was truly scary working with some people who had no security sense whatsoever or those who truly didn't care.

Soon after the event at the outside hospital, the younger female guard switched positions from guard to counselor. She left the Elmira Correctional Facility for just a short period before returning as a full-fledged counselor. Come and think about it, the female counselor who was attacked in shop 5 never returned to the Elmira Correctional Facility.

Compensation, I would imagine, comes in many forms. With the counseling staff, you either had good or bad. There was no in between. Either they were competent or incompetent. Like I said there were those who did their jobs to the best of their ability and stood out from the rest.

As I worked the unit, there were hardly ever any problems with the inmates fighting or becoming unruly. I was lucky to be able to have rapport with a lot of the inmate population, where we had a understanding that fighting around me would involve me in unnec-essary uses of force, also known as a UI, to help break up the alter-cation, which I didn't want. That rapport and understanding was achieved through mutual respect. The inmates hardly ever fought around me. That respect was given to me by the inmates also for the way I did my job.

The old saying "Don't start nothing, would be nothing" went a long way with the inmates, but not so much with the out-of-con-trol staff. For example, working my daily mess job where I would be standing smack dab in the middle of the mess hall, I was usually the only black officer. I remember a few times as I exited the mess hall and started my way back to the block escorting my group of inmates, as soon as I would start down the corridor and the door slammed behind me, a fight would break out in the mess hall I had just exited. There was one time as I stood watch in the mess hall, one of the inmates on my left kept calling my name to get my attention. After he had called my name a number of times, I turned to order him to stop. One of the other inmates jumped up and punched his buddy inmate in the eye. It was basically a two-hit fight—the inmate who hit his buddy and his buddy's eye hitting his fist. It was quickly ended, and I turned and started to speak and asked the inmate why the hell he kept calling my name. All the inmates laughed and said, "You know we didn't want you to see it, so that way you had nothing to do with it, no paperwork." The two inmates that fought were buddies. You would see them out in about at rec and chow. You wouldn't see one without the other, but evidently, the love affair was over.

In all the years I worked the service unit, there was only one fight in the outside waiting area on the unit. The fight involved two Hispanic inmates, which was quickly broken up by my partner, who was worked the rear of the unit and myself. I grabbed one inmate, and my partner grabbed the other, and we literally yanked them from each other's grasp and pulled them apart. The inmate that I was restraining was face down on the floor. I asked him what the hell was he doing as I lifted him from the floor. As he stood up, he then said, "Man, Brown, I'm sorry for fighting up here, but that guy's a piece of shit." He was trying to join the Latin Kings, one of the Spanish gangs in the New York state prison system. The inmate went on to say that the service unit callout was the only place he could catch him, and the inmate that he had assaulted had a hit out on him by the gang to all its members to get him if they saw him anywhere in the facility. The hit was over—the other inmate trying to join the gang and the gang had asked to see his commitment papers (the court papers that have the inmate's charges and sentencing information), which he hadn't produced, but it had been found out by other sources that the inmate was in for child molestation. The Latin Kings had been disrespected by the child molester trying to become a King, so he was assaulted for it. The apology for carrying out the assault in the service

CURTIS BROWN

unit was from the mutual respect that fighting was prohibited while I was on duty. That was the only fight on the unit while I was on duty. Now when I wasn't there and I was off, there were a few fights which all took place during my absence.

One of the reasons the inmates showed me so much respect was for the way I did my job, which was care, custody, and control of the inmates within the prison. Also it was because I was fair, firm, and consistent with all the inmates, which meant if the inmates were entitled to something by the department, that is what they got from me—no more, no less. Many of the guards would place inmates on what they called the burn for some reason or another and would deny the inmates even the basic human needs to satisfy their thirst for revenge over some minor rift they had with the inmate.

I would watch as many of the guards seemed to suffer from a slave-master mentality. They would talk to grown men like children even though the inmate would be respectful to them. There was one guard—if you could call him even that—he was more like the slave master or overseer. He was an older guy. He had snow-white hair. He was even given a nice old cheerful Christmassy nickname. His all-white hair shed dandruff the size of snowflakes. I kid you not—the back of his coat or shirt would be piled with the white flake mess. He was one of the worst examples of a human being I have ever seen—his demeanor, attitude, and personality were all pure evil. Hell, the man smelled evil. He seemed to be Satan the devil himself. He would show everyone he worked around he truly had zero humanity. I had witnessed the devil verbally and mentally harass, intimidate, threaten, and belittle inmates for no reason or for the littlest or most smallest of things they may have done. During an inmate's forced interaction with him—I say forced because the inmates tried to avoid this out-of-control racist nutjob like the plague—some would even avoid looking the devil in the eyes because just eye contact with the devil could get you locked up or beaten up. He truly was an overseer. The slaves could not look the overseer or the master in the eye unless given permission to do so. Violating that could result in the slave having his skin savagely removed from his body by a whip.

On more than a few occasions, I would observe the interactions that the devil would have with the inmates, and the way he talked to the inmates was very inflammatory and would be on the level of inciting a riot. He would fan that low-burning flame within the inmates, hoping to cause a negative reaction, which could result in others around him being seriously hurt. The officers that worked around him would complain about his toxic attitude, but the guards would cheer him on and encourage his unprofessional and inflammatory rhetoric. There would even be some supervisors that turned their heads the other way, giving this sad, miserable excuse of a human being carte blanche to do as he would unchecked for his reckless behavior.

There came a time it seemed that the dandruff-packing devil had finally disrespected the wrong inmate. There was a hit placed on the devil. An inmate who had just transferred into the facility was the hitman. He must have been given a description of the devil and his work location, which was the block the inmate locked in.

There was another older white officer who was a good soul of a man. He was quiet, well-mannered, and seemed to just do his job to the best of his ability. I had never seen the man act anything but professional, but he too was an older white male with white hair like the devil had. The inmate set his diabolical plan in motion to carry out the hit on the racist, evil devil. The hit took place in the block where the inmate savagely and brutally assaulted his victim by stabbing the officer multiple times. The inmate had hit the wrong officer. It wasn't the racist devil but instead it was the officer who was just doing his job. No, it wasn't the hateful, evil devil who had ill feelings toward the inmates; it was the officer who just did his job to the best of his ability and was respectful. So you see, the hateful and dangerous way the devil was allowed to do his job almost cost a good man his life.

Some time later, the devil's offspring, his stupid and just-as-ignorant son, showed up as a guard at the Elmira Correctional Facility. Right from the get-go, he showed just what his ignorant, racist, devilish ass father had taught him. The son was a mess of a young man. His body type resembled an old man. He had no muscle mass. His arms looked frail and weak, and his stomach stuck out. You know some clothing say "athletic fit"? Well, he wouldn't be shopping for that. He would be better fit for the "old man fit." He was short and dumpy looking. The first time he was in my presence and he opened his mouth to talk, I was like, *Oh my goodness.* The boy's mouth was hideous. Most of his teeth were a rotten brown color. I have seen the homeless and the less fortunate with better dental hygiene. It was obvious that good dental care was very, very low on his priority list. It would also appear that basic human hygiene was lacking. I believe he had a year or less on the job when he arrived from the facility he had transferred in from. It didn't take long for him to start spreading his racist hate.

One day in the mess hall/kitchen area, it was told that he was trying to exit a door that was next to the serving line where the inmates lined up, and when he went to use the door, it was blocked by an inmate standing in line. It was the mental hygiene block line, which is H block. When he could not exit the door, he said to the black inmate blocking the door by no choice of his own, "Nigger, get out of the way." That didn't go over well because it was told and told often that the inmate had cold cocked him upside the head, causing him to be sprawled out on the floor down for the count. Now remind you, he had a year or a little more on the job, and his ass had already been served up an ass whipping by an inmate that he had disrespected. It would appear that the young devil was taught to be a racist by the devil himself but was never taught to fight. They said there were two hits—the inmate hitting the racist and the racist hitting the floor. He was a mirror image of his racist father who had no knuckles either and was filled with the same hate and anger. The racist dandruff-packing father was allowed by the administration and the security supervision staff to run amok without paying any consequence for the racist behavior. There were staff members who were appalled at the behavior he was allowed to display. Some would talk ill of him. Many were mad at the attack or hit that was meant for him and the fall of a good officer who in no way desired it. After that incident, many started to show more dislike for him. I heard some staff even make the statement, "I wish that would have been his ass, he would have deserved it."

Others started to talk of his outside life and where and how he lived. I for one have never been to his house or on his property, but others had, and it was said it looked like something straight out of the classic movie *The Deliverance*, banjo and all. It was said the property was out a ways from Elmira. it was in the sticks, a.k.a. the country, and the property was littered with discarded items, which was a true reflection of "One man's junk is another man's treasure." The house itself was in disarray. His life seemed to be a mirror image matching his attitude and disposition, which was also a mess.

As I said, in the service unit the chaplains were also located in the rear of the unit. They each had their own offices. The Catholic and Protestant chaplains seemed to have the most problems with acknowledging the fact that the poor souls that had found God or were searching for God were still convicted felons. Over the years I worked the service unit, I witnessed this firsthand. You would have multiple chaplains from these two faiths who were fired for things that were highly inappropriate and highly questionable, or even criminal in nature. Some would help inmates break rules to cover up for the inmates. They were even accused of assisting inmates obtain escape paraphernalia.

I remember one—he was the Protestant chaplain. He was being watched closely and was accused of liking inmates a little too much. There were two protestant chapels or service areas in the facility. There was one in the gym basement for the general population and a second in the reception area where the new inmates are housed, and that too was located in the basement area in the reception center. Since my desk area was located at the front door area on the service unit, I watched everyone that came and went during my eight-hour shift. The front door was three feet from my desk. I had heard staff make derogatory comments and innuendos toward the frail, timid man while he was in my presence such as "There is a toucher" or "Man, he looks gay." Then the rumors would fly that he was being watched closely in the recaption center because some thought he may be getting way too close to some of the inmates. He was allowed to take inmates from the reception center to the basement chapel to clean the area. I started to watch his demeanor and movement as he came and went throughout the day.

On one particular day, as I sat at the desk, the reverend announced he was on his way to the recaption center if anyone was looking for him. Many of the staff would inform me of their travel because when they were being sought out, I was one of the first people they called to find out their whereabouts. The Reverend passed by and exited the door en route to his said destination.

After around an hour or so, he returned to the service unit, where I let him in by pushing the button that controlled the door. Once he entered, I locked on him like a heat-seeking missile. He posed at the drinking fountain that was located directly across from the desk. As he bent over to drink from the fountain, I noticed his clothing was disheveled. One side of his long-hemmed shirt was pulled from his tightly belted pants, which gave the appearance of someone dressing in a hurry. After he finished his long drink out of the drinking fountain, he looked up to find me looking at him. He smiled and I said loudly, "Reverend, your shirt is hanging out of your pants."

His reaction to my statement was truly priceless and telling. He was startled and seemed to be stunned at my statement about his clothing being out of place. His feet stood frozen in place as he hastily tried to put himself back together in front of me. Before walking away, I asked him if he was all right and he said yes, but if I had to guess by the Reverend's nervous reaction and where he had just come from, which was the reception center basement with an inmate, I would have to say something was up. I told my newfound suspicion to the service unit sergeant, who advised me that the Reverend was indeed being clocked, meaning others were watching him closely.

There was another Reverend—we will call him Reverend Buzzard. He was a womanizer and a snake. I would watch as this married Reverend took a liking to this poor soul of a woman who was one of the hardest-working civilian staff members that worked at the Elmira Correctional Facility. She would go above and beyond her job. I would watch as she would do her job and that of others. The Reverend grabbed hold of this poor woman and was under her at every opportunity he had. You would see him at her work area, hovering over her with smooth talk and sweet nothings. All day long he was sprung. The Reverend was even accused by others as to having a special liking to the hardworking woman, which he would sheepishly deny. This filthy buzzard even helped an inmate that was caught giving another inmate a BJ in the back area of the service unit, where the chaplains' offices are located. That took place on the 3–11 shift after I had left for the day. It was told to me and my partner that two of the inmates that were registered as Catholic were at the weekly call-out called the rosary group, which gathered in the back of the service unit during the 3–11 shift. One of the inmates was white, the other black. There is only one officer on the unit on the 3–11 shift because the majority of the callouts were done on the 7–3 shift, so the officer who was working said in his own omission that he went back to the rear of the unit to make rounds and found the two inmates together. The white inmate was on his knees in front of the black inmate, facing him with his head at waist level. The black inmate stood at the ready when the officer walked up on them. Both inmates were said to be startled by their discovery. They were both questioned about their actions, and the white inmate said, "I was just checking his bellybutton." Yes, that was the inmate's response to the sexual act he was about to perform before they were interrupted by the officer on rounds. The black inmate also tried to use the bellybutton defense when questioned, which would also fall upon deaf ears. Both were locked up and written up for the act. The buzzard Reverend would soon come to the aid of his two beloved inmates and fully supported the bellybutton defense, questioning whether the incident happened like the officer had reported. I then started to ask around some of the inmates that knew of the two inmates in question, and all whom I asked called them gay names and confirmed that the two inmates enjoyed spending time with men, so the two of them being caught together was no surprise. It was therefore a safe bet that the officer was indeed correct in his assessment of the two lovebirds he had caught. But the Reverend continued to fight for the release of the two inmates to no avail.

After the inmates served their time for the incident, the white inmate, who was the Reverend's clerk, was fired from his job in the rear of the service unit where my partner was located. The Reverend went out of his way trying to bring the inmate back to the service unit to work. My partner, who was very security-minded and did his job was having none of that. My partner even started his own investigation after the buzzard Reverend continuedly called the inmate up to the area on a call out to see him. Even though the inmate had been fired for his sex act, the Reverend seemed he couldn't do without him. My partner and I complained to the sergeant about the Reverend's refusal to stop calling the inmate up to the area.

Also, my partner was still deep into his investigation. One day, while searching the area, my partner decided to search the computers that the inmates were allowed to use. On it, hidden within a file was a document that the Reverend's sex-hungry clerk had authored that falsely accused me and my partner of misconduct for our adamant refusal to allow the inmate to return to his clerk position after his dirty, nasty, foul attempt at a sex act while on the unit, which we were having none of. The inmate was then written up again for unauthorized use of the computer. The computers that the inmates used for clerk work intended for whatever area they were clerking for personal use was prohibited. During the investigation, it was also learned that the Reverend was aware of the inmates' unauthorized usage of the area's computer located in his office. Everything the buzzard Reverend was doing brought into question if he was even a practicing man of the cloth. His attitude, common sense, and poor behavior and judgment should have been a warning sign to all around him to what was to come next.

The buzzard Reverend continued his out-of-control behavior with other inmates also. There was one inmate that locked on G-7 gallery, the gallery I was assigned to. He was white and was said to be a military vet. He would tell his story of innocence to all that would listen, including me. His story was he was in a bar fight with an individual outside in the parking lot, and the guy he was fighting fell and sustained a serious head injury. He seemed to think that his military status and the medication he claimed to be on should have precluded him from being held responsible for his actions; therefore, he proclaimed to be innocent and felt he shouldn't be incarcerated in prison, all of which sounded like a bunch of BS. He would try to sway all the staff members with his sad song. I would watch as some staff would allow themselves to be sucked into his delusional thoughts of innocence. Some staff would allow him to perform special tasks throughout the facility to get him out of his cell. The buzzard chaplain even made him his new clerk. Knowing how the out-of-control chaplain had no common sense and very poor judgment, a close eye was kept on the chaplain and even a closer eye on the inmate. I and my partner who worked in the rear of the service unit were watching.

One day. I observed the Reverend rushing into the service unit with a worried look on his face. He was clutching a Kentucky Fried Chicken sack just as it was time to send the inmates back to the blocks for the afternoon count. The Reverend hastily made his way toward the rear of the unit though the inmates heading in the opposite direction from which he had just come. The delusional vet was not with the other inmates that had all come from the back to ready themselves to exit the unit, so I immediately knew what was going down. The Reverend was running late with his delivery to his new clerk, the delusional vet. The rush was because the Reverend knew exactly what time they went back for the count, and he was late. His tardiness bought to light what he was up to.

After a couple of minutes, the Reverend's new clerk emerged from the back, walking fast in my direction, carrying his net bag, which is the bag in which inmates are allowed to carry some of their authorized items in. I immediately stopped him in his haste and questioned him on his tardiness in exiting the back of the unit along with the other inmates. When I stopped him, his look was priceless. He was so shaken and was startled by my questioning. For me, both were admissions of some form of guilt. I allowed him to exit the service unit, knowing he was going to the gallery.

I had to count. I made rounds on the unit to ensure it was clear of all inmates and I locked up and headed to G block to perform the afternoon count. As I made my way down the gallery of thirty-eight cells, when I was in front of the chaplain's clerk's cell, I looked in and found him sitting on the bed. I then begin to inform the inmate that I was well aware of the inmate's dealings with the shady buzzard Reverend. I then told him about what I had suspected—that the Reverend had hand-delivered him an order of KFC, which to my surprise he fully confessed to. I informed him that the Reverend was out of line and his close behavior with the Reverend was a problem. Even though the incident was reported to the area supervisor, the inmate was still allowed to remain the Reverend's trusted clerk.

Following the KFC caper, a few weeks later, I sat at the officer's front desk area monitoring and securing the area with the callouts and workers waiting in the waiting area until the turn out of the afternoon programs was completed and my partner returned to his post. As I sat there, I noticed the chaplain's clerk sitting on the bench just across the large observation window looking in my direction as the other twenty-plus inmates mingled with one another. The delusional vet came to the window area and spoke in the two-way slot and made a bold and absolutely ridiculous request. He asked me if he could be let in to go to the back where the Reverend was at. Now I must remind you the purpose of the inmates that worked in the back, in the waiting area, was the lack of security. Since my partner was not back at the unit yet, I asked him why he thought he could be allowed in the back with no security staff present. He then went on to tell me it would be all right. That was the day I knew my assessment of the vet being delusional was spot on. I then also knew this inmate was leaving this area and relocated somewhere else to work. After speaking with him to drive the point home, I clicked on the microphone to speak over the speaker system in the waiting room, and I said, "Have you lost your rabbit-ass mind? What—you think you're better than the other inmates forced to wait?" I then ordered him off the window area. I told him he was not special or privileged.

The whole waiting area got quite as the inmate sat back down to ponder the rejection to his ridiculous request. See, that was the thing—some of the white inmates didn't see themselves as inmates. They thought of themselves more as staff because staff had empowered them to do so by treating them differently—by giving them things and doing stuff for them that they weren't doing for the other inmates and fraternizing with them. This inmate was a prime example of the staff misconduct that created this problem.

The Reverend's new clerk was soon fired from his job, but the real problem still remained and that was the out-of-control Reverend, who was being allowed to be unprofessional, unethical, and a security threat to all around him. That was now more than a few things. I had alerted the all-white supervisor staff regarding the rogue, buzzard Reverend, none of which he was disciplined for.

The buzzard Reverend's next caper would be his last. The Reverend later was locked out of the facility for it was said he was dealing with an inmate and his sister, passing information to his family and something to do with money. He helping the inmate plot a plan to escape while the inmate was on an outside medical trip. Man, you talk about staff being out of control. It was spread all over the facility.

Both guards and civilian staff would be charged with a host of crimes while dealing with the inmates at the facility, but none I'm aware of ever did a day in jail for any crimes they had been charged with. Some staff were worse than the inmates themselves. Some staff that had been entrusted with the care, custody, and control of inmates in the New York's state prison system were themselves criminals. There were more than a few working among us. What empowered and emboldened them was all the head turning and the cover-ups, which gave them the freedom to do as they wished. So many felt comfortable going rogue.

There was one civilian—he was a maintenance man who would walk around with his small crew of two or three inmates to assist in whatever work needed to be done. He had a large, oversized work wagon or cart that was only supposed to contain tools, but this self-proclaimed peddler turned his work wagon into a store on wheels. He peddled what started off as baseball hats even though it directly violated the facilities policies and procedures that specifically prohibited this sort of behavior. The peddling maintenance man peddled on. I would observe him stop in the middle of the corridor to open up the rolling store to show off and offer his goods to potential customers, which was a security risk. The tools in the cart could be used as weapons if in the wrong hands. Everywhere he traveled throughout the prison, he would peddle his goods. I watched as his hat sales went from just hats to include T-shirts, baseball and hockey jerseys, and watches. Hell, he could even place a special order for a particular jersey on request from one of his customers. He wasn't an authorized vendor nor did the department issue peddlers' licenses to its employees. I would watch him whenever he appeared in the area where I was. I would observe his overzealous behavior as he would push his goods to all that inquired about his items for sale. I never observed any supervisor or higher-up stop him or inquire into the unauthorized activity.

After about a year or more of peddling his goods successfully, the maintenance man expanded his operations by including more items in his inventory. It was found out that the maintenance man wasn't only peddling items to the staff but he was also selling items to the inmate population. He was selling women's undergarments to the inmates. He was a rolling Victoria's Secret on wheels. It was said that the gay inmates were buying the bra and panty sets to strut around in, and the other inmates were said to be buying them to have a women's connection as they relieved themselves of their built-up pressure of their detachment from not having a woman's touch. It would seem that some felt closer having the women's undergarments to reference a women. It was said that an bra and panty set was discovered by an officer during a frisk. It was also told that it didn't take long for the inmate to reveal where and how he had obtained the items.

After an investigation, they found out that the maintenance man would handle the staff sales and his small work crew handled the sales to the inmates for items that were requested that he brought in for them. Only the peddler and his crew knew what other contraband was brought into the facility by the self-proclaimed peddler. After the investigation, the maintenance man was fired, and his sales associates, the inmate crew, were also fired. You have to remember the peddler had been doing this for a year or more. No one knows how much contraband or what kind of contraband was brought into the facility by the peddling maintenance man.

Man, the facility was so out of control you literally could not even do anything positive to help the facility look positive here in Elmira, New York. We have a community center that is named after the late great Ernie Davis, the country's first black Heisman trophy winner. He received the trophy in 1961 during the civil rights era. His life has been memorialized on the big screen, and his life and story has been talked about here in Elmira, New York, for years. He is legendary. He was truly one of Elmira's greatest residents. It wasn't just Ernie Davis's athleticism—it was also said it was his persona. He was a true scholar and statesman. He was loved by all who knew him.

So one day, while speaking to one of the center's directors, we spoke of the need for new signs for the center. Knowing that we had a sign-making shop at the facility that was putting out good work, I suggested I would talk to the higher-ups at the facility to see if the sign shop could make some signs for the center. So I went to the dep of security and superintendent. Even though I knew I wasn't one of their favored few, I asked if they would help the local community center by allowing the facility sign shop to make some signs. Surprisingly, the facility administration was on board with the idea. The only thing required would be for the center to purchase the material.

After I got the green light or go ahead, I contacted a local hardware/lumber store that donated the material to do the job. Next, I sat down with the civilian carpenter/sign maker and discussed what the center needed. He and his crew of inmate workers then came up with a design that was agreed upon, and the making of the signs went ahead.

Approximately a month or so later, I received a call at my post. It was the civilian carpenter/sign maker informing me that the signs had been completed. I was later shown the completed signs that looked amazing. If one would have paid for them, they would have cost hundreds of dollars. I thanked the civilians and the inmates for doing such an amazing job and assured them that their work and hard effort was much appreciated. The sign shop informed me the signs would have to still sit for a while to ensure that the paint dried completely. I then thought that the good deed shouldn't be overlooked, so I contacted the local newspaper and told them about the amazing signs that the facility had made for the local community center, and the news reporter thought it would make a good story, so a date and time was set up for the newspaper to be on hand for the dedication of the signs to the center.

When that day came, I, the dep of programs at the facility, the carpenter/sign maker, and the members of the center were all on hand to take photos with the large amazing wooden signs. A photo and story were published in the local newspaper. Man, it felt good helping to bring something positive to the Elmira Correctional Facility that seemed to have a black cloud hovering over it and no one seemed to want better. It was a win-win for everyone. The center got some amazing signs, and they were profoundly grateful for the good job and donation. They sent thank-you cards to the administration, and the inmates assured them that they were thankful. The facility was thankful for being able to have something positive to display to the public. Albany was also happy. They displayed the photo that was in the local paper on their state web site for all to see. The inmates were happy to be able to help the local community by being able to contribute to it. Man, all was good in the neighborhood. The facility had a bright, shiny light beaming on it that was shining bright.

But in true negative, evil fashion, the Elmira Correctional Facility's shining light was eclipsed, and the facility was placed back into darkness and gloom. A black cloud reemerged that hovered over the facility. This came from the new startling revelation that the civilian carpenter/sign maker was also a drug dealer and was dealing with the inmates. I was stunned by the announcement. It was said he was accused of being connected with some inmate's family member that was supplying him with cocaine and he was selling and bring it into the facility. The story that was being told around the prison was the carpenter/sign maker/drug dealer was brought up on charges and fired from his position. The good deed and the shining light were both extinguished just that quickly by this selfish, rogue act of criminality, which made the facility as a whole look bad. Man, I told all that would listen, "You cannot even do anything positive around this place." Albany immediately took the photo and article off the state web site from the shame the civilian carpenter/sign maker/ drug dealer brought upon the department. That's how a good deed is undone at the Elmira Correctional Facility.

While still working the front desk area in the service unit, some of the councilors ran around like they were in a sorority club instead of working at a state job. I would watch as some would refuse to do their jobs, saying they felt overworked, when in all reality, they spent much of the day hanging out and playing grab ass all day. Hell, they had it so good they got a full two-hour lunch break. They took it each and every day. Now what damn job besides the president of the company or a self-employed person gets two hours for lunch? You would think not a state job, but think again. These privileged people were being allowed to do whatever they wanted, including wasting state time. Most only did the bare minimum, and some wouldn't even do that. There came a time when there was a need for one of the councilors to volunteer for the job of signing marriage licenses and be deputized by the city of Elmira to carry out that function of signing marriage licenses for the inmates. All refused, saying, "It's not my job. I have enough to do. They can't make me do it." They even said, "I'm reporting this to the union."

After the senior counselors didn't get a volunteer to carry out the task of signing marriage licenses, the counseling staff was threatened that one of them would be picked to do the job. That's when the counselors ran to the union and complained about someone requiring them to work and sign marriage licenses. A grievance was filed, and the defining line was drawn in the sand.

Months went past, and the inmates were being denied the right to marry even though the state had granted them the right as long as they qualified. The longer the stalemate went on, the more complaining the inmates started doing. The inmates filed their own complaints regarding the right to marry. I sat and watched the drama unfold as the civilian staff refused to do what had been asked of them, and they remained defiant. Then you had the inmates who felt let down and denied their rights because no one cared, and many felt it was being done purposely. After this continued, the inmates threatened to sue the department and the Elmira Correctional Facility for violating their rights.

As the battle intensified, I was dragged directly into the middle. I thought, *Yep, why not the only black officer around? Who else but me in the middle of all this craziness?* A couple of the older inmates who were in the service unit on callouts one day with their counselors to discuss just that—not being able to get married because the counselors were refusing to do their job. They came to the desk before leaving and pleaded their case as I was allowed to sit in judgment to their compiling argument of why they should be allowed to marry. Before I sent them back to the location from which they had come, I told them some of their points were well taken. After the inmates had gone, the counselors were muttering around, talking about the inmates complaining about not being able to get married. Both sides, the inmates and councilors, were at a stalemate.

One day, during the morning callouts, as the inmates came and went, I had a few of the inmates that were doing long-term sentences approach me and asked why I couldn't sign marriage licenses. Now I knew that this wasn't something they had just come up with. It was something that the inmates had come up with to bypass the roadblock that was in front of them.

I answered their request of me becoming the deputized clerk to sign the marriage licenses with "I don't think they would allow that."

One of the inmates on the inmate liaison committee (the inmates that meet with the administration to address problems) said, "Well, when I see the dep of programs, I'm going to ask."

After that, the inmates went on a campaign to make me the new deputized clerk. The idea soon got back to the senior counselors by way of the administration that was facing a potential lawsuit for not allowing the inmates the right to marriage at the facility. One of the senior counselors came to me one day and informed me that he had been told about the idea.

I responded with, "I never said I was going to do that," and told him the inmates had suggested it. Either way, he thought it was a good idea for the administration to avoid the inmates filing a class action lawsuit. At first I was hesitant, but once the complaining continued on both sides, I gave in to the idea. Most of the counselors didn't care one way or another. They were just happy that they themselves didn't have to be the one to take on the extra work. And then there were the ones who felt like their job was being infringed upon—you know, the job that they didn't do in the first place. I was then pulled aside and told about the position and what it required and asked if I was interested. I thought, *What the hell? I'm not here to be liked. I'm here to do my job.* So I said yes. I was then sat down, and everything was explained to me, and I was showed how to file the paperwork required.

After that one afternoon, I and one of the senior counselors went down to city hall in Elmira, New York, and I was sworn in and deputized by one of the city clerks. It was official I was now the person signing the marriage licenses on behalf of the Elmira Correctional Facility. My newfound position was immediately met with security staff complaining about my new title and position. After being given a briefcase to carry the documents for the marriage licenses, the guards lost their everlasting rabbit-ass minds. They were so upset they went to the union and complained about my new position. Now I wasn't the only officer participating or helping to facilitate nonsecurity matters within the facility. Others as well did so, and none complained. They would stare and make off-the-cuff comments about me being allowed to sign marriage licenses, and the briefcase seemed to bother them even more. They were like little kids in the sandbox, and I had the shovel and the bucket and they only had their hands to work with. I thought the briefcase made me look important because it really aggravated those that hated me, despised me, harassed me, and discriminated against me. they all seemed to be beside themselves. If looks could kill, I would have been killed a million times.

The inmates started to file for marriage certificates, and at first, there were a lot because of the backlog of inmates that were waiting when the councilors refused to do it. Some of the inmates seemed to be marrying for different reasons. Some would marry to benefit themselves for the opportunity to have trailer visits, which is known as the family reunion program. Some would be marrying just for the opportunity for sex, and then others would marry for the purpose of having someone bring them packages and place money in their inmate accounts. Others would marry to benefit the outside spouse in obtaining benefits from state and governmental agencies. And then you had some that would marry for love. I will admit I had fun in finding out the reason behind the inmates' desire to tie the knot. I would ask questions of the inmates about their reasons for marriage, and surprisingly, many would open up and be upfront and seemingly truthful about their intent. I would have the opportunity to talk to the inmates one on one while discussing their application that they were filing, and then I would have the opportunity to talk to them and their bride in a closed setting when I would request for them to sign the necessary paperwork to file for their marriage. This would take place in the visiting room in a small room just off the large visit room area. Usually, I wouldn't know what the bride-to-be looked like until meeting on the day to sign the application for the license, but sometimes, the inmates would have previously showed me photos of the bride-to-be. During those meetings, I'll just say this: Sometimes I would be stunned and surprised at the two people that sat across from me waiting to sign. I would have fun with some of the people that you could obviously see were using the system to their advantage. I would ask questions like "Where did you two meet? How long have you been knowing each other?" to even "Do you love each other?" Most of the inmates knew I talked open and freely. My communication skills was one of my best fortes.

Some of the inmates would in no way pass my test of marrying for the right reason, but they qualified and meet the state standard. Some of the inmates that had applied and were waiting for their marriage licenses would never receive one. Their request would be voided or denied for any number of reasons. One of the more notable reasons would be from being placed on keep lock by a staff member. Some would get written up for legitimate reasons, and others would be set up by a rogue staff member out to ruin the inmates' plans of marriage. After the inmate would be denied, I would find out the reason he was denied and hear the reason—some would be legitimate and some would just be retaliatory reasons. The staff might have something against the inmate. Either way, the inmate would be denied and unable to get married.

After clearing the facility backlog of marriages, I was stopped by the administration from continuing, citing that the union NYSCOBA had filed a grievance against me, one of its own members. That's right—the union I belonged to, NYSCOBA, had filed a grievance against me. I thought to myself, *How is that even constitutionally possible?* The union I was paying dues to could be allowed to work against me, filing a grievance against something that I volunteered to do. The union didn't file grievances against the almost all-white staff that was allowed to volunteer to do other nonsecurity functions throughout the prison, but they chose to file one against the black officer who had chosen to volunteer. This is a prime example of the white privilege that the majority of all white-staff had, and all they had to do is complain about the black officer. The same union I paid dues to would violate my union rights to please the almost all-white staff by filing a grievance against me and the administration.

After my dismissal from my deputized clerk position, a few weeks later, one of the councilors was made to do it. As I continued to work the front desk area in the service unit, the officer's position in the IGRC or grievance office changed four times. The position was like the last stop for a number of officers who would retire after relinquishing the position. The position usually went to an officer that had twenty-five years or more on the job, seeing that the post or position had weekends off, which was something that many correctional officers and guards desired. Out of the four IGRC officers that had the post while I worked the service unit, all had their own style of doing the job. One was laid back, one was a go-getter, one was all over the place, and one was a stickler.

When not busy at the desk running callouts, I would sit and watch everything that went on around me, taking it all in. Some of the civilians would involve all around them in whatever was going on in their life. Many would complain about problems they were having and some would create problems to talk about. Sitting there watching was like watching real live TV, and the station was turned to "*How the Hill Turns.*" The Hill is a nickname that was given to the

Elmira Correctional Facility years ago because it sits on a hilltop. It was a real-life soap opera that would play out every day. I and others would often say that the old HBO television series *Oz*, which was about prison life and was chaotic and crazy didn't have shit on the Elmira Correctional Facility because this was worse than the tv series itself.

You see, the public has no real idea what goes on in prison. What most of the public knows is what the prison officials reveal or offer up as information to the media. The media is not allowed to access or interview inmates or staff. All the information is filtered through the department's own system that controls what information is allowed for the public's consumption, and if the information was a plate of food, you would starve to death from the amount they were feeding you, which is very little. Anytime that an incident accrued and it was newsworthy, the story was controlled and driven by the department and union to ensure that the narrative was controlled by them and not reported thoroughly, honestly, or objectively. Most of these prisons in the upstate New York area are located in small rural areas that have small news outlets that have no desire to find out the truth about what is really going on behind the walls of the large human warehouses located in their backyards. So many are content to report only what the union and state officials tell them, and they never even try to use their investigational reporting skills to find out the true story or the true reason for some incident that may have occurred in their communities. Long before fake news was termed *fake news*, the Department of Corrections was already disseminating fake and misleading news to cover up wrongdoing and misconduct by staff members and others. Over my twenty-eight years of service, I have observed this over and over again. The prison system is truly veiled, shielded, and hidden from the public's eyes to protect its own interest.

As I continued working the service unit desk, I would work G block 7 gallery on the weekends as part of the bid job, and the situation in the block remained the same. Every officer or guard in the block could be found downstairs, hovering around the main desk area, playing cards and eating the groceries that had been allowed to be brought into the facility and prepared by the facility's short-order cook. It almost reminded you of the cowboy days when the Old West was being explored. The short-order cook was like the old chuck wagon cook cooking up the vittles for the other cowboys. The area sergeant could be found either playing cards with the others or he would be locked in his office sleeping. This all was allowed to go on for years with no one questioning the outright dereliction of duty that seemed to be more of the norm then abnormal. These guys truly were allowed to do whatever they wanted, when they wanted. Most of the time, I would be the only officer on his post sitting just off the gallery I was in charge of. When the mess hall run would take place and the inmates would be escorted to the mess hall by the gallery, much of the time I would also stand alone in the mess hall as others grouped up or stood along the sergeant, who entertained them with foolishness or was up to some kind of shenanigans.

Later in the afternoon, when the facility count was clear, the inmates would then be run out to recreation, which would take place in the large fieldhouse structure or in the gymnasium during warmer weather. The outside yard was used, where I would sit alone monitoring the large inmate gathering as the usually all-white staff would group up in numbers. As they would sit and entertain themselves, I would have a couple of officers that sometimes felt comfortably sitting with me who seemed to harbor no animosity toward me.

As months went by, after winning a very large out-of-court settlement due to the state's desire not to have a court trial, during an afternoon mess hall run, I escorted G block 7 gallery to the mess hall, and as usual I posted myself in the middle of the mess hall. As I watched what was going on all around me, a young guard was posted at the door. The young guard was one of many who had money problems—from what was said, child support and other financial problems, which he had seemed to bring on himself by out of control behavior like so many others at the facility. As I stood, the other officers in the mess hall were distracted by idle conversation with one another and lost to what was going on in front of them, including the sergeant posted in the mess hall. As the young, troubled guard started to clear the mess hall, he would step into the mess hall though the large steel door and try to get the attention of the guard. He wished to exit the mess hall. For the most part, he would have to call their name because the other guards were distracted with idle conversation. He would then throw his hand in the air and spin his hand around in a lasso-type motion that was universal in prison to run the inmates in or out of an area.

As the young, troubled guard continued to clear the mess hall, I waited my turn. As I stood in the middle of the mess hall, moments later, I heard *boom*, *boom*, *boom*. I looked around, and the young troubled guard stood clinching his state-issued baton, looking in my direction with a snarl on his face. He then hit the large steel door three more times with his baton and pointed in my direction. Since we were an earshot away from one another, I asked him if he was ready for me to unseat the inmates. His snarl or grimace became more intense by my question asked. He then raised his hand in the air and gave me a quick lasso motion, which was followed by me motioning to the inmates to exit the mess hall. Once the inmates were clear of the mess hall and in the corridor, I too stepped out into the corridor. I observed the young troubled, savage guard standing about twenty to twenty-five feet down the corridor, glaring in my direction. I then immediately said to the young guard whom I had more than fourteen years more on the job than him, "Hey, you don't have to beat on the door to get my attention. You can call my name like you do for everyone else."

My comment sent this young, troubled savage of a guard into a rage. He immediately ran in my direction, where I stood approximately twenty to twenty-five feet away. As he ran up on me, I was ready for what was to come he ran up on me and started yelling "Don't tell me what to do!" and he then pushed me. The push was a gentle push to my shoulder area. It was almost like he didn't want to push me or feared pushing me too hard. The push was so gentle it didn't even move me off the spot where I stood. The push was the push felt around the world as far as I was concerned. I immediately thought to myself, *Did this crazy-ass savage just put his damn hands on me?* To me, that was a no. No, I wasn't around here putting my hands on anyone. My protest was always one of nonviolence. After he placed his filthy hands on me, I told him, "Touch me again," which he refused to do by backing up off me.

The inmates were all watching this go down, as well as other guards that stood idly watching the young savage guard lose his rab-bit-ass mind over my statement of "You don't have to beat on the door to get my attention, you can call my name as you do everyone else." No one in their right damn mind would react to that the way he did unless there was something else going on. As this young savage stood now feet away and no longer on top of me, I told him, "Don't ever put your hands on me again," and if he had a problem with me, which he seemed to have, he could see me after work as I put the savage back in his place.

The sergeant and a lieutenant got involved. The door had then been opened as the savage guard was still talking to me. I then informed the sergeant and lieutenant this wasn't the place for this. "See me walking down the street after work since you like touching people." The all-white staff that were in the area immediately came to the savage guard's defense by literally standing in back of him as he continued to yell idle threats of putting his hands on me.

The inmates had been let go to start walking back to the block, and I walked down the corridor as they rounded the corner of the block. As I walked them up the stairs to lock them in, the inmates were all yelling in my direction, "Brown, we were waiting for them to jump you! We were all going to jump in to help you!" Some were yelling, "Brown, they're trying to set you up." Some even yelled out, "Brown, f——k them rednecks" or "Call me for a witness." As I went down the thirty-eight cell gallery, all the inmates said that was bullshit—what was allowed to happen.

You see, most of the almost all-white staff treated me just like they did the inmates. After locking the inmates in, I exited G Block to return to the service unit. All the guards I walked past glared or stared at me with discontent and hate. As I walked through the cor-ridor where the incident had just taken place, there were a number of guards in a pack that looked like a huddle, and they were getting ready to run a play or, in this case, get their lie straight. As I contin-ued through the door, I observed the young savage guard talking to one of the head racist union guards, who seemed to be giving him some advice. I made my way back to the service unit and my post. I sat at the post after the chow run was completed and the turnout to afternoon programs was completed. The area sergeant came to me and informed me that I was wanted in the executive office where the superintendent and dep's offices were located. I gathered my things together and waited for my relief from my post.

After being relieved, I made my way up front to the executive office. Now, I have to remind you this is six months after receiving the largest out-of-court settlement by one person against the Elmira Correctional Facility. As I waited in the executive office, I was called into the dep's office and informed that I was being accused of threatening the savage guard who ran up on me and pushed me for saying something to him. Yes, I was being accused of threats, not the savage white guard who had assaulted me with a push but me—the one that told him not to put his damn hands on me again. As I tried to explain to the racist dep who seemed to be elated by telling me I was being charged with false accusations, he didn't want to hear none of what I had to say. He said that the sergeant and lieutenant verified the story that was being told, which was a lie but the administration was accepting it as the truth. After getting nowhere with the dep, I was ordered out of the facility.

Days later, while at home, waiting to hear from the administration on March 10, 2010, I was notified via a phone call informing me to report to the facility. Immediately, once there, I was escorted into the dep's office and ordered to turn in my badge and ID and informed I was suspended without pay. The racist dep had a smile on his face as he requested my badge and ID that I nicely placed on his desk and informed him as like many times before, "I'll be back." I was then escorted out the front door through the double-gated area into the inside sally port and shown the front door. I was being suspended over a savage racist guard who had assaulted me just because he could.

I remember the date of this suspension well because it was the day of our wedding anniversary. As I had said earlier, the facility and state used birthdates, holidays, and special occasions to harass me and my family and bring discord. The evil, hateful people making these decisions showed me a long time ago they cared nothing about me and even less about my family.

After being suspended, I contacted my attorney, who had just reached the large out-of-court settlement on my behalf six months prior. He was shocked the state had chosen to continue to allow the employees at Elmira Correctional Facility to harass me. I informed him of the trumped up charges I was being accused of and the penalty the state was seeking, which was termination from the department. That's right—they were seeking my job for just telling a savage that used a baton to beat on a door because he refused to call my name, and he was the one that ran up on me and pushed me, which amounted to assault, but the white savage guard was being charged with nothing. I was actually charged for being assaulted and harassed by a savage, racist guard. And the union which represented me, NYSCOBA, the administration at the Elmira Correctional Facility, the department in Albany, and the employee relations board all thought that it was a good idea to charge me with misconduct for this young troubled, savage racist guard's out-of-control behavior. I was being held responsible for his actions. All had to be either sincerely ignorant, or they would have to be claiming conscientious stupidity for their involvement in allowing the facility to charge me with a NOD, or was it a conspiracy and they were all working together to ultimately get rid of me? It had to be one or another. I had just been given a very large cash settlement so the state could avoid going to court and being exposed publicly for what it really is, so any reasonable person could see it was retaliation.

After informing my attorney about the NOD, I told him I had reservations about being represented by NYSCOBA or its legal team. My attorney suggested that I use the union to represent me and I should be requiring them to do what they were paid to do, which was represent its members. We both talked it over, and my attorney and I agreed that the union would represent me until I felt that they were truly misrepresenting me. As the weeks went on, I started talking to the union's lawyer, who was out of the Buffalo, New York, area. We will call him Attorney Duck. One of the first questions I asked him was how he was going to represent me against another union member who was lying. His response was made to try to assure me he was going to represent me fairly, which sounded more like I was in trouble of losing my job over the lies that were being told by other staff members. I in no way after our first conversation felt any more comfortable being represented by the union that had turned their back on me than the racist guards that were lying about me, so I played along with Attorney Duck and the union representative out of the western district office that oversaw the Elmira area. I know a duck when I see a duck, and believe me, I also know when I'm being bamboozled and hoodwinked by a bunch of racist idiots out to protect the guilty at any and every means necessary. The union and the union's lawyer were fully aware I was the only officer or guard that was being charged with NODs at the Elmira Correctional Facility, and it had raised no alarms or protest to the many NODs I was charged with. It never would be accepted by the union had it been one of the white officers or guards.

I tried to obtain evidence to clear my name. There were video cameras smack dab in the corridor where the incident happened that would show the savage guard push me in retaliation for my verbal protests of him beating on the door savagely with his baton to get my attention, treating me like some kind of animal rather than call my name like he had done for everyone else he was trying to summon. He was allowed to antagonize me with his state-issued baton and then assault me for just my verbal protest. Now that is pretty damn privileged to not have to even hear someone telling you they thought you are wrong and your out-of-control behavior is acceptable by the masses, so much so they would lie to cover up your wrongdoing. I requested the video from the camera system in the corridor, and I was quickly told there wasn't any video of the incident. The administration even went as far as to say that the cameras didn't record, which was a lie also. I then thought long and hard and said, "Well, let me have the video of the mess hall." They questioned my need for that since the incident took place in the corridor, at which time I mistakenly told them the opposition or team that wanted to get rid of Brown at the Elmira Correctional facility that I wanted it to show the savage running up to me from outside the door area. Since some of the mess hall cameras were amid at the doorway, this request was made to the western union rep. After making the request I thought, *Man, I just showed my hand,* but after thinking about it for a while, I thought it was more to my advantage. The reason was I was afraid they would tamper with the video, but at the same time, it would be a telling sign I was being bamboozled and hoodwinked by the union, NYSCOBA, and Attorney Duck.

After my request, a few weeks later, I received a copy of the video, and sure enough, the video was tampered with. The video was clear with the exception of the door area that had been brightened to the point it was blurred, the area I had told the union rep I was looking for. I now had evidence that they were trying to bamboozle and hoodwink me. One of my Masonic Brothers had a brother that owned a video equipment business that he used for editing videos. He would shoot for people at parties and events. When he saw the video, he immediately could tell it had been altered to hide the area in question—the front door area of the mess hall. He then took the video and tried to undo what they had done, which resulted in a little better copy of the incident, and you could just barely make out the savage guard running past the door in my direction. I then informed my attorney down in New Jersey and told him my fear of the union representing me had been fully recognize and proven to be right by the manipulated video. We then spoke about my alternative, which was having him come to Elmira to represent me in the NOD hearing I was facing. We discussed the pros and cons of having my personal attorney versus the union representation.

After our conversation, I and my wife sat down and looked at our finances and tried to figure out how we would pay for the attorney fees, the stenographer fees, and state arbitrator's fees. We also weighed in the outcome of the hearing if we were to stay the course with the union's lawyer, Attorney Duck, who was looking out for the best interest of the union and its almost all-white staff at the Elmira Correctional Facility, having already shown themselves to be in cahoots with the state in hoodwinking and bamboozling me. The outcome would have been my termination from the department most definitely, bringing with it financial hardship in the form of my job lost and having to wait six years until I reached age fifty-five to collect on the pension for years credited for service. Now going with my own attorney came with a risk also. I could lose and face the same termination from service. Going with my own attorney was also going to cost us a lot of money. We decided to take our chances with my own attorney, seeing that my pension was at stake, and when it all boiled down to it, that is what truly mattered—retirement and collecting my pension that the state and union seemed hellbent on taking.

After I and my wife decided on the course we were taking, which was my own attorney, I contacted my attorney and signed what papers were needed to retain him. It was still months away before the hearing would take place, but my attorney asked that I keep an open dialogue and channel of communication open with the union and Attorney Duck to give the appearance that they were still representing me moving forward. As the months went on, I continued to try to gather information to prove my story or side of the event. I had contacted the department's IG office, which is the office of the inspector general, who interviewed me and asked if I had any witness to the event or incident, to which I told them the guards that were present and all the inmates had witnessed the whole altercation from start to finish. Now remined you the inmates were all in a uproar after the incident and verbally denounced the treatment I received from my fellow staff members. Remember, some had even said they wished to be called as witnesses.

After my interview with IG a few weeks later, they said they went in and interviewed the inmates and they said nothing and they also backed up the administration's lie that there was no video in the corridor. As for the Department of Corrections IG office, it was later dismantled and reorganized for being corrupt to the core, so I had a corrupt IG office investigating nothing on my behalf. They were looking for evidence against me to booster the state and union's claim to rid me of the department. I thought to myself, *Would you expect anything different from the Department of Corruption?* As I waited, I continued to play along with the union and its paid attorney,

Attorney Duck, as they continued to try to pull a hood over my head with lies and mistruths to cover up the misdeed of the savage guard. I played along for many months as they fed me their story of what was happening with the case. I relayed the information on to my attorney, who was preparing my defense after being locked out of the Elmira Correctional Facility for approximately six months without pay, waiting for a hearing.

My beloved sister passed away. I was now dealing with a great amount of grief from the loss of my sibling. My heart was crushed. I was truly overwhelmed. I can truly say if it wasn't for the love of the Lord, I don't know where I would have been. Perhaps lost and in the wilderness with no hope. That's one thing God gives all of us—hope. On the evening of my second sister's wake at one of the well-known funeral homes, the wake was filled to capacity with the many family and friends that had come out to mourn and pay respect to my sister, who was a quiet, loving soul of a person. She was truly loved by many. As I mingled with the many family and friends, I looked up to find the dep of security from the prison entering. The look on his face was tense and very nervous. As he made his way through the crowd of people, I heard some speak out and object to him being there. Many of the people there know the history of the Elmira Correctional Facility and how I was being allowed to be discriminated against and harassed, so as he made his way through the crowd in his gray uniform toward my direction, I heard some yell out, "What the hell is he doing here?" and "Here comes the devil."

It truly took everything I could do to keep from grabbing this man by the back of the collar and the back of his paints and literally tossing his ass out. The reason was when my beloved mother passed away, I didn't even receive a card from the facility or union like other officers and guards did when their mothers died. They were sent cards, and collections were taken up by the union, and they sent a large flower arrangement to show their respect and condolences. I received none of this. Remember, I received harassment by the head racist guard in the kitchen after the passing of my mother. The head racist guard, along with the administration, had me arrested on fake charges that they filed with the New York State Police. When my father passed away, I also didn't receive a sympathy card from the facility or the union or any other form of condolences. So why would the dep of security from the Elmira Correctional Facility show up at my sister's wake unannounced while I'm suspended without pay on false charges for the last seven months? Why?

I kid you not, as my blood boiled at the sight of him, a calming feeling came over me. By the time he reached me with his outstretched hand, which I shook like a gentleman and graciously accepted his condolences that spilled from his mouth after speaking, he then walked up where my sister's body was resting and paid his respects and left. After he departed, I thought to myself, *God is truly good*, because if it wasn't for the love of the Lord and the respect I have for my family, I would have knocked his ass out, but you see, that is why I believe he showed up. He seemed to be that sacrificial lamb. Neither he nor any other person from the Elmira Correctional Facility had shown up at any of the other family member's funerals but this one, the one where I was suspended from work without pay. They thought it would be a good one to be at. I didn't take the bait.

Soon after putting my sister to rest weeks later after being out of work for almost eight months without pay, it was time for the arbitration hearing. My attorney arrived the day before for preparation, we booked a room for him at the same hotel where the hearing was taken place in downtown Elmira. After he arrived and checked in, I took him out to dinner, where we discussed the case and my defense against the lies being told. It was hard to believe that I was on trial for telling an out-of-control, raging guard to not bang on the door to get my attention and he was allowed to assault me by pushing me, and this was enough to constitute an eight-month suspension and a NOD, which was seeking my immediate dismissal from state service. The white raging, out-of-control guard wasn't charged with anything. It was just like the saying we have in the black community, "If you're black, get back," and "If you're white, you're right," because this was so wrong on so many levels. It would seem that the state would have rejected the ideal as constitutionally and morally wrong, but because of the conspiracy and cover up to conceal the harsh discriminatory harassment I was being subjected to by the New York

State Department of Correctional Services along with the administration at the Elmira Correctional Facility and the union NYSCOBA felt charging me with a false NOD would better fit their needs even though the almost all-white staff at the Elmira Correctional Facility would be allowed to violate rules and regulations every day and none would face disciplinary charges.

You had guards that would have dragged out fights among themselves. There was one incident where two sergeants had a bloody fistfight on the cage floor in front of the watch commander and other high-ranking officials. Neither was charged with anything. Other guards would fight all throughout the jail in front of both staff and inmates, and none were reported to Albany for NOD charges to be brought against them. I kid you not—I was the only officer being charged with NODs one after another, and no state official questioned the facility and union's agenda. I was being charged for being assaulted and for telling this racist guard to stop antagonizing me with his baton, which resulted in him assaulting me, and I was charged for telling him, "If he wanted to see me, see me after work." That statement was enough to constitute a NOD under the state's so-called standards that I was the only one subjected to obey and adhere, to which was obvious.

After going over the case that my attorney was going to present, my attorney suggested that I wear a suit if I had one. I told him I had a couple; he requested that I wear one to the hearing. The morning of the hearing, I and my attorney met hours before for breakfast at the hotel where he was staying and also where the hearing was taking place. As we sat and ate breakfast, we strategized to come up with helpful ways to defend me against the lies that were about to be told. It seemed that many of the employees in the department had no problem lying or telling half-truths to support one another or the agenda they supported. Now remember the union has no idea I had retained my own counsel to represent me, so when the time came to start the hearing, I entered the room escorted by my attorney. The union and their attorney, Attorney Duck, were seated along with the arbitrator, stenographer, and a state representative from the state employees relations board that was bringing the false charges against me. All seemed too consumed to even realize I had brought a friend with me into the lion's den. They seemed to be itching to go. As we entered, I paid close attention to the union representative and their lawyer; both seemed to be all giddy and excited. I then looked at the judge, who was in a conversation with the stenographer, and the state representative was looking over paperwork.

As we entered, none were aware what was happening until Attorney Duck looked up and my attorney introduced himself to the room. That's when the union rep and Attorney Duck lost their rabbit-ass minds in unison. Their giddy, upbeat mood switched to anger, and they seemed upset, and Attorney Duck looked at the arbitrator to ask him to prevent or stop me from having private representation. They were more than taken aback. Their looks were of pure surprise, stunned by the newfound revelations. They could hardly believe what was happening. It was Attorney Duck that piped up first, saying he didn't know what was going on, then the union rep echoed his comment. It was then nicely explained to the two desperados by my attorney that he was there to represent me. I call them two desperados because they were both desperately out to get my job. After my Attorney said his piece, the arbitrator asked me if my attorney was the counsel I was going with. I responded yes, and the union rep and there lawyer got up from the table, voicing their dislike as they packed up their belongings. Remember, it had been at around the second month of this so-far eight-month suspension that I had gotten evidence that the union and their lawyer were out to bamboozle and hoodwink me with misrepresentation by the request of the union. Their plan had backfired. The union, the Elmira Correctional Facility administration, and Albany were all stunned by the new turn of events. The union's lawyer started making threats, saying, "You better not be trying to sue the union."

Now why would he say that? I thought he must be feeling guilty for what they were trying to do, and then I thought also, Why are they so mad? If anything, I was saving the union money because the cost of the arbitration was now going to be my sole responsibility and not the union's, and what difference would it make? See, the difference was this: if the union had the opportunity to represent me, they were going to make sure that representation was misunderstood, lacking evidence, and miscommunicated to the arbitrator, all adding up to misrepresentation to ensure my immediate termination from the Department of Corrections. By using my own attorney, I still had a glimmer of hope that I would keep my job as he represented me against the coming onslaught of lies, untruths, and deception that they had baked up.

As the union rep and their lawyer continued to gather their belongings after they had been hoodwinked, bamboozled, and horn-swoggled, they were dismissed by the judge. As they left the room, the union rep led the way with Attorney Duck in tow who stopped and again seemed to feel it necessary to threaten or warn me about suing the union with another "You better not try to sue the union." This time, his comment was met by not only a look of disgust by me but also my attorney. As he tried to linger in the door, he was wangled along by the union rep, who seemed to want to get away from the situation quickly. I'm sure he had to go notify the administration at the Elmira Correctional Facility, mainly the superintendent, who was helping to facilitate this whole thing.

After the union and its lawyer were dismissed, sent down the road back to the western New York area of Buffalo, New York, the arbitrator quickly went on the record to acknowledge my private counsel. He then informed me that all cost was now my responsibility. After that was handled, the IG investigators there to testify were quickly brought in to testify to the information or what they had found while doing their investigation. When I say they were quickly interviewed by the arbitrator, I mean it was quick. There was no doubt they had to hurry to catch there ride back to the western New York area along with the union rep and Attorney Duck.

As soon as the arbitrator started asking them questions, they started lying. They claimed to have had signed statements from the inmates who witnessed the altercation that was started by the raging, out-of-control, troubled young guard. Almost all the statements were all in the same handwriting, as well as the signatures. Now this might had been acceptable if the union's paid lawyer was allowed to misrepresent me in this hiring, but with my paid attorney, the two lying IG investigators and there fraudulent statements were quickly dismissed and their testimony was stricken from the record by the arbitrator. The two scallywags were then dismissed and sent to catch up with the two desperados who had been hornswoggled. I sat there picturing the four of them scurrying to their vehicle and hustling their way out of town, hitting the dusty trial back to western New York.

Months before the arbitration hearing, when I was speaking to the union lawyer, I had asked him, "How are you going to effectively represent me against another union member that has been allowed to assault me and not be charged with anything?" I also let him know that I didn't trust the union for allowing this to take place, and I told him nowhere in an arbitration hearing would you see the state and the union arbitrating an incident with two white officers' or guards' involvement in anything. Their false misconception of me allowed them to fall victim to being hoodwinked, bamboozled, and hornswoggled. They became entangled in their own web of deception to rid me of the Department of Corrections with lies, false statements, and a coverup of administration's refusal to do their job correctly and fairly. The superintendent at the time was a well-known guard from the Attica Correctional Facility, where it is well documented that discrimination and abuse is a way of life for all that work and do time there, and the superintendent and his attitude showed he supported the Attica way of running a New York State prison. In 1971, the Attica riot took place some forty-eight years ago, and ill feelings are still felt by prison staff that unleash their hate and anger on the inmate population and anyone else they fear as a threat to their white privilege and power. They have been allowed to have using fear and intimidation as tools of control. Hell, I think there may be a couple of black or minority employees allowed to work there. Can you believe that they are allowed to work at Attica by those controlling the prison with fear and intimidation, which also takes place at other state correctional facilities. They are given power to harass and intimidate those they have chosen to be undesirable and unwilling to submit to their ideology. This is the mentality that the superintendent at the Elmira Correctional Facility had coming out of Attica Correctional Facility. Yep, there was no doubt he was helping to fuel the effort to rid the Elmira Correctional Facility and the Department of Corrections of me.

Some of the harassment I was subjected to as terms of my employment was having drawings of monkeys on the wall with my initials placed by the drawings. Talk about disrespectful. Being black and thought of as a monkey or less than human is totally disrespectful and hurtful and hateful, but if my harassers were referring to looks, someone looking like a monkey, they didn't have to look far because the superintendent from Attica had more of a primate look than myself. He had thin lips that curled at the top like a monkey, and they were shaped like a monkey, his hairless lip, and his small beady round close-set eyes—all made him look more primate than me, and he was white.

The arbitration hearing was now on its way, and all had been informed that my private attorney would be representing me. Right from the start, the arbitration hearing was a dog and pony show. The arbitrator was well aware I had just won a large out-of-court settlement just six months earlier before being charged with the NOD I was now facing. He himself had seen the fraudulent evidence that was offered up by the IG investigators who were out to mislead and outright lie to protect the guilty and cover up the truth. Remember, this is the same IG office that a year or so later after this NOD hearing was found to be corrupt from the top to the bottom and had to be cleaned up by firing many of the people within, and they then had to revamp the IG office, which included bringing in new people to rid the office of widespread abuse and corruption.

After the first day was done and not much was accomplished in the terms of testimony, a second day was scheduled. Every day of this hearing would cost me thousands of dollars. On day 2, the state presented its case and started calling in witnesses to testify against me. They called one clown guard who was a training officer who testified to training officers and guards to use their baton to summons someone by using it to bang on something to get their attention that the judge seemed to take in as being truthful testimony. Remember during the incident with the baton, I was standing in the mess hall closest to the door. He was calling other officers and guards by name who were further away. I was the only one he antagonized. The idiot training officer that testified to training the guard was a trouble-maker in the prison. When he worked the reception center area of the prison, he would walk up and down the gallery yelling, "Dead man walking!" Then he and others would pull inmates out of the cells and walk them down the gallery out of sight to abuse them. He was one of those loudmouth punks that had no knuckle game when alone but with a bunch of his buddies he was Superman. He would also stay with his nose up the higher-ups' butts. He was an ass kisser. The arbitrator who was dressed in his flannel shirt and jeans seemed to hang on every word that came out this idiot's mouth. The idiot was also friends with a sergeant that was of a different race, whom he abused with taunts about his race, calling him "pan face" and other derogatory remarks that the sergeant allowed himself to be subjected to so he could get along with the racist clown. A lot of times, whenever the two of them were in my presence, they would put on a show with the idiot verbally abusing the sergeant.

After the idiot training guard was dismissed, the state called one of the raging guard's good friends that wasn't even in the area when the incident took place. He just happened to walk by as it was ending, but the state let him testify mostly to basically what this man thought of me. He was another young, troubled guard himself who was having marital problems after becoming smitten with a young woman at work. He was also teased by other guards and officers about his naïve ways and the strange things he did at work. He testified and lied to what he had witnessed, which did nothing to help bolster the state's case against me. The hearing was stopped by the arbitrator, and another hearing date was scheduled.

The state seemed to be stalling, knowing I was paying for the arbitration proceedings. Also I would be off without pay. We were now financially hemorrhaging, and to make matters even worse, our daughter was starting her first year in college. Approximately a month later, another hearing date was set again. This is hearing number 3. This arbitration hearing should have been over after day one. After the state offered as evidence false and misleading statements, they started calling supervisors in to testify against me. One of the first was a lieutenant who while testifying seemed to have remorse for what he was being made to do. He sat across from me at the table and couldn't look at me as he testified to the state's liking. His testimony was both damning and supportive. During his testimony, just as all the rest, I tried to read his body language, which was emitting nervousness. I knew the lieutenant, and unlike many of the other staff members, he had respected me and I respected him. He seemed to be forced to help the state in their diabolical plan to have me fired from the department. He was quiet and laid back. He truly seemed like he didn't want to be there and in no way wanted to be forced to lie about me, but he did.

After he was finished, next came the dep of security who basically lied to help cover up the administration's wrongdoing. The arbitrator seemed to believe everything that came out of his mouth as he lied about the facility's tolerance on violence. He himself, the dep was well aware that staff would have knockout, dragged-out fights among themselves, some in front of inmates, and the almost all-white staff would never be charged or disciplined for their actions. Now remind you, I didn't hit anyone. I had just told an out-of-control guard after he pushed me to keep his hands off me and this wasn't the place. If he had a problem, he could see me walking down the street. The Dep of security, during his testimony, acted as if I was a threat to the facility when he himself was aware of guards that had commented much, much more real and serious offences that the administration he was a part of helped cover up or turned their heads away from. Once again, I was the only employee being brought up on charges that would result in suspension and sent to a NOD hiring for litigation on trumped-up charges and lies authorized and supported by the Elmira Correctional Facility administration, NYSCOBA, and higher-ups in Albany.

There is a word that is used when a group of people have a secret plan to do something that is unlawful or harmful, and that is *conspiracy*. Yes, they were all conspiring to rid the Department of Corrections of me, and the lying dep who was testifying knew it, and he was doing his part to try to solidify and bring truth to the lies that were being told. After the dep finished telling his pathetic lies and falsely accusing me of being a threat, the arbitrator sent him off with a parting question. The arbitrator said to the dep of security, "Hey, dep let me ask you a question."

And the dep responded with, "What's that?"

The arbitrator then said, "What makes the inmates do what you tell them to do?"

The dep of security at a maximum-security prison's response was, "Well, when we tell them to do something, they do it because they know we are in charge."

The arbitrator said nothing in response to his foolish response. He, the dep of security then got up and left out of the room. It must had been the look that was on my face—you know, that look you make when someone says some dumb shit that makes no sense at all. The arbitrator turned to me after the dep of security was gone and asked me the same question. He said, "Now let me ask you, Officer Brown, the same question. Why do the inmates do what you tell them to do?"

I responded with, "The inmates allow us to run the prison because we are outnumbered. For instance, if I were standing in the mess hall with 150 inmates and 6 officers or guards, the inmates allow us to be in control because we are outnumbered."

The arbitrator looked at me and said, "I like your answer a lot better."

This arbitration hearing was over, and yet again, another date was made for another hearing. This was, I believe, day number 5 of a hearing that should have been one day. After every hearing, I was subjected to writing large checks for the arbitrator that would have his short, stubby arms and small hands outstretched with a cheesy smile on his face. He was more than happy to continue to allow the state to call witness after witness as they used the arbitration system as a tool to harass and intimidate me. As the legal system was used as an ATM machine to try and bankrupt the bank of Brown. I also had to pay the stenographer thousands of dollars as well that she would graciously expect while doing the stenographer work, and while in my presence, she voiced her opinion about this hearing as being a charade. I then had to pay my attorney, who was now working at a prestigious law firm in New Jersey. He was also paid thousands of dollars after each of the scheduled hearings. During the course of the lengthy hearings, the state would call witness after witness to prolong the hearings. Out of all the witnesses called, none were requested by my defense. All were requested by the state, and all lied. They all either covered for the out-of-control, raging, troubled young guard or lied out of the animosity and hate they felt toward me.

A sixth day was scheduled for a hearing date, so again as months went on, I was still out of work without pay for being assaulted and antagonized by a raging, out-of-control young guard. I was now moving into over nine months without pay, and I was still being forced to foot the bill for the state as they use the legal system as a tool of harassment. Yes, this was our state government harassing a New York State resident that was standing up for justice, the same state government that would go after a private company and fine or sanction them for doing what they were doing. There was even a field trip to the facility by the arbitrator, my attorney, and the state rep to the scene of the crime, which I was being charged for. The arbitrator was shown how close I was standing to the young raging guard who had chosen to antagonize me with his baton rather than call my name like the rest of the guards and officers. He was also shown where and how far I was away from him before he ran up on me and pushed me.

The sixth and final day of the arbitration hearing. That's when the instigator, the raging, troubled young guard walked into the hearing to testify. As I sat quietly at the table, the raging, troubled young guard entered the room. He had a half snarl on his face. His clothing was a pair of dirty jeans and a wrinkled shirt. As he looked around the table, he was directed where to sit. He then took his coat off and threw it on the floor in the corner like a discarded rag. After doing so, he looked over at me as I sat quietly dressed in a suit and tie. I'm sure that the rest of the liars that had all come before him had told him how I was dressed. My attorney had insisted that I be in a suit for the dog and pony show. Most guards don't care about their appearance, which is obvious by their dirty, sloppy uniforms they wear every day, and the young raging guard was one of them.

As soon as the state rep started asking him questions, he started telling lie after lie that flew from his mouth freely as he tried to make the lies he was telling become true and factual to what had taken place on the day in question. It is truly hard to remain silent as someone is allowed to lie about you over and over. The lie he told wasn't even close to what had transpired. His use of his state-issued baton, which he had beaten on the door to summon and antagonize me seemed to be acceptable and explained away with the misconception that the practice of doing so was taught during weapons training once a year. The only problem with that was I also had weapons training yearly for the last twenty-eight years, and I had never been taught to use my state-issued baton to antagonize an officer or guard or another employee. But the troubled young guard and the others that the state had paraded in front of the arbitrator all told that same lie of being taught to use there baton to summon someone standing twenty feet away. He totally and categorically denied putting his hands on me, as did all the liars that testified before him.

After his lie-mony was given to the arbitrator, I testified to the truth, which was on the day in question, I was posted in the mess hall halfway away from the door and the raging, troubled young guard had pulled out his state-issued baton and beat it against the door to summon me to escort the group of inmates. After exiting the mess hall, I told the troubled young guard who stood in the corridor staring in my direction with a snarl or grimacing look on his face that it wasn't necessary to use his baton to get my attention and he could call my name as he had done for everyone else. After informing him of that, he was allowed to assault me by pushing me, which was all captured on camera and hidden to cover up for him and the wrongdoing that was allowed to take place at the Elmira Correctional Facility. The arbitration hearing was finally over it went on longer then a murder trial and cost as much or more as one. It was now in the hands of the arbitrator for him to make a decision on my guilt or innocents, and the penalty if any.

Now remember, the arbitration judge is handpicked though a selection that both the union and the Department of Correctional Service approve him together. After the hearing, the arbitrator rendered his decision. He found me guilty but allowed me to keep my job. Also, there would be no back pay for the lengthy suspension without pay. The total cost of the suspension and the lengthy arbitration hiring was more than eighty thousand dollars. It was truly longer then a murder trial and as costly. This is what I paid for getting antagonized and assaulted by a raging, out-of-control racist nut, and both the state and the union I was subjected to pay union dues to NYSCOBA were still unsatisfied with the results because I was able to keep my job. The department was still attempting to refuse the arbitrator's decision and terminate me, and I was more than sure the union was backing it also. That was proof that the union and the state were in cahoots with one another in the arbitration hearing. If the union would have been allowed to represent me, I would have lost my job and kept some of our money, but by having my own attorney, I kept my job and the ability to retire but lost eighty thousand dollars doing it. Either way, the union and the department along with the administration at the Elmira Correctional Facility were allowed to violate my rights and abuse the arbitration system and use it in a way other than what it was intended for. Instead of using it as a disciplinary tool to fix the real problems that plagued the department that have been allowed to fester and overrun the department to the extent that the department has morphed into a criminal enterprise, what the state and the department of correctional services did to steal our money was no different than someone writing a fraudulent check or someone running a scam to defraud someone out of money, eighty thousand dollars for an arbitration hearing, knowingly lying to do so. The union NYSCOBA and the administration at the Elmira Correctional Facility, and higher-ups in Albany all participated in the coverup and fraud and colluded together to rid the Department of Corrections of me. Hell yes, that's a criminal enterprise by all means. The same fraud and deception by another entity not connected with the state a private company doing business in New York state would face the iron fist of our state attorney general, who would bring down the law to protect the rights of the citizens of New York from being subjected to this kind of abuse. But seeing the Department of Corrections is a state agency, even though they say they fall under the same laws and protections that are outlined in the state constitution and affords state employees protection under our human rights laws both federal and state, there is nothing further from the truth. In fact, they do just the opposite. They themselves participate in practicing in conscientious stupidity and sincere ignorance to justify the injustice that is allowed to plague the Department of Corrections from the top to the bottom. Think about all of the injustice that happens in society in plain sight. Now think about what goes on behind closed doors in a department that is off limits and veiled from the public's sight. They are allowed to have absolute dominion over the Department of Corrections and subsequently answer to no one.

After being suspended for almost nine months and dragged through the mud once again and robbed of eighty thousand dollars by the union NYSCOBA and the administration and higher-ups in Albany, I was ordered to report back to work. My first day back, I wasn't in the prison for thirty minutes when a good officer who had always talked to me no matter what and stayed out of the hate campaign that was allowed to be waged against me came to me, welcoming me back with a handshake and quickly informed me I wouldn't have to see the guard that had lied on me and had been the cause of the state and union allowing false charges to be brought against me.

I quickly asked, "Why not?"

He then said, "Man, he got the shit beat out of him." He then went into detail explaining the troubled young guard's new problems, which he had gotten himself into. He went on to tell me how he had been severely beaten up. There is a saying, "He got the breaks beat off him," but this was more than the breaks. He had a black eye, bruised ribs, a broken ankle, and a broken jaw. I would dare say he got the engine beaten out of him. Rumor had it he had put his hands on his girlfriend, and the brother disassembled his lying ass. Well, you know what they say: "Karma is a bitch." This was truly a troubled young guard who was raging out of control, unable to control his own emotions, evident by the way he went off. After I had told him to call my name and not use his state-issued baton to try and antagonize me and was allowed to run up on me and push or shove me, I was charged with an offence, risking my job. The idiot superintendent who helped to bring the false NOD charges against me was gone. He had gone back where he came from. He was rewarded with a superintendent's job back home in western New York at the infamous Attica Correctional Facility where hate and discrimination is a way of life, obviously by the mistreatment of black and brown people and a facility that employs a all-white staff. This has been all well documented and concealed for many years, and the powers to be have done little or nothing to correct the problem. The union NYSCOBA that also claims to follow the state's human rights laws and state and federal discrimination laws also violates the rights of black and brown people by allowing a prison to be exclusive and cater to the majority of their members, which are white males, denying the same rights to its minority members.

It was true when my uncle, a correctional officer, told me to make sure you always have money up for an attorney. It was true then and it's true now. The union doesn't care about its minority members in these upstate prisons. We are no more than dues to them, no more, no less. I wasn't the only one happy to see the arrogant, self-serving, pitiful excuse of a superintendent gone. Others were also glad to see him go. He was what we called a guard's superintendent—that meant he would help protect the guilty and hide and conceal the truth. He would be just the opposite if you were looking for someone to do the right thing. These are the types of people that the Department of Correctional Service put in charge of prisons throughout New York state. They are usually picked by someone in the position of commissioner whom they had worked with at some other prison, where they had done questionable things together.

There was one commissioner who was the superintendent at the Cayuga Correctional Facility when I was working there. When he first came to the facility and I was the only African American officer, he attempted to intimidate me, threatening me with disciplinary actions if I reported discrimination. His threat was well-taken and reported to Albany. The man hated the sight of me as much as I hated being threatened for reporting wrongdoing and discrimination. He was laughed at and mocked for looking like the Purdue chicken guy from the advertising commercial, and he was later picked to be a commissioner in Albany within the department. There are actually way too many commissioners in the department for it to be in such bad shape. Many cannot even justify the title of commissioner.

After returning to work, I resumed my duties in the service unit. Some welcomed me back, and some despised seeing me. Either way, I had three years till I would be eligible to retire. I resumed working at the front desk area. I was still going to G block on the weekends to work, where they were still not doing the bar and hammer check, to check the integrity of the cells to make sure the inmates haven't been sawing at the metal or chipping away at the concrete with a plan to escape. No, they were still being allowed to spend that time playing cards and cooking and eating breakfast or lounging in a chair, sleeping off a hangover. They did any and everything but their official job functions. I was still the only one along with the officer or guard that worked 8 gallery doing the bar and hammer check.

Every weekend, I worked. The sergeant, and the watch commander brought breakfast and lunch from the G block short-order cook/guard along with and the union rep who participated in the card games in the G block casino area were all aware that the staff in G block were all refusing to do their jobs and I was the one doing my job, but I continued to be the most written-up employee at the Elmira Correctional Facility. I continued working in the service unit at the desk area and G block, counting down the days to retirement.

It had been about a year and a half after my suspension when the guards in G block started to feel slighted because I would go up in the officers' small office on 7–8 gallery and refuse to eat breakfast and play cards with them, so what they started doing was refusing to give me the key to the office area on 7–8 gallery, and if they did give it to me, they would refuse to take it back. When I went to exit the block, they would then make a scene over the key. A lot of these grown men would act like little kids and they acted as if they were in grade 13 instead of prison. This went on for a few weeks until one of the young racist guards that was a known heavy gambler and was said to be having marital problems decided he would refuse to take the key also and took it one step further and falsely accused me of calling him "Whitty." he then had this other out-of-control, troubled young guard who had just gotten divorced lie with him to bring truth to his story. They then reported the lie to a sergeant who was one of the most racist supervisors at the Elmira Correctional Facility. This sergeant's face and neck were so red he looked like he was always boiling. The sergeant was happy to run with the lie and wrote me up and accused me of calling a white guard "Whitty."

When the sergeant accused me of this, I assured him if I was going to discrimint against a white guard, there were a whole lot of other derogatory racist names for white people. I would have chosen to use the troubled young guard's cartoonish first name and his sidekick who lied with him, and the racist sergeant that had never written up any other officers or guard were all looking stupid. I didn't even flinch over the absurd accusation. The facility was using troubled young staff members to intimidate me with lies and deception.

The guard that was accusing me of saying this had a brother who was just as stupid or stupider than him. He had gotten into a dispute with a female neighbor, and just because he didn't like her, he took an object and went down the side of her car. Now this is how stupid he is. He did it in a store parking lot that had cameras, and there were signs all over the parking lot that stated this lot is monitored by video surveillance, and think about it—this man was antagonizing a single mother that was out here in the world trying to make it. What a punk. His way of thinking was like so many of these punk guards. They would beat your vehicle up and then cower behind their badge. Both he and his brother were good examples of what was wrong with the Department of Corrections. I know for a fact that the inmates had reported to me that the older one was dealing with the inmates, and the younger one was heavily in debt over gambling, which the inmates had overheard. You can never trust someone that has a bad gambling habit because there is a good chance they will gamble away their integrity and more.

After the incident with the cartoonish name guard, I was approached by a guard who suggested I bid on the IGRC job, the grievance officer in the service unit. The job had weekends off. He was sent to me with the suggestion. I was close to the twenty-five-year mark. The thought of having weekends off was enough to make me decide to put in a bid for the job. Like I had said, it was like a retirement job that most officers and guards took right before they retired. After the bid came down, I was awarded the job. I was now the IGRC officer. I was now changing my desk from the desk at the front door to the desk in the IGRC office. The inmates that worked in the office were all familiar to me because I interacted with them on a daily basis.

The civilian that ran the office was another story. He was a miserable short, little man who didn't like himself. I had never seen a person that was so miserable. He became even more miserable when I got the job in the IGRC office with him. He was friends and drinking buddies with a lot of the guards that were harassing me. He would yell at the inmates that worked for him and also to other employees when he decided to blow his top. One of the first things I made clear to his disrespectful little ass was that he wouldn't be talking to me in the tone he used for most people, which put him on the defensive. He would then sit in the same room all day and refuse to talk to me in defiance to my statement about him not talking to me like he talked to most people, although when one of his drinking/card-playing guard buddies came around, he would smile from ear to ear and then start speaking loudly. This went on for months until finally he started speaking to me and trying to explain what was going on in the IGRC office, which amounted to nothing I didn't already know.

One of my jobs in the office was to sit in on hearings, which happened twice a week. He would try to limit the information about the rest of the grievance department by concealing information and not including me in on what was going on, but little did his miserable, disrespectful self know the minute he left out of the office to go play cards in the blocks with the rest of the gamblers while he was supposed to be on rounds, I would go through all the grievances that had been filed or were going to be filed. Also seeing I was security, I would also rummage through the desk area to check for contraband. I would obtain a lot information about the grievance department from the inmate clerks and the two reps that assisted the inmate population in filing grievances.

After he would return to the office, he would find me sitting at my desk like I hadn't moved. His way of running the grievance office was just to file every grievance that came across his desk instead of picking up the phone to try to resolve some of the problems through communication and coming to some form of understanding.

One day while I was out of the office, some young woman from Albany visited the facility to check on the counselors and other matters. When she went to cut through the grievance office to the other side of the unit, the miserable short, little man that seemed like he didn't like himself went off yelling and screaming at her for cutting though the office instead of going around. This time, he had picked the wrong one. The young lady's family member was some big shot in Albany.

When I returned after he had disrespected the young lady from Albany, you would have thought we were long-lost buddies. Before he gave me his side of the story, I had already gotten the story from an officer, a counselor, and a couple of inmates, and all were saying he had disrespected the young lady that was at the facility from Albany and her relative in Albany had called the facility and he had gotten in trouble. So now that the little loudmouth, disrespectful, miserable man was in trouble, he wanted to talk to me. I listened to him cry to me about what had transpired with him complaining about people cutting through the office to the other side. I ignored him and laughed inside, thinking he finally had gotten caught disrespecting people. I had previously warned him about his mouth, months ago prior to him going off on the young lady over nothing. He was now trying to communicate with me trying to find a sympathetic shoulder to cry on.

After a few months went by, the day finally arrived—the day that all correctional officers, and guards wait for. The day you start counting down from day one. It was finally here—the twenty-five-year mark had finally arrived. I now had twenty-five years on the job. I could retire at any time. My pension was now etched in stone. My pension or retirement that had been used by the administration at the Elmira Correctional Facility and the union as well as Albany as a tool to harass and threaten our livelihood for years was now off the table. All my harassers who had been enabled by thus in power, giving them the right to harass me were all silenced. My twenty-five years was like kryptonite to them. It wrecked all the power that they held over me. They could no longer use fraudulent, illegal NODs and the justice system as a tool to harass me by threatening to take my pension. I now had the power to literally walk out the door and receive my full pension. It was officially *game over* for my harassers. The harassment I had been receiving for over twenty-two years was now over. I mean, right after getting twenty-five years on the job, the harassment stopped. The ace in the hole, my pension, was now my hold card. I was in control of my destiny. As far as them taking it from me was concerned, it was now 99.9 percent impossible. Hell, we had ex-correctional officers and guards that were doing time at Elmira for murder that were collecting their state pension after having worked twenty-five years or more. During my career that is one thing I have seen staff serve time for—that and child molestation.

There was a guard at the Elmira Correctional Facility that had been charged with this hideous offence. He worked at the Elmira Correctional Facility, and so did his wife. She was a counselor for the inmates, and she herself had been charged with questionable behavior, and she was counseling inmates that need help. Unlike the murderous staff, the child molester was a young guard that only had maybe ten years on the job. His retirement or what he would be entitled to, he would have to wait until he reached fifty-five years. So yes, after reaching that milestone of twenty-five years, it was the end all to the harassment I had faced. Their game was over.

As I continued to work in the grievance office with the miserable civilian who now felt slighted by being told about the way he was speaking to people after the encounter with the high-ranking Albany official's relative that he had spoken to recklessly and disrespectfully, he was now even more miserable and angrier than I had ever seen him. He started spending less time in the office. He would leave, saying he was going on rounds, which was a lie. He would go to the blocks and hang out with the guards and gamble. As I would be left alone in the grievance office with the inmates who continued to tell and show me what was going on in the office, from what I could see and from what the inmates were telling me, the miserable civilian seemed to be a stumbling block and the problem why the office was filling a large number of grievances and why even minor grievance issues weren't being addressed.

A couple of months later, the little miserable civilian that was the head of the grievance office, the IGRC supervisor, who was both mad and miserable, went on vacation and never returned. He retired. He left the facility the administration and the grievance office high and dry. It only takes a two-week notice to put in for retirement, so while he was on vacation for two weeks, he used his retirement power and did so. He gave no notice whatsoever. If I would have to guess, that was payback for being spoken to or chastised for his rude and disrespectful attitude.

After the department was left abandoned with no supervisor, the grievances all still had to be filed which meant they were either given a hearing in front of the sergeant, me, a civilian employee, and the two inmate grievance reps at the hearing. The inmate that had brought the grievance forth would ask for his grievance to be granted by attempting to show preponderance of evidence showing where the state may have violated a policy or procedure by denying him some access to anything from medical treatment to a package item that had been denied. A hearing was conducted and then decided by preponderance of evidence. After the inmate has his hearing and if he is unsatisfied with the results, he could appeal the decision to the superintendent. That will give the last opinion from the facility level. Once again, if the inmate isn't satisfied with the superintendent's decision he can appeal it to the grievance department in Albany, which is called Central Grievance, where the denied grievance would receive consideration to be overturned in the inmates favorite, these procedure also had its own appeal process After the Civilian IGRC Supervisor left without warning I had two choices to make either sit and watch as chaos and confusion breakout in front of me as the IGRC/grievance department imploded, or I could step in and keep the ship afloat as they searched for a new supervisor. But with that scenario it would cause me to have to assume the role of the IGRC supervisor and still do my job as a correctional officer.

Over the years, I would watch as some would consciously help to bring chaos and confusion to whatever they could when they couldn't get their way. From the security staff refusing to follow policy and procedures because they felt the inmates weren't deserving of some new change in the policy and procedures that may benefit the inmates in getting some new privilege or staff helping to fuel some ongoing rift among the inmates. My decision was to step up and assume the role of the IGRC supervisor because ultimately, I would be the one stuck in the office dealing with the chaos and confusion.

After setting some ground rules with the administration regarding my new rule as the acting IGRC supervisor/correctional officer, the first thing I set out to do was to lower the number of grievances that were flooding the office. The largest number of complaints were coming from the medical/dental department. The complaints were anything from the inmate claiming to be denied treatment for an illness, refused medication, denied sick call, to being harassed by medical staff. The dental department was being grieved constantly for its lackluster ability to provide adequate dental care. There were inmates that had been complaining about teeth that have been hurting them for well over a year. Others had been seen and placed on a list for extractions that never happened. The dental department was a mess. There had been a dentist or dentist assistants, both male and female that had been bought up on charges for inappropriate behavior with the inmates, so it was hard for the facility to retain and keep staffing to run an adequate dental department. There were many inmates that were complaining for over a year about toothaches that were causing them sever pain that seemed to be heightened to the level of cruel and unusual punishment. The dental department was held together by a thin, cheap piece of dental floss that had long been discarded. The almost all-female nursing staff would mimic the guards and officers and not pay homage to the oath they had so humbly and graciously taken and accepted.

There were inmates that would abuse the system for many different reasons—some to gain access to drugs, some with legitimate complaints, other with self-diagnosed issues, and some were trying to just see the nurse for their personal pleasure, using the nurse as a substitute to fill the void of lack of a female's companionship. A lot of the time, the officer or guard would influence the nurse's judgment by the way the guard or officer talked to the inmate while the nurse and officer were on rounds. If the guard or officer had deemed the inmate a troublemaker of undesirable to be seen by the nurse, the nurse would oblige the guard or officer's wishes to deny the inmate treatment by refusing to stop at the inmate's cell and document his issues or refer them to medical so he could be seen by other medical staff. This seemed to be a problem throughout the prison as staff would stand in solidarity in refusing those inmates they deemed unworthy of medical treatment. The bond between some of the almost all female nursing staff and the officers and guards would be so close they would be connected as one. These relationships generated marriages and untold love stories between the two groups of employees.

When speaking of medical, this includes the mental health department as well. Another area in the prison that received a lot of grievances was the Special Housing Unit, a.k.a. the box, the S-H-U, or the hole. It has even been called the dungeon. You would have inmates complaining about a lot of different problems they claimed that were going on. You would have the same inmate grieving the same issue over and over again. You would have inmates having psychological breakdowns and staff that were uneducated or unwilling to offer assistance because they had no true training on how to deal with the mentally ill and had no desire to be trained. Hell, some of the staff themselves suffered from mental illness, so it was literally the crazies watching the mentally ill, and it was a mess.

You would have inmates grieving over and over about the desserts being taken out of their meal trays or not being given salt with their meal. Over time, there was hundreds of grievances about staff refusing to give the inmates everything on the statewide menu they were entitled to because of some riff the guards was having with the inmate that was locked in his cell for twenty-three out of the twenty-four hours of the day. They had an SPCA commercial talking about the abuse of animals, and it shows how animals suffer from the extreme cold weather when not provided with the proper shelter. It is surely sad to see animals suffer from abuse, but what is also truly sad and heart-wrenching is to watch human beings suffer at the hands of other human beings.

In the Special Housing Unit, the inmates are only issued a set of sheets and a thin blanket. The guards and officers would open up the windows in the box in the winter time to punish the inmates by freezing them. It would sometimes happen when the temperature dropped dangerously low outside. The staff would open up the windows and leave them open as they would find refuge in the office area the sergeant and the administration would be well aware of what was going on but no one would stop the unlawful abuse of power. Even though the Special Housing Unit had cameras and was also wired for sound, none of this would stop or prevent the staff from the brazen abuse.

There was one guard—he was among one of the most abusive with his mouth and his hands. he had more time than the rest of the young staff in the box, but his time on the job didn't exceed more than eighteen years. He had been in the box for some years and helped train the young staff on their jobs in the box. He was approximately 5'11" and medium built. His face was scarred and pitted from what appeared to be severe childhood acne. His skin tone was red in color. His hair was blond and looked translucent. It was thin, and it was cut short to try to compensate for going bald. You could see his scalp, which was also red. When mad, the man's whole head would be red. His knees were knocked; his knees bent inward, causing him to walk awkwardly, so much so his shoes in the heel area wear uneven on the inner heel area, causing a noticeable difference as they leaned to one side. It was told to me by a few his father, whom I was blessed to not have ever had the pleasure of working with, was one of the most racist guards to walk a beat at the Elmira Correctional Facility. If true, this could be the reason that this evil individual existed. I could just imagine what this man was subjected to as a kid as his father would come home from work and unleash his racial hate-filled day upon his family to relieve his built-up frustration, telling stories of his interaction with the inmates. He no doubt must have boasted about his domination and authority that he had over them, giving him the power to abuses the inmates. I had heard similar stories of other father-son careers where the sons became correctional officers because of their fathers. The evil young offspring of the racist retired guard would seem to be a chip or a chunk off that same stone because he was filled with hate and anger that he would subject all around him to. He seemed to play a major part in the chaos that would erupt in the Special Housing Area.

There were staff that seemed to thrive on putting their hands on inmates, subjecting them to beat ups, and beat downs. For example, if an inmate and a guard had a verbal dispute over one thing or another—and believe me, it would always be one thing or another—that dispute would usually leave the two feeling slighted, which would then put the two at odds with one another, turning each encounter into a dispute. These disputes in SHU, the special housing unit, would then turn into the guard violating the inmate by denying him of anything that he could, such as food, rec, writing material, medical treatment, showers, and mail. The inmates would then file a grievance to rectify the wrong. The staff would usually allow themselves to fall prey to an inmate having a mental breakdown from being confined to the area, and then there were the inmates that were just troublemakers and caused problems. Either way, most staff were untrained to tell the difference. The racist guard who worked the SHU area was an agitator and would purposely cause problems with the inmates in the SHU area with hopes of being able to put his hands on one of the inmates. I didn't directly work in the SHU area, but I was told of his actions by both inmates and staff which would occur while talking about the prison in general.

I also would later find out more about the problems in SHU by having to make weekly rounds in the area after assuming the role of the acting IGRC supervisor, who was responsible for making rounds in the areas where inmates were kept locked in such as SHU, and PC. I block had a number of galleries dedicated for keep lock inmates. Inmates are placed on keep lock for violating a rule in the inmate rule book or a facility rule or procedure. PC was another area where the IGRC supervisor was responsible to make rounds. PC is protective custody, where inmates go when they fear for their safety.

My first time on rounds on those units, I was told by both staff and inmates that the IGRC supervisor doesn't and hasn't made rounds on these units. In one unit, staff even offered to tell me when the old supervisor came to the unit. He usually came in and sat and play a few hands of cards and never made rounds. Many of the grievances filed came from these areas each and every day. After finding out the troubled areas that were generating the largest number of grievances, I tried to lower the number by trying to communicate with the area supervisors regarding some of the more notable problems that were under the control of the staff, which we had the ability to stop because we were the ones causing the problem by allowing our emotions and feelings to get in the way.

A lot of staff, for example, fall prey in the special housing unit to the out-of-control racist guard who had gotten his training and received his upbringing from one of the said-to-be most racist guards to walk a beat at the Elmira Correctional Facility in SHU. The racist guard showed the younger guards how to abuse both the inmates and the system by putting his abusive power on full display, where it would be unchecked by either the area supervisor or the facility administration. The younger staff felt his actions were acceptable, as he would deny the inmates even the tiniest bit of respect and human decency. He denied them food, rec, and other items they were entitled to and subjected them to extreme conditions by opening windows in the winter and closing them in the summer months. It seemed the more he could abuse the inmates, the happier he was. He seemed to be a hit with the young, impressionable officers, who would follow his lead and adopt his reckless, unprofessional way of communicating or dealing with the inmates, which caused chaos, confusion, and cause problems with both the staff in the special housing unit and the inmates. It would be a scripted play that went on 365 days a year. The guards and the officers that worked the SHU area had long adopted the mind-set that the box or special housing area was a place of punishment and felt that the inmates placed in SHU were there for that.

When I first started in 1988, that punishment was loss of most or all phone privileges. Locked in for twenty-three out of the twenty-four hours in a day, inmates were also limited to property. The inmates got three showers a week and one hour rec. There were other things they could have and couldn't have. Over time, I watched as the special housing unit morphed into a mental health unit run by untrained guards who were supervised by unequipped supervisors unable to lead. You would have inmates that would shove things up their rectums only to be retrieved later. You had inmates that would swallow sharp items. You had inmates that were shit throwers, and you had the writers that wrote grievances on the staff that worked in SHU. Most of the grievances were on both the guards and the nurses. The inmates would complain about them every day to the grievance department, about being denied medical care or being harassed by medical staff and the guards. Knowing the staff and watching the interaction that most of the staff had with the inmates, I could almost assess if the problem truly existed; 70 percent of the time, staff were at the root of the problem. The reason for that was staff was supposed to have a higher level of professionalism and training, but some staff would stand in front of an inmate's cell and literally have a full-blown, outright argument with an inmate having a psychotic breakdown, screaming and ranting and yelling abusive language, when all staff had to do was walk away. Like the racist guard, some would rather dump gas on the flame so they would be able to stomp it out later after the flame roars on, literally. Some staff were truly instigators and troublemakers and only helped to overwhelm the grievance office, the IGRC, with senseless and unnecessary grievances that were caused by their unprofessional behavior that goes unchecked and overlooked by those in charge, using conscientious stupidity and sincere ignorance as a means of justifying their not knowing about the ongoing problems plaguing the Department of Corrections.

Many of the other grievance problems came from all over the prison—inmates complaining about missing property was a big one. It would seem that a lot of the missing property came from inmates that had some problem or another at another facility and were transferred to the Elmira Correctional Facility. Upon arriving, the inmate would be told his property was missing. The inmate would then be forced to go through a lengthy process, which would require them to file a grievance for their missing property that would never be located. The inmate would then have to put in claims that would go unanswered due to the large backlog of missing property claims that usually involved staff either throwing the property out or allowing inmates to mysteriously gain access to the property of another. This happens in the block where the guard would allow the inmate porters in the block to pack the inmate's property that is being moved or sent out of the block to SHU, the special housing unit, or another keep lock area or transferred. The porters would ransack the property, taking anything they could sell or keep worth value, or the property would be discarded. A lot of the times, this could also include the inmate's legal work, which could contain legal papers for an appeal or some other sensitive material that could have cost the inmate hundreds if not thousands of dollars to obtain. They say statewide, the amount of money spent to reimburse the inmates for missing, stolen, or damaged property was astronomical as were the grievance claims filed and the missing property claims by the inmates for reimbursement, and much of the time, it was the staff's fault for being either careless or vindictive when required to handle the inmates' property.

The food service was another highly grieved area in the prison. The inmates would complain mainly about not being allowed their special diet meals that all the inmates seemed to want. See, the inmates had long learned that as the system evolved and the food source was changed from less fresh food to processed food, which contained high amounts of soybean byproduct, it is said when consumed daily, the side effects are many. So a large number of inmates, when seen in the medical department, asked to be placed on the dietary restriction list, affording them the opportunity to receive food with less or no soybean content, such as boiled eggs, canned fish like tuna and sardines, as well as fresh fruit and other items. The inmates would file grievance after grievance against the food service administrator and his staff, the cooks that worked under him, for refusing to provide the inmate with his special dietary meal that had been granted from the medical department.

Back when I started in 1988, the inmates didn't have the choices that they have now on the serving line. They can have the regular meal that is being served or they can ask for the alternative. The regular is usually a meat meal, and the alternative is a meatless meal. Or the inmate, if he has an authorized diet, gets his diet meal. In 1988 and into the mid-nineties, there was no alternative meal or special diet. The only alternative on the menu was a peanut-butter-and-jelly sandwich or don't eat. Through the inmates complaining about the poor choice of food offered, over time, they were ultimately successful in having the statewide menu changed to offer a wider variety and a healthier menu. This change only lasted a short time because in early 2000, the state went to quick chill, which resulted in the food being supplied in large plastic bags that are boiled in large vats of water. The bags contain stew, sauces, chopped meats, and other baggable, boilable food items that were high in soybean content. This made many of the inmates chose an alternative or diet meal through authorization from the facility medical department.

The inmates' diet meals program can only be described as a chaotic, dysfunctional mess. The food items for the special meals would come into the facility. During that drop off of that delivery, items are usually stolen by both staff and inmates, who receive and put the items away, then the inmates that work in the kitchen who would put together the special diet trays would steal items like the canned sardines and the fresh fruits and vegetables, either for themselves or to be sold for profit to the inmate population. Then when the trays are set out during mealtime to be distributed to the inmates, there would be a problem with the inmate even being allowed to receive a special diet tray off the serving line. This was usually because of many different reasons. One, the inmate had missed picking up a number of trays that would automatically remove him from the diet list. Two, the tray is missing because someone had stolen it. Three, the tray was never made because there wasn't enough to go around after the shipment was hijacked. Four, the inmate cannot get the diet tray because the guard, civilian, cook or others working in the area and the inmate requesting the tray may be having a beef, and the individual refuses to allow him to have his tray. So that drama created a lot of grievances from the food service area just over the diet meals alone, not counting the many other grievances over other issues that plagued the food service area.

The maintenance department was another troubled area. This department would also be plagued with grievances from the inmate population. The problems would be about the condition of the inmates' cells such as the toilets and sinks being clogged or inoperable. Each cell was equipped with a wall jack that the inmates could plug a set of headphones into to listen to music and television that the administration had chosen for the inmates' listening pleasure. Many of the jacks in the cells were broken, and so was the choice of stations offered as fare as the inmates were concerned by the number of grievances filed by the multicultural inmate population. There were two ways the inmates could put in a complaint or work order regarding repairs. One would be to write it on the work report sheet located next to the officer's desk in each block or inform an officer or guard. Neither of these options worked. The work order list that was in each block would never make it back to the maintenance department into anyone's hands that cared, and then informing an officer or guard usually fell on deaf ears. The only time security staff would take notice to a repair was if water was involved with it, spilling onto the floor, causing a flood. So the grievance office was used as a way to file a work order for cell repairs, which the inmates did in high numbers.

The security staff had many grievances filed against them—the officers, guards, sergeants, lieutenants and above would have grievances against them for many things. There would be as many grievances as there were issues, which were many. The inmates would complain about security staff physically assaulting them by putting their hands on them. Some inmates would even accuse staff of sexually assaulting them.

There was an inmate that came to me pleading for help. He was in his early thirties and black. He locked in I block. He came to me and reported he was sexually assaulted by staff. His story was he was in I block in his cell on the 3–11 shift when he was called downstairs

While the inmate is usually waiting for the grievance to go through the process, the item in question, more times than not, is lost, stolen, or missing from the package room. If the inmate had decided to send the denied package back, many times it would never make it to the destination intended.

After becoming the IGRC supervisor and seeing where the largest number of grievances were coming from, I worked to try to get the numbers down. The inmates in the IGRC office also helped. A lot of the grievances were first investigated by making calls to the areas where the inmate was grieving to see if there was another resolution to the situation, and if the situation could be rectified without going through the grievance process, I would call the maintenance department and inform the supervisor that the maintenance department had grievances filed against them and we would talk about the issue at hand, which the inmate was filing the grievance about. Many times, the supervisor would make sure the issue was fixed and the inmate would sign off on the grievance.

I would also call the infirmary area to see if the inmate who was grieving was on a list or if he could be put on a list to be seen by the doctor regarding the inmate's complaint. The head nurse in charge of the infirmary would check the inmate's file and, if eligible, would place the inmate on a list to be seen by the doctor. The medical department is usually overwhelmed with inmates waiting to be seen by medical staff. Many of the people in the public seem to think that the inmates receive great medical care—that isn't true. Most of the time, the care seems to be just at the level of acceptable. The waiting list to see a doctor was long due to the inadequate staffing of doctors and others, just as the dental department had a long waiting list due to staffing and other problems that prohibited them from providing adequate care to the inmate population. Remember, the dental department's waiting list had inmates waiting well over a year for extractions and other serious dental procedures. But at the same, inmates were routinely admitted to the local hospitals for treatment of different ailments and sickness. Many of the inmates had to use the grievance department to even get on a list to see the doctor after being refused by the nursing staff and security during a sick call interview. Like I said, some of the medical staff were deeply aligned with the rogue guards who would deny medical treatment to the inmates based on how they felt about the inmate.

The staff in the facility, the guards and officers who had grievances against them, really didn't care because there was no way that anyone was going to take the word of an inmate over a guard or officer, so grieving staff was like wasting paper and time. In my twenty-eight years, I myself have never seen a staff member disciplined over any allegation brought against them by an inmate in a grievance. No matter how brazen and obvious the guard's offensive behavior may have been, the undying proof of assumption is always bestowed upon the guard or officer like a crown of divine righteousness, never finding them guilty of any misconduct. The same crown of divine righteousness was also honored as I sought justice and they attempted to harass me into submission and quiet my plea for justice.

Over my twenty-eight-plus years as a correctional officer, the grievance system is like many of the other systematic systems that the state has put in place and used as a smokescreen to give the illusion that there is actually a system to help prevent abuse within the system. While acting as the IGRC supervisor and having to file, review, log, and report the many grievances filed, I could see the system was flawed, from the facility's handling to the central grievance office in Albany. For example, the inmates in SHU would grieve the same issues over and over, and even though there were cameras on the unit, neither the facility nor Albany would do any kind of true investigation into the inmates' allegations, once again giving the staff the undying proof of assumption, no matter what the inmate claimed. During my twenty-eight years, I can say that there was usually a 25 percent chance that the inmate was lying about the officer or guard and there was a 75 percent chance that the guard or officer was truly guilty of the said violation reported by the inmate. The grievance against a guards or officers was investigated by their immediate supervisor, the area sergeant, who was usually their friend, who then helped the officer or guard cover up the misdeed. The responses to the grievances from the administration and Albany were usually generic responses. It would be the same answer for the same problem that they, the administration and Albany, refused to address and rectify. Sometimes it would be the higher-ups being grieved for something they may have done or said, and they too would cover their tracks or, as they say, CYA, which stands for "Cover your ass." When this was said back in the eighties, it meant make sure you do the right thing to avoid a problem later on, but as the years went on, it stood for telling a lie to get out of trouble or cover yourself and others with lies and deception.

The grievances that were appealed by the inmates that were unsatisfied with the superintendent's decision went to Albany, where it would most often be affirmed. Out of the thousands of grievances I proceeded, Albany may have overturned two superintendents' decisions. Those determinations were usually affirmed and reaffirmed by Albany, certifying it, giving a nod or an okay to the officers or guards who have chosen to do as they wish and warning the inmates that they are just complaining to the same entity that is harassing them or denying them. It was a perpetual system set up to give the illusion of a fair of impartial system, which was far from the truth. It seemed to be no more than a job creator in the prison system and a smokescreen in compliance with some federal or state law.

For six months, I continued to do my job as a correctional officer and the job of the IGRC supervisor. I would also attempt to reach out to the many supervisors, some of which were responsive, while some would brush off the inmates' complaint, not caring one way or another.

While running the IGRC office and acting as the IGRC supervisor, none of the guards or officers complained about me being the acting supervisor as they had complained to both the administration and union when I became the deputized clerk for the purpose of signing marriage licenses. I don't know if it was because this position didn't come with a briefcase to carry around, which had seemed to offend and upset so many when I was the deputized clerk. No one complained, and there was no thank-you for doing the IGRC supervisor job.

After I did two jobs for over six months, the administration filled the position. The new supervisor was a female. She was more less dropped in the office as the IGRC supervisor with no knowledge of the grievance department. In an ideal situation, she would have been trained by the former supervisor, had he not performed a Houdini act and disappeared. It was a good thing for the administration that the young lady caught on quick and was a fast learner. I and the inmate IGRC workers helped to familiarize her to her new supervisory position. Also, reps came down from Albany a couple of times to give instructions. After the new supervisor took over, I continued to work with her in lowering the high number of grievances being processed. I continued making calls, as did she, trying to resolve some of the grievances. The new IGRC supervisor was more into doing the job at hand than playing cards and gossiping on the telephone. The old supervisor had been worst than an old cackling hen on the phone, trying to get an earful of some new drama that was unfolding in the facility or elsewhere, which seemed to be his main concern. Also the new supervisor had no problem making rounds as we would do on a regular basis as required. The old supervisor would say he was going on rounds but would go and spend time in the housing unit blocks playing cards with his guard buddies, neglecting his duties.

After the arrival of the new supervisor and the cooperation and help of the inmates working in the IGRC office, the office was running like a well-oiled machine. There was one problem that the new supervisor did have, and that was her boss pressuring her about grievances that she herself was responsible for. The grievances were supposed to be answered in a timely manner, but even the administration would drag their feet in responding to grievances, and when pressure her boss, the dep, would get on her about some said missing response. A lot of the time in prison, I noticed the ball would be dropped right from the start, and it would continue to be fumbled and mishandled as it moved along the way, and after it stopped in its path, there would be left uncertainty and misinformation. That would leave those holding the ball misguided, which usually resulted in chaos and confusion, which left problem after problem. It seemed as if it was a repetitive action that couldn't be stopped or prevented.

The boss of the new IGRC supervisor was a ball dropper. The grievance system was never designed to benefit the inmates. The grievance system is just a way the state can cover their ass and be in compliance. The administration or those ultimately in Albany do not care about an inmate's grievance or complaint, no matter how the inmate is being treated. Rather, it's an inmate being denied a package or an inmate complaining about physical abuse. When the inmates were filing a grievance, they were complaining to their harassers and enablers, who truly didn't care.

It had been over a year since the new IGRC supervisor had taken over. I had reached my twenty-eighth year of service working in the New York State Department of Corrections. I was fifty-three years old. Like I had said, the IGRC officer's job was like a retirement job. All four of the officers who had worked the job prior to me with the exception of one had retired from the post, making it their last bid job. Now I too was eyeing the goal line. The old timers would say they were contemplating pulling the trigger to their retirement.

I went to the next retirement seminar and listened to the information disseminated and then prepared myself for the day I myself would choose to leave the Department of Corrections and retire. After the seminar and getting my retirement calculations for how much I would be receiving and the cost of medical insurance, the only thing left was for me to go and sign my retirement papers and pick a date to retire. As a state employee, this is one of the only times in your career when you are in total control of your own destiny, the captain of the ship, the boss.

I then sat down with my wife, and we picked a date for me to exit hell. After picking a date, I still hadn't signed anything. The date I had picked was a few months away, giving me plenty of time to ponder my decision. As I waited, the department decided it was going to make some changes to its security system at the front entrances and elsewhere at all facilities. One change called for limiting what could be brought or carried into the facility by limiting the size of bags that were allowed into the facility by staff. This all came in the wake of the escape from the Clinton Correctional Facility that was facilitated by staff. A letter was issued notifying staff in the New York state Department of Corrections and community supervision that they would all be required to carry a small clear, see-through plastic bag that was going to be supplied by the state itself. This would hopefully limit the amount of stuff being brought into the prisons. Over the years, some staff would carry large duffel bags big enough to put a week's worth of clothing in it. Hell, the security at the front entrance was so relaxed in the morning time you could literally walk into the prison with a bag of guns, money, or drugs with no one asking or knowing the difference. Others would have oversized thermal coolers big enough to hold a full case of beer or soda, much larger than what was needed for a traditional lunch, and no one would stop or ask these guards or officers about their need for such large lunch containers. The state during my career was never proactive about anything, including security, a problem seemed to never get rectified until it caused some form of problem that resulted in paperwork and/or liability, affecting the facility.

After, the inspector general found that longstanding systemic failures in management and oversight by DOCCS was the contributing factor to the costly escape that cost some twenty-three million dollars. It was said that it cost a million dollars a day for the twenty-three-day manhunt. The Union NYSCOBA should have also shared the brunt of the blame. It helped to cover up and shield this same type of correctional officers and state employees who helped to contribute to the systemic abuses of power and coverups that was the contributing factor to the escape. The union helped to shield the guilty from being brought to justice when rules and policies were broken by its members. I have witnessed in the past even the most obvious and most abusive and outrageous abuses of power, and this human abuse is covered up with the help of the union, shielding its members from being held responsible for their outrages and lawless acts and behavior.

As the state announced the many changes it felt necessary to implement statewide after the escape from the Clinton Correctional Facility, the union pushed back once again, trying to shield its members from their responsibility for their lapse in security and unprofessional behavior, which was now being brought to light statewide in the Department of Corrections. In no way was the Clinton Correctional Facility the only state prison ravaged with systematic abuse of power and run or controlled by rogue management that allows its employees to go unchecked or challenged, which has made many of the state-run facilities more dangerous and less secure. It also makes them more prone to just what happened at the Clinton Correctional Facility.

As I continued to work waiting for the day to come I had chosen for my exit, I watched as the guards and the officers started to lose their rabbit minds about all the changes that the state had coming down the pipeline. Their feelings regarding the changes were all the same—they felt singled out, and the new changes were a form of harassment for the escape. What I saw were a bunch of privileged people who felt they themselves couldn't and wouldn't be told what to do by the New York State Department of Correction heads in Albany.

Over my twenty-eight years, the state had attempted to bring change. This change would always be received in the same manner—the staff would resent those at the top for implementing the change, the union would get involved, and the change would be grieved or protested. This would include even common-sense changes that would enhance security. Change was unwanted and rejected, it sure was nice being able to now have the option of walking away from all the bullshit. And walk away is what I did.

March 23, 2017, ended my twenty-five *years of hell* as a correctional officer in the New York State Department of Corrections. I will never forget that date. When I arose that morning, it was just like any other morning, getting up and readying myself for work, coffee, shower, and that is where it ended. When it came to putting on my neatly pressed uniform, the light-blue shirt with the American flag and the state patch with the state seal displayed on it along with my name tag and the dark blue colored pants, that's when my normal day became surreal. I was dressing for the last time in my twenty-eight-year career. My uniform, the uniform that I had sacrificed so much for the traveling up and down the many New York state highways from one prison to another, the family sacrifice of being away from home on the holidays or having to work on many holidays, the sacrifices were many, but none seemed to be more costly than being the sacrificial lamb for all of those that wear this uniform after me. I wore my uniform with pride and dignity. I wore my uniform with respect and respected others. I performed my duty just as was asked of me, which was care, custody, and control of the inmate population in the state prison system and I did it being fair, firm and consistent. Every day I walked my daily beat, one of my uncles, who was a man filled with wisdom and knowledge, used to say, "Someone has to lay on the barbed wire while the rest of us slip through." All this weighed on me as I dressed in my neatly pressed uniform for the last time. I was struck with the realization it was truly over. I had my retirement—that winner's trophy that all correctional officers strive to get. This chapter in my life was over.

As I finished readying myself for my final day as a New York state correctional officer, I made my way to work. No one knew this was going to be my last day working. I told no one. Your last day of work is spent with nothing but lasts. For example, right from the start, this was my last time punching in, last time reporting to the sergeant to let him know I was here, last time walking through the gate to go to my post. The whole day was spent doing and performing my duty as a correctional officer for the last time.

During the day, I went about my daily tasks just as if it were any other day in the grievance office. The new IGRC supervisor had been advised by me months ago that I was getting close to retirement. My official retirement date was March 31, 2017, which was still over a week away, so on March 23, 2017, after my tour was done for the day, I got up from my desk, gathered my belongings, and wished the new IGRC supervisor goodbye and good luck. I notified her this was my last day.

After saying goodbye, I walked out of the office just like any other day, walked up front, punched out at the time clock for the last time, and walked out the front door to the front gated area. As the steel gates slammed behind me, I walked toward the final gates. The first gate opened and closed, and then the second one opened, which allowed me to walk free from my twenty-five years of hell.

# CONCLUSION

The New York State Department of Corrections and Community Supervision, along with NYSCOBA, the union that represents the state correctional officers, both have a systemic racism problem and use discriminatory practices to guide those under them. Both have systemic abuse of authority. These two entities continue to allow the Department of Corrections to go unchecked and unchanged, enabling some staff to be unprofessional, inhumane, racist, and dangerous. Those working in the system are well aware of what truly exists behind the walls of the many state prisons located in New York state, but the ones at the top that are able to bring meaningful and lasting change seem to rather—as Joe Madison the Black Eagle would say using the quote from the late, great Martin Luther King Jr.—"justify their actions with sincere ignorance and conscientious stupidity." Either one seems to work well for them, as they have no problems turning their heads the other way as chaos and confusion erupts all around them. The unchecked and unchallenged acts of abuse and discrimination that are allowed to happen cause great harm to many. The staff, the inmates, their family members, and others all suffer from the abuse that goes on behind the walls. The New York state prison system as a whole has been allowed to be taken over by a union, NYSCOBA, that has used its power and money to control the prison system. Many times during my career, I would have to ask myself who was in control of the system because the union seemed to have more power than our own state government. In my twenty-eight years, not much has changed in the way that the state has tried to stop the systematic and systemic abuse of power. It was something in the nineties to hear about the abuse in our war prison at Guantanamo Bay, the inmates supposedly being waterboarded.

259

But it was a realization that the inmates in the New York state prison system were subjected to far worse abuse, and some, I would imagine, would rather have been waterboarded than be beaten so severely they were barely recognizable and then thrown into a SHU, the special housing unit, hidden from view until their wounds were healed. Like the old saying, "If only the walls could talk." In a lot of the prisons throughout the United States, this same systematic and systemic abuse happens.

Here in the United States of America, the prison system was set up or was first introduced right after the abolishment of slavery in the South. It was a system designed to place black people, African Americans, back into bondage, and from its conception, it has been doing just that—placing young, mostly disadvantaged black men behind bars. The lack of meaningful rehabilitation makes it a revolving door. Many of the young men that leave out of prison system are only soon returned, some for violations to the terms of their parole and others with new charges. Either way, the system and society have failed, or have they? The communities that are affected with poor education, high unemployment, no job training, and poor health care are usually minority communities made up of black and brown people that live in the ghettos, slums, and urban areas throughout the United States. Many young African American men born or raised in these areas have a greater chance of going to jail than going to college.

Now the flipside of this is the winners in the bondage of black and brown people are the people that usually live in rural America. They are usually mainly white. They have access to good schools, jobs, job training facilities, and excellent health care, in some of these area's prisons are the only real form of employment in places such as Elmira, New York, where the Elmira Correctional Facility is located; Dannemora, New York, where the Clinton Correctional Facility is located; Attica, New York, where the Attica Correctional Facility is located; and Auburn, New York, where the Auburn Correctional Facility is located. All of these are some of the oldest prisons in the upstate New York area. Without the prison system operating in these rural upstate locations, there would be nothing, but with the confinement and incarceration of the many black and brown disadvantaged New Yorkers who have fallen victim to the intercity decay and find themselves incarcerated, the mostly white population in these rural upstate areas are able to find gainful employment at these facilities, earning a decent wage on the backs of the disadvantaged. They are able to live the true American dream. They are able to buy homes, cars, and even send their kids to private schooling and college in place of the factories from what seems to be an era gone.

The factories in these rural areas have been replaced with human warehouses where black and brown people are stored and usually watched, guarded, and abused by a predominantly white staff that has been indoctrinated in a culture that has been misguided, misinformed, and uneducated on common human decency. They themselves are usually trained by someone who has harvested ill will, hate, and contempt for many years. This resonates in the way that these employees perform their jobs. Even though each and every employee receives many, many hours of training a year on the way to perform their duties and receives updates on their responsibilities, few or none are usually held responsible for their sometimes careless, reckless, or abusive actions because those in charge remain complicit and in solidarity.

As they continue to hold on to tradition and power over these prison system and the many prisons that have been placed in their backyards, the recklessness, lawlessness and abuse at many of the state facilities are contributed to conscientious stupidity and sincere ignorance that those at the top continue to use as a justification for not doing what is right. And thus they empower those at the bottom to be more likely to be lawless, reckless, and abusive as they perform their duties.

Being a New York state correctional officer for twenty-eight years was both trying and rewarding. When I first embarked on my career, I had grand aspirations of becoming more in the Department of Corrections than just a correctional officer. I had hoped to achieve a higher rank then what I was ultimately forced to settle for, but I was subjected to the discriminatory practices by the department and union. I informed those who were in charge of the department and the state agencies that protect people from discrimination, but they themselves refused to help by turning their heads and denying my claims to protect the guilty. Making any kind of advancement in the department was impossible for me also. For reporting the wrongdoing, I was subjected to years of relentless harassment and abuse at the hands of state employees who were empowered by those in charge, who failed to address the department's rogue employees. There is indoctrination of many of the employees to believe that lying and abuse are an acceptable practice used to perform one's duties as a New York state correctional officer. Some of my fellow correctional officers might have thought it was all right to lie to cover up the truth, but I didn't. My fellow correctional officers might have thought it was all right to assault and harass the inmates we had been entrusted their care, custody, and control of. I didn't. Some of my fellow officers might have thought it was all right to discriminate against a minority employee, which I didn't. There still remain dedicated employees in the Department of Corrections, men and women who go into these state prisons day in and day out to earn a living, but many of these trusted and loyal employees are themselves subjected to the lawlessness and corruption of the system and have chosen to remain mute. What wrong doing you allow to go on around you and you don't report or address, you empower. The New York state Department of Corrections and Community Supervision has been emboldened and empowered by what seem to be rogue employees at the top and bottom who have been allowed to harass and intimidate anyone who comes up against their ideology. For example, if you're a correctional officer and you watch as a group of correctional officers assault an inmate and you do or say nothing, you have helped to empower wrongdoing, which plagues the Department of Corrections.

Even though I retired in 2017, as I had mentioned, on October 6, 2018, I and my wife were accosted and harassed by a correctional officer from the Elmira Correctional Facility who had screamed racial hate and anger at us by screaming, "You motherfucking nigger!" over and over as we waited at a red light. This was reported to local law enforcement, the Department of Corrections, and those in charge in our state and local government. To date, March 1, 2019, we have yet to hear back about the state correctional officer being held responsible for his actions. The longstanding stand that the state has opted to take was he will never nor will anyone be held responsible for their discriminatory actions.

Again, any and everything written here is the truth. To anyone who doubts any of this, I am willing to take a lie detector, polygraph, voice stress test, or any other lie-detecting technology we have in the now or in the future.

# ABOUT THE AUTHOR

Curtis Brown was born in 1963 in a small town nestled in upstate New York in the Finger Lakes region called Elmira, New York, and raised in a blue-collar household where he was taught early on about respect for others and hard work. While growing up in a predominantly white small town of approximately twenty-two thousand residents, life was full of challenges. There were obstacles, roadblocks, and many trials and tribulations for him to overcome. The majority of his young childhood was spent living in the public housing. His education experience, though, was different from those he lived around. He attended both public and private school while living in the predominantly black housing projects. Those exposed him to both sides of the track, giving him a unique and different experience from those standing on either side of the track. That unique experience helped to mold his life, placing God and family above all and adapting a strong desire for fairness and justice for all. Over the years, he has been able to give back to the same community he was raised in by coaching youth sports and volunteering through church and local clubs and community centers. He continues to believe we are all solely responsible for ourselves and must never allow ourselves to become the responsibility of society in general.

CPSIA information can be obtained
at www.ICGtesting.com
Printed in the USA
BVHW070928070721
611349BV00006B/110